Springer Texts in Business and Economics

Springer Texts in Business and Economics (STBE) delivers high-quality instructional content for undergraduates and graduates in all areas of Business/Management Science and Economics. The series is comprised of self-contained books with a broad and comprehensive coverage that are suitable for class as well as for individual self-study. All texts are authored by established experts in their fields and offer a solid methodological background, often accompanied by problems and exercises.

More information about this series at http://www.springer.com/series/10099

Shaun West · Paolo Gaiardelli ·
Nicola Saccani

Modern Industrial Services

A Cookbook for Design, Delivery, and Management

Shaun West
Institute of Innovation and Technology
Management
Lucerne University of Applied Sciences
and Arts
Horw, Switzerland

Paolo Gaiardelli
Department of Management, Information and
Production Engineering
University of Bergamo
Dalmine, Italy

Nicola Saccani
Department of Industrial and Mechanical
Engineering
University of Brescia
Brescia, Italy

ISSN 2192-4333   ISSN 2192-4341 (electronic)
Springer Texts in Business and Economics
ISBN 978-3-030-80510-4   ISBN 978-3-030-80511-1 (eBook)
https://doi.org/10.1007/978-3-030-80511-1

© The Editor(s) (if applicable) and The Author(s) 2022. This book is an open access publication.
Open Access This book is licensed under the terms of the Creative Commons Attribution 4.0 International License (http://creativecommons.org/licenses/by/4.0/), which permits use, sharing, adaptation, distribution and reproduction in any medium or format, as long as you give appropriate credit to the original author(s) and the source, provide a link to the Creative Commons license and indicate if changes were made.
The images or other third party material in this book are included in the book's Creative Commons license, unless indicated otherwise in a credit line to the material. If material is not included in the book's Creative Commons license and your intended use is not permitted by statutory regulation or exceeds the permitted use, you will need to obtain permission directly from the copyright holder.
The use of general descriptive names, registered names, trademarks, service marks, etc. in this publication does not imply, even in the absence of a specific statement, that such names are exempt from the relevant protective laws and regulations and therefore free for general use.
The publisher, the authors, and the editors are safe to assume that the advice and information in this book are believed to be true and accurate at the date of publication. Neither the publisher nor the authors or the editors give a warranty, expressed or implied, with respect to the material contained herein or for any errors or omissions that may have been made. The publisher remains neutral with regard to jurisdictional claims in published maps and institutional affiliations.

Illustrations in the book by Annick Holland. Cover Picture © Kudryashka / shutterstock.com

This Springer imprint is published by the registered company Springer Nature Switzerland AG.
The registered company address is: Gewerbestrasse 11, 6330 Cham, Switzerland

Foreword

> Services are important and that is why it is essential to have practical approaches to help managers deliver service strategy.
> —Peter Alexander, former President Sulzer Rotating Equipment Services

Many industrial manufacturing companies struggle to develop their service businesses. I was a first hand witness to this as the President of an independent service division in a corporation with three sister manufacturing divisions. My team and I often struggled to get my fellow Executive team and Board members to grasp that we were fundamentally different than a manufacturing-based organization.

I do not know how many times we introduced our business to new CEOs and Board members that we had to answer and defend the same set of questions:

- "How can you work on other manufacturers' equipment?"
- "Why do not you sell more spare parts?"
- "Why do you need so much capital expenditure as a service group?"
- "Why do you see a reduction in orders and sales during economic downturns, service is supposed to be near immune in these times?"
- The one thing they could not argue with was our consistent, high level of profitability.

Facing these questions and searching for growth when developing a mid-range plan, we decided to fundamentally explore our service business's nature and identify key characteristics that we could use to build and grow our business. At the time, this was criticized as "navel-gazing," but the ensuing growth proved our exercise's value. We were able to double the size and diversify the business over the next 2 years and near doubled it again over the next 5 years. (In the interest of full disclosure, (Prof) Shaun West, one of the authors of this book, was my Business Development Manager and did the donkey's work of the research to support the creation of the plan).

Service, in many companies, is still regarded only for the provision of high-margin spare parts. These parts' profitability is often used to mask operational inefficiencies in manufacturing and can be considered a dirty little secret. It is really only in recent years that many industrial companies began to see beyond this perspective and widen their view to more comprehensive service models. As competition increased and costs were driven down, companies were forced to seek new income streams to offset the competitive pressures in selling products. Many companies with long and glorious histories in the industrial sector have failed miserably when developing new service models, while others have profited spectacularly.

Many factors have been identified that can lead to the design and implementation of a successful service strategy. However, in this age of artificial intelligence and smart software, in service, perhaps more so than any other industrial sector, it boils down to people. There are some very key elements, both objective and subjective, that need to be developed to have highly effective service personnel in sales, engineering, and operations.

As with all behavioral development programs, it takes training, commitment, and consistency to accomplish the goals established. The correct guard rails and levels of authority must be defined, and personnel trained on when and how to recognize the need to act and then act appropriately.

This book serves as a how-to guidebook for managerial staff training in how to understand their service model and implement actions when deploying a service strategy. There are key and identifiable plans, actions, and metrics that can be developed to fit the many diverse service business and business models deployed. It is not a theoretical treatise and is written by people who have burned and calloused fingers from their experience.

I wish you the best on your service journey. I found it to be, on a personal level, a highly rewarding career path. I am a much better person for having traveled this road with all the customers and co-workers I encountered, all over the world.

Sulzer Rotating Equipment Services
San Antonio Texas, USA

Peter Alexander

Acknowledgments

This work has been built up from over 10 years or more of research and 20 years or so of leadership experience in many aspects of service excellence. Shaun would like to thank three people for their direction with services: Stuart Brooks who led Operations and Maintenance Services at National Power, Ian Hall who was the leader for Contractual Services for GE Energy Services in Europe, and Peter Alexander who was the president of Sulzer Rotating Services. Academic inspiration for the approach taken with the work comes in a major part from Larry Leifer at Stanford University. Testing of many of the methods and tools was by Oliver Stoll, Dominik Kujawski, Marika Østerlund, Linus Bächler, and Philipp Hamm, among others.

The core of the work has been from interviews with people at the "sharp end" of service delivery. We have worked with the contributors to anonymize the cases we have used, nevertheless we would like to acknowledge the following people (or firms) for their input in whatever form it was made: Alexander Schlaepfer, Ali Z. Bigdeli, Andrea Gombac, Andrew Harrison, Andy Neely, Andy Polaine, Askold Falkenberg, Christian Kowalkowski, Christopher Ganz, Colin Brewster, Daniel Bischofberger, Daniel Weltin, David Hart, David Romero, David Selway, Felix Keiderling, Giuditta Pezzotta, Hans Rauber, Heiko Gebauer, Herbert Müller, Iain McKechnie, Ian Hall, Ian Harper, Jason Smith, Jim Baston, Jim Spohrer, Job Kamphuis, Julian Gorniok, Kenneth MacKenzie, Klaus Hermes, Lothar Heinrich, Marc Stickdorn, Mario Rapaccini, Mark Homer, Henk van den Berg, Martyn Fisher, Matteo Zironi, Oliver Stoll, Pascal Schweitzer, Petra Müller-Csernetzky, Philipp Schmitt, Renzo Sigrist, Scott Nicol, Stefan Andres, Stinson McElhinney, Stuart Brooks, Sven Siepen, Sven-Hendrik Wiers, Thierry Mariot, Thomas Sautter, Kris Oldland, Tim Baines, Tudor Davies, Veronica Martínez, William Jeal, and Zied M. Ouertani.

We also need to thank Anet Mathews, a talented student from HSLU who through her MSc studies carried out many of the interviews on which some of the cases in this book are based. We have also published academically with Anet.

We need to recognize the contribution of Annick Holland for the visuals in this book. She is great to work with and has lifted the quality of the graphics in this book to another level. A talented designer who understands innovation, she was able to transform our messy sketches into something much clearer, and in many cases simpler to understand. We also need to thank for her patience our proofreader Lisa Jones.

Annick Holland, who created all of the great illustrations in this book

About This Book

We have all worked in industrial service business or researched servitization for over 20 years and we wrote this book to help managers to make the move into services. Services are based on intangibles like relationships and trust, and product businesses are based on physical objects with clearly defined requirements. Product businesses are, on the whole, separated from the customer, while a service is often delivered with the customer. This means that senior management deciding the strategic objective is to "move into services" can lead to failure unless there is guidance for the management team, which is where this book comes in as it is designed to help middle management take actions to support the servitization strategy. We recognized that there are many good strategy books on why service can be good for a product-focused business, but few provide actionable concrete examples of how, say a service shop manager, can improve their performance.

The final reason for the book came from the fact that many service leaders come from the shop-floor workforce. Now, while this has many advantages, such as the service leaders really understanding the pains of their customers, it can mean that the leaders view them more as partners or friends than traditional customers. Service leaders often need more support with the "change management" aspects of transitioning the business to focus on services, as there can be a tendency for operational action to overtake strategic thinking. This book is constructed of three chapters:

- Chapter 1 sets out the barriers to servitization and provides the impulse for the organizational changes.
- Chapter 2 describes the seven categories of barriers and gives insights into how people overcame them.
- Chapter 3 provides tools that you could use to help you overcome the barriers and build your own service excellence roadmap within a servitization strategy.

The work is based on a series of papers about our research, should you want more depth and a more academic approach.

Contents

1 **Understanding the Barriers That Slow Firms Shifting from Products to Services** 1
   1.1 How This Book Works 1
   1.2 Product-Service Systems and Servitization 4
   1.3 The Journey to Services 10
   1.4 Learning to Understand Complex Systems 11
   1.5 Seven Barriers Stopping Firms from Moving to Services 13
   1.6 Further Reading 15
   References 15

2 **Overcoming the Barriers to Service Excellence** 19
   2.1 Customers 19
      2.1.1 How Do We Get Our Sales Team to Be Effective in Services? 23
      2.1.2 How Do We Coordinate with Our Customers/End-users? ... 26
      2.1.3 How Can We Reach the End-User When the Equipment Is Sold via an Installer/External Partner? 29
      2.1.4 How Can We Promote a Solution to the End-User When the Equipment/Service Is Delivered via an External Partner? 33
      2.1.5 How Do We React When Our Customers Ask Us Explicitly for New Services? 36
      2.1.6 How to Manage Delivery When Our Customers Want to Perform Some of the Tasks Themselves? 40
   2.2 Organizational Structure and Culture 43
      2.2.1 Some Managers Do Not Think of Service as a Real Business. How Can We Educate Them? 45
      2.2.2 How Do We Get R&D to Consider the Whole Equipment Lifecycle? 49
      2.2.3 How Do We Get Top Management Involvement? 53
      2.2.4 How Do We Get the Firm to See Service as a Real Business Unit with a Profit and Loss? 56
      2.2.5 How Can We Reduce Resistance to Developing Service Business? 59

		2.2.6	How Can We Educate HR/Employees?	62
	2.3	Knowledge and Information		66
		2.3.1	How Do We Share Know-How?	69
		2.3.2	How Can We Better Share Service Feedback with the Equipment Designers?	72
		2.3.3	What New Project Management Skills Are Needed for Services?	75
		2.3.4	How Can We Learn More About the Equipment Operation?	78
		2.3.5	How Can We Mix Know-How from Installers and Customers?	82
	2.4	Products and Activities		85
		2.4.1	How Do We Understand the Installed Base?	89
		2.4.2	How Can We Professionalize Service Delivery?	92
		2.4.3	When Can We Start to Design and Deliver Advanced Services?	95
		2.4.4	If Customers Ask for Digital Service, Where Do We Start?	99
		2.4.5	How Can Services Support New Equipment Sales?	102
	2.5	Competitors, Suppliers, and Partners		106
		2.5.1	How Can We Expand Our Capabilities?	109
		2.5.2	How Do We Coordinate Cooperation in the Supply Chain?	112
		2.5.3	How Can We Transform Agents and Distributors into Service Partners?	116
		2.5.4	How Can We Transform Our Partners into a Service Force?	119
		2.5.5	How Can We Develop a Common (Business) Language?	123
		2.5.6	How Can Both We and Our Partners Manage Performance Measurement?	126
		2.5.7	How Do We Work with Installers?	130
	2.6	Society and Environment		134
		2.6.1	How Can We Convert Free to Fee (Change the Internal and External Mentality)?	137
		2.6.2	How Can We Deal with the Conflicting Demands to Standardize (for Efficiency) and Localize (for Effectiveness) at the Same Time?	141
		2.6.3	How Can We Manage Long-Term Contractual Commitments Made at the Corporate Level with Local Laws?	144
		2.6.4	What Are the Main Legal Implications for Our Organization?	148

		2.6.5	How Can We Understand Tax and Transfer Pricing Issues?..................................	151
	2.7	Economic and Finance...............................		154
		2.7.1	How Do We Move away from Cost-Plus/Hours-Based?...	157
		2.7.2	How Should We Consider Margins? How Do We Price Effectively?.................................	161
		2.7.3	Spares Have High Margins, More Service Will Reduce the Margins, How Do We Manage This?..............	164
		2.7.4	How Can We Develop Our Service Business When We Have No Cash to Invest?.......................	167
		2.7.5	How Can We Manage Dealer Discounts Better?........	170
	References..			173
3	**Methods and Tools for Overcoming the Barriers to Servitization and Service Excellence**....................................			**175**
	3.1	How to Build Your Service Excellence Roadmap.............		175
	3.2	Service Methods and Tools............................		176
	References..			201

About the Authors

Shaun West gained a PhD from Imperial College in London, then worked for over 25 years in several businesses related to industrial services. He started his industrial career with AEA Technology before moving to National Power, where he developed and sold services to external businesses. After studying at HEC (Paris) for an MBA, he moved to GE Energy Services, modeling and negotiating long-term service agreements. At Sulzer, he drafted the strategy that led to the service division tripling in size over 10 years and executed part of the strategy by acquiring a 220M CHF service business. Now at the Lucerne University of Applied Sciences and Arts, he is the Professor of Product-Service System Innovation. He focuses his research on supporting industrial firms to develop and deliver new services and service-friendly business models. He is a member of the advisory board for the ASAP Service Management Forum and a member of the Swiss Alliance of Data-Intensive Services. He lives close to Zurich with his wife and two children. He climbs, skis, and runs.

Paolo Gaiardelli is an Associate Professor at the Department of Management, Information and Production Engineering of the University of Bergamo. His teaching and research mainly focus on Production and Service Management, with a specific interest in Lean Management. Recently, his research interests have extended to exploring lean management's role within operation and service management. He is mainly involved in understanding how the adoption of lean paradigms increases Product-Service System design and development, as well as its impact on management's efficiency and effectiveness. He is the European Chair of IFIP Working Group 5.7 (Advances in Production Management Systems) and coordinator of its Special Interest Group in Service Systems Design, Engineering, and Management. Paolo is also a member of ASAP Service Management Forum, an Italian industry–academic initiative that aims to promote service management's culture and excellence through research projects, practice, education, and technological transfer.

Nicola Saccani is an Associate Professor at the Department of Industrial and Mechanical Engineering at the University of Brescia (Italy). He is part of the RISE Laboratory (Research and Innovation for Smart Enterprise, www.rise.it). He is a member and past coordinator of the ASAP Service Management Forum, a community involving academics and practitioners to develop the culture of excellence in service management and servitization (www.asapsmf.org). His research concerns service and supply chain management. He studies the impact of digital transformation, servitization and circular economy on business models, supply chain configuration, and operations management. He is the author of several scientific publications in these fields. He has also taken part in several company transfer projects on these topics.

Shaun West, Paolo Gaiardelli and Nicola Saccani, (Illustration by Annick Holland)

List of Cases

Case 1	Learning to Capture Relevant Operational Information to Support Pro-active Sales	24
Case 2	Splitting Sales Teams to Focus on Either New Equipment or Service	25
Case 3	Learning to Identify Customers' Service Trigger Points	28
Case 4	Learning to Understand Its Customers' Buying Process	29
Case 5	A Firm Sells to an Installer Yet Was Able to Develop a Relationship with the End-User	31
Case 6	The Installer Wants to Provide Services to the OEM's Customers (the End-Users)	32
Case 7	Learning to Understand Installers as Well as End-Users	35
Case 8	Sharing the Sales Leads and Getting Rewarded for It	36
Case 9	New Service Development Is Different to New Product Development	38
Case 10	A Firm Has Been Asked by Customers to Deliver New Services	39
Case 11	Building Field Services in Collaboration with Customers	41
Case 12	Working with the Customer to Make Them Part of the Solution	42
Case 13	Sales in Services Take So Much Effort and Yield Too Little Value	47
Case 14	With Clear Aftermarket Targets, the Firm Started to Grow Services	48
Case 15	NPD Only ever Considers the Newest Technology	51
Case 16	Using the Lifecycle of the Equipment to Discover New Services	52
Case 17	A Cost Center is Always Under Pressure to Reduce Its Budget	54
Case 18	Service Is Now Headed by a Senior Manager	55
Case 19	Service Helped to Deepen the Customer Relationships	58
Case 20	Running a Business Means Every Service Shop Has to Make Money	58

Case 21	The Firm Needs to Show Real Success: Not Just Financial Numbers	61
Case 22	Creating a Protected Service Business as a Single Unit	62
Case 23	Taking Time to Work with Human Resources Pays Off	64
Case 24	Moving People Between Locations Can Be Disruptive in the Short-Term but Pays Off in the Longer Term	65
Case 25	Sharing of Know-How Comes from Collaboration	70
Case 26	Developing Field Service Behavior in Product Development Engineers	71
Case 27	Information Can Only Be Shared Effectively Through Trusting Relationships	73
Case 28	Learning to Share Long-Term Equipment Operational Information	74
Case 29	Commercial Project Management Is Just Different to Project Management for Product Development	77
Case 30	The Service Team Needs to Be Coached in Project Management	77
Case 31	Using the IoT Provided Insights into the Performance of the Equipment	80
Case 32	Learning to Share Knowledge About Equipment Performance Within the Firm	81
Case 33	The OEM Needed to Learn from Its Installers	84
Case 34	Learning to Use Customer Know-how	85
Case 35	The Installed Base Is a Key Asset for Service Business	90
Case 36	Learning to Understand the Market from the Installed Base	91
Case 37	Learning About Customer Value	94
Case 38	Improving Warranty and Creating Extra Work	95
Case 39	Being Pulled into Advanced Services by Customers	97
Case 40	Delivering Advanced Services	98
Case 41	Digitally Enabled PSS Is Really Complex	101
Case 42	Using Digital to Transform a Business	102
Case 43	Using Service to Support Product Sales	104
Case 44	Working in a Razor/Razor-Blade Market	105
Case 45	Broadening Capabilities Through the Ecosystem	110
Case 46	Working with Partners to Get a Win-Win Solution	111
Case 47	Enhancing Supply Chain Learning to Support Service	114
Case 48	Build Supply Chain Collaboration	115
Case 49	Building a Framework to Get More Value from Agents and Distributors	117
Case 50	Learning to Share Value and Risk with Service Partners	118
Case 51	Developing Agents to Become The Extended Service Force	121
Case 52	Transforming the Business to a Service Business	122
Case 53	Three Acquisitions Later: We Have Four Different Languages	124
Case 54	Developing a Common Approach to Customer Feedback	125

Case 55	Legal Team Was the Barrier to New Value Propositions that Aligned with Outcomes	128
Case 56	Measuring Performance Is More Than Just Financials	129
Case 57	Cleaning Up the Mess that Installers Leave Behind	132
Case 58	Using Installers to Extend the Sales Force	133
Case 59	Learning to Charge for Free Services	139
Case 60	First Steps of Changing for Services	140
Case 61	Standardizing Service Modules to Provide Flexibility	142
Case 62	Developing Competencies and Capabilities for Modular Services	143
Case 63	Cleaning Up the Mess that Corporate Created	146
Case 64	Tax in Service Is Really Hard to Get Right	147
Case 65	Sales Needs to Learn to Negotiate Service Terms and Conditions	149
Case 66	Service Risk Management that Creates Opportunities	150
Case 67	Learning to Deal with Political Risks from Brexit	152
Case 68	Building Transfer Pricing that Is Competitive and Compliant	153
Case 69	Teaching Buyers that "Cost Plus" Does Not Deliver Value	159
Case 70	Working with Finance to Build New Revenue Models	160
Case 71	Deal with Premium and Budget Pricing Models	162
Case 72	Introducing Proactive Spares Pricing	163
Case 73	Spares Sales with New Equipment Belong with the Service Business	166
Case 74	Focusing on Service Cash Generation Not Just Return on Sales	166
Case 75	Investing in Service Without a Clear ROI	169
Case 76	Getting the Customer to Pay for Innovation	169
Case 77	Global Business but Local Process	172
Case 78	Dancing with Ambiguity by Having Transparency	172

Understanding the Barriers That Slow Firms Shifting from Products to Services

1

Just in case you have any doubt about the importance of services to a manufacturing business, Fig. 1.1 shows the contributions made by equipment sales and service sales for typical manufacturing firms (producing durable goods for business-to-business – or B2B – markets). In absolute terms, the total margins are very close in size to each other. However, due to design and development costs, there are much larger risks associated with new equipment than with services. This makes it all the more important to make the shift to services and capture new sales as well as learning to combine products with services to create a product-service system (PSS).

There is also a virtuous circle, where improved service experience increases the chance, that the customer will buy from you again. It means that development teams can get more relevant feedback from the customer, either directly or indirectly, through the field service teams. Services are also generally less impacted by the economic cycles than product businesses, because product sales are often driven by "boom-and-bust" CAPEX (or capital expenditure) cycles, whereas services are driven by gross domestic product (GDP) cycles and firms' OPEX (or operating expenditure) spends. This means services can give a firm a more stable long-term cash flow based on servicing the products sold in the past (Gebauer, 2007; Kowalkowski et al., 2017).

1.1 How This Book Works

Before moving on, we think it is worth explaining how this book works. It does not have to be read from beginning to end. In fact, we could not imagine many people doing that. It is a cookbook that uses actual cases to offer approaches to overcome individual barriers that can slow the move to services. Indeed, there is no single journey to services for firms, as each approach is context specific. Because of this, we focus on the barriers and provide some examples of how they were overcome. We have also included the tools that we think could help managers and practitioners

© The Author(s) 2022
S. West et al., *Modern Industrial Services*, Springer Texts in Business and Economics, https://doi.org/10.1007/978-3-030-80511-1_1

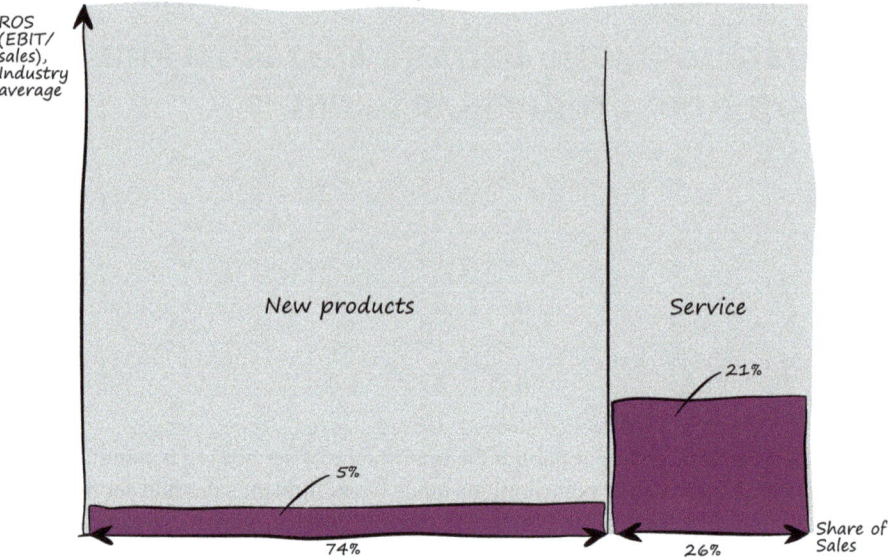

Fig. 1.1 The contribution to sales and margin for typical manufacturing firms (illustration by Annick Holland, adapted from Schmiedeberg et al., 2010)

analyze a specific situation and deal with the seven distinctive categories of barriers (Fig. 1.2) that have been found by research (Hou & Neely, 2013):

1. Customers
2. Organizational structure and culture
3. Knowledge and information
4. Products and activities
5. Competitors, suppliers, and partners
6. Economics and finance
7. Society and environment

The individual barriers have been identified from surveys and direct observations we carried out in several companies experiencing a servitization journey. Over the 3 years we spent on this research, we had the opportunity to talk to many operators and collect hints and tips from over 200 different discussions and chats, as well as over 30 complete interviews (West & Gaiardelli, 2016; West et al., 2014). This was backed up with our own personal experiences and interactions with service leaders as well as the frontline people who are often the most visible aspect of delivering a service (Fig. 1.3). Of course, we published and presented the results of our research in scientific conference proceedings and journals (we are academics), but we also want to make what we have learned accessible to managers who face these barriers on a daily basis, which is why we have collected all our findings in this book.

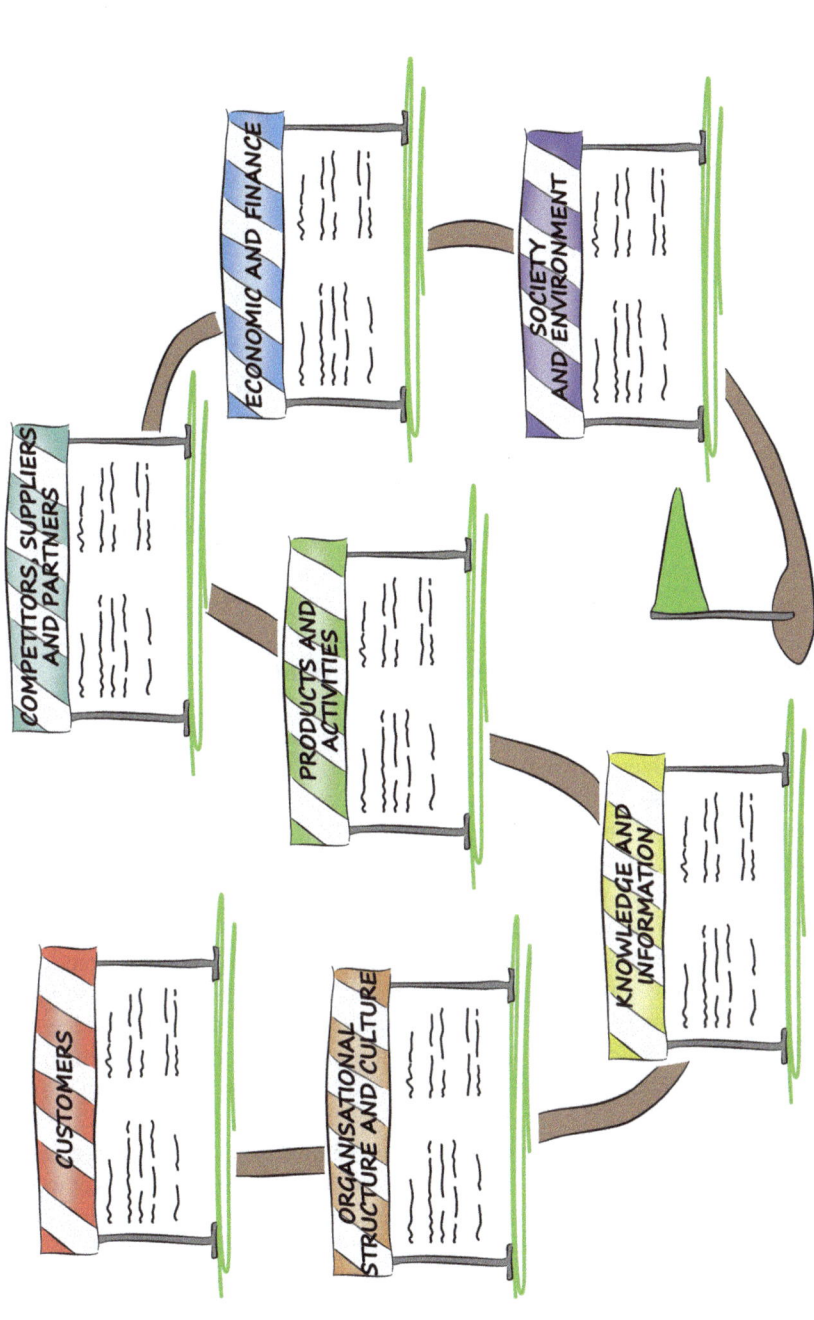

Fig. 1.2 The journey to services: seven barriers that prevent manufacturing firms from shifting to services (illustration by Annick Holland, adapted from Hou & Neely, 2013, West et al., 2018 and West et al., 2019)

Fig. 1.3 Experienced service leaders contributed to this book (illustration by Annick Holland, authors' work)

1.2 Product-Service Systems and Servitization

In the past, many firms focused only on the value related to products, and they often provided services for free, viewing them as a cost or a "necessary evil" (Mathieu, 2001; White et al., 1999). Over the years, an increasing number of manufacturing companies have begun to understand the importance of services as a source of profit and a way to differentiate one company from another to gain a commercial advantage. This has led them to propose increasingly sophisticated, integrated product-service solutions. In research, literature and practice, the concept of "servitization of manufacturing" has become the common term to describe the business model's continuum from a pure product orientation toward an integrated product-service system (or PSS) as shown in Fig. 1.4. Many firms continue to consider service as a cost and make the customer happy "tool" to ensure other sales or the performance, whereas others are moving from "free" to "fee" and, in doing so, journeying along the servitization transition.

Today, several manufacturers are designing and selling complex product-service systems. Notable examples are Rolls-Royce with aeroengines, Hilti with power tools for construction sites, Ricoh with photocopiers, Caterpillar with construction machinery, ABB with ship turbo compressors, and GE with power plant. With each of these examples, the manufacturer's products and services are bundled together in one form or another.

1.2 Product-Service Systems and Servitization

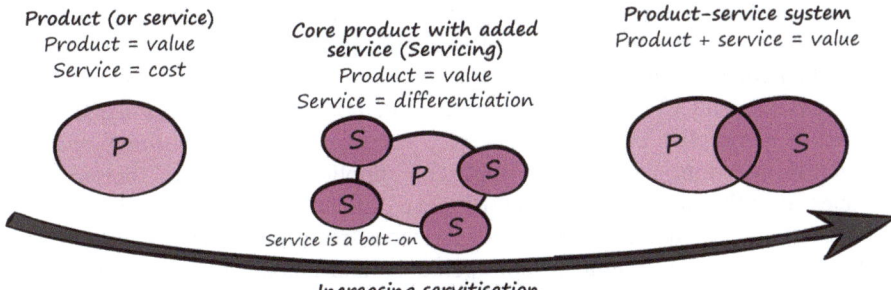

Fig. 1.4 The stages of the product-service system continuum (illustration by Annick Holland, adapted from Vandermerwe & Rada, 1988)

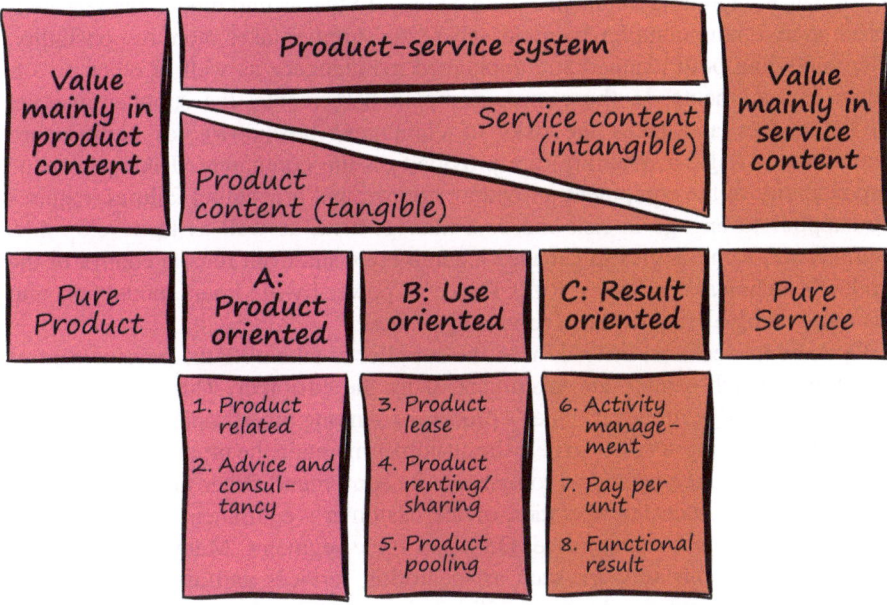

Fig. 1.5 The stages of the product-service system continuum (illustration by Annick Holland, adapted from Tukker, 2004)

Many researchers have tried to describe the characteristics of product-service systems through several models, frameworks, and schemes. Tukker's (2004) model shown in Fig. 1.5 is probably one of the most famous and widely used. Created to describe types of PSSs and their revenue models, working from left to right, this model shows a service transition. It also gives different perspectives (e.g., the role of the asset owner, the manufacturer, the operator, the service provider).

Many product-service system-based business models today are still product oriented, as companies are still geared to selling products and providing services during their lifecycle. In this case, services fall into two general areas: (1) maintenance services and (2) operational services. In both cases, services are usually bundled as a complete package in a service contract, where the customer and the supplier form a long-term relationship. The supplier still receives transactional revenues from the sale of the product. However, under this business model, instead of transactional onetime revenues for the services, recurring revenues are received for the bundled services. Often, both operations and maintenance services can be packed together.

Also, maintenance services fall into two different models. In the first model, maintenance is provided through a simple model based on a call-off contract with pre-agreed fees for parts and services, where the customer takes responsibility for performance, including unplanned maintenance. In the second model, the service is based upon a more complex scenario, where the supplier takes more responsibility, often including both planned and unplanned maintenance as well as other performance commitments. In these more complex agreements, the supplier receives use-based fees and takes the risks of equipment breakdown, as performance commitments (e.g., availability) are provided on the equipment. Taking over the responsibility of the equipment, providing uptime, and preventing failures, requires the supplier to engage in risk and cost management, as well as to develop new methods and technologies to enhance a continuous and even remote control of the product's technical conditions. Rolls-Royce's "power-by-the-hour" model falls into this more complex maintenance service agreement.

Operational services, instead, need the supplier to take over the management of operations, which usually are taken care of by the customer. This calls for more detailed knowledge of the customer's processes. Among others, operational services may include training services to help the customer maintain the product correctly and required maintenance personnel to manage the equipment. Other firms extend this, yet further, to include the operation of the customer's equipment, which is often called operations and maintenance (O&M) in some segments. Many hybrid models exist with operations support, such as mentoring services and asset management support, where the roles and responsibilities of the traditional manufacture/customer deviates considerably from the traditional relationships.

In the case of "use-oriented product-service system," the product is no longer sold to the customer, as its use is delivered to the customer, without the responsibilities of ownership. This means that the supplier does not sell its product; rather, both product and services are integrated into a package based on the actual usage or availability of the equipment to the customer. The supplier is fully responsible for the correct functioning of the product, since it still owns the product. In this situation, the supplier must have the financial resources to own the assets. Hilti provides a good example of this.

In a more sophisticated product-service system, such as a "result-oriented product-service system," the customer and supplier agree on a certain functionality or outcome, with the supplier maintaining full responsibility to deliver this.

1.2 Product-Service Systems and Servitization

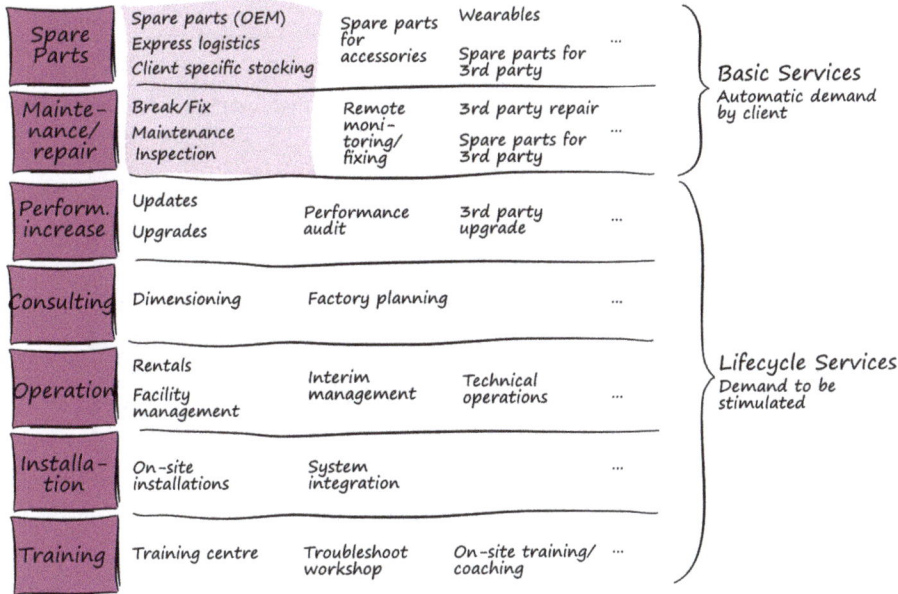

Fig. 1.6 Types of services: a set of basic services needed to keep equipment operational and different lifecycle services where demand needs to be stimulated (illustration by Annick Holland, adapted from Schmitt & Sipen, 2017)

Ownership of the equipment required for delivering the service remains with the supplier, so it is closely related to "use-oriented PSS." An example is the delivery of a "pleasant climate" as a service, instead of selling heating, ventilation, and cooling equipment.

Services can also be classified in relation to how their demand is created. Indeed, some of the services can be automatically demanded (e.g., planned inspections), whereas others require a callout service (unplanned events), and others need the owner or operator to be encouraged (e.g., training services or upgrades). However, too often, companies focus on the basic services without considering the product and/or customer lifecycle. Figure 1.6 provides a list of services that may be required over the operational life of the equipment, based on Schmitt and Sipen (2017).

A complementary perspective on Tukker's (2004) model is provided by Kowalkowski and Ulaga (2017), who consider the nature of the value proposition and the service recipient. Specifically, services can be classified by the supplier's promise to perform (input based) instead of the customer aiming to achieve a target (output based). Moreover, they can be oriented toward the supplier's goods instead of the customer's processes of the services, as shown in Fig. 1.7.

A further interesting perspective on product-service systems (PSSs) can come from considering a traditional product lifecycle, where there are many people providing many services to many different pieces of equipment or products (Fig. 1.8). During the operational life of a piece of equipment, spares, consumables,

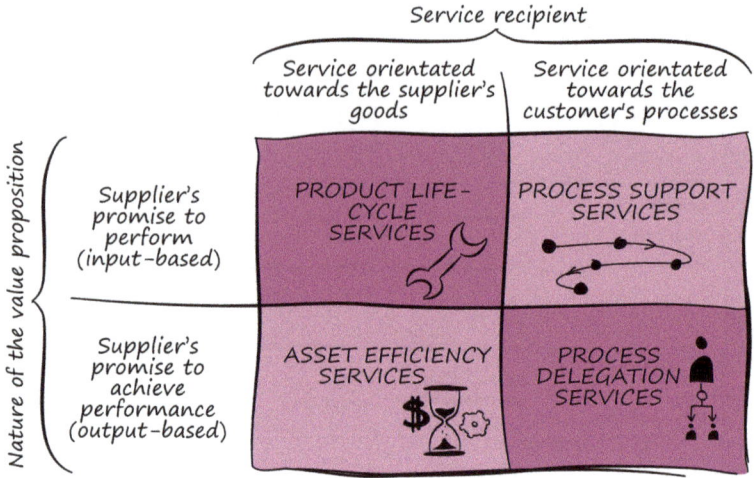

Fig. 1.7 Service classification (illustration by Annick Holland, adapted from Kowalkowski & Ulaga, 2017 and Kowalkowski & Witell, 2020)

and services are needed to ensure safe and reliable operation of the machine. Generally, these are based on a planned maintenance schedule; however, there are also unplanned events that can mean the plan has to change. Late in the operational cycle of the equipment, upgrades may be offered, which change the status and the capability of the equipment. This is in effect a very complex model.

Perspectives are always important, and with servitization it is fundamental to understand how they fit together. Figure 1.9 shows this for a coffee machine manufacturer (what we call the original equipment manufacturer or OEM) and its customer. The owner/operator's view is shown horizontally as the supply chain from beans to coffee. Here, the main value creation processes are based on transforming the coffee beans into a drink, which they sell. The coffee shop's key outcome (or purpose) is to provide good-quality coffee, and the OEM can support them in several different ways. The coffee machine manufacturer (OEM) can provide the following: consumables, spares, and maintenance when requested, machine process parameter monitoring to ensure consistency of coffee quality, and even fleet monitoring to allow optimization of machines based on production volumes.

Instead, the OEM's product perspective is shown as a vertical silo. Here, the owner of the coffee machine buys it to make coffee, which s/he sells. By considering the different perspectives and the different service classifications along with the detailed types of services, new value propositions can be imagined, as in the example here. Similar considerations can be made for trains, planes, and automobiles as well as ships, oil refineries, power plant, and photocopiers... *the different types of products with services and their markets are endless.*

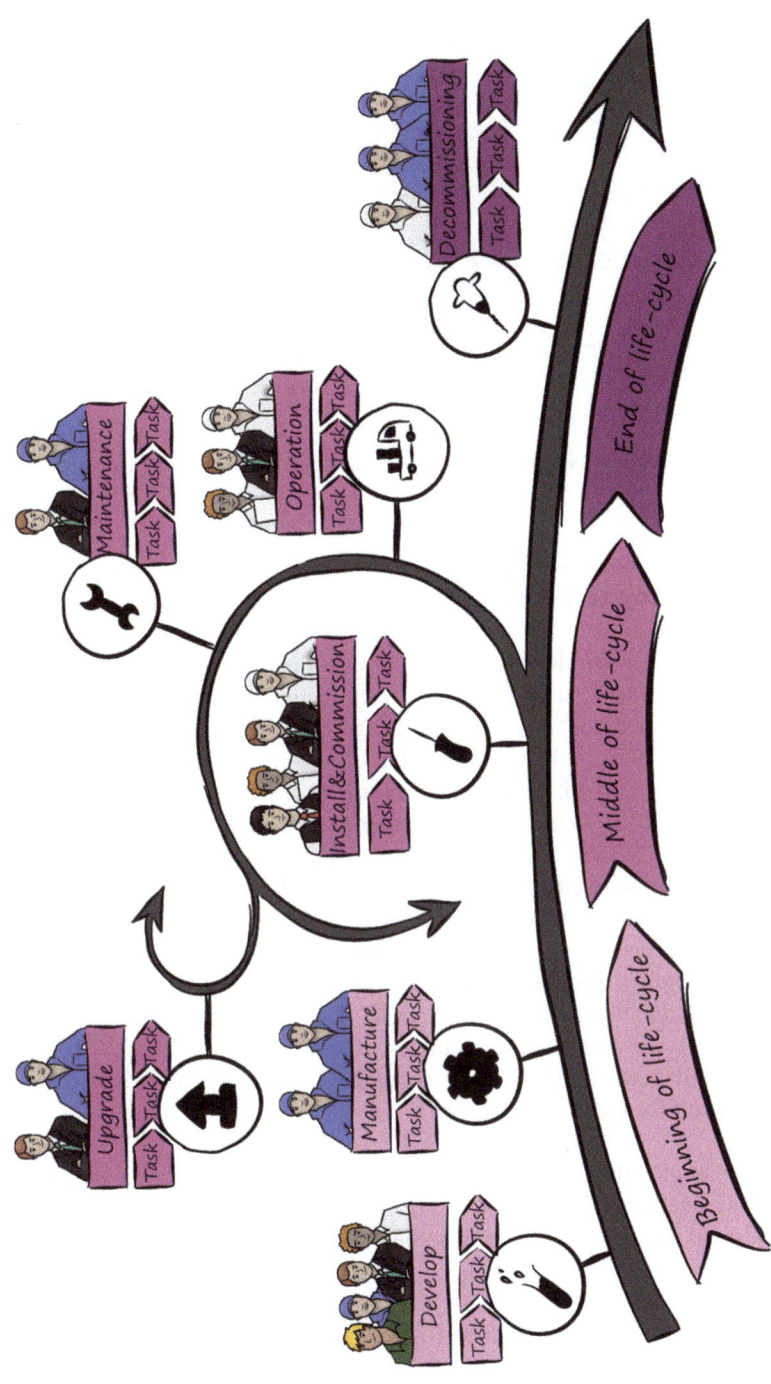

Fig. 1.8 The cradle-to-grave lifecycle showing many of the services needed (illustration by Annick Holland, adapted from West & Pascual, 2015 and West et al., 2020)

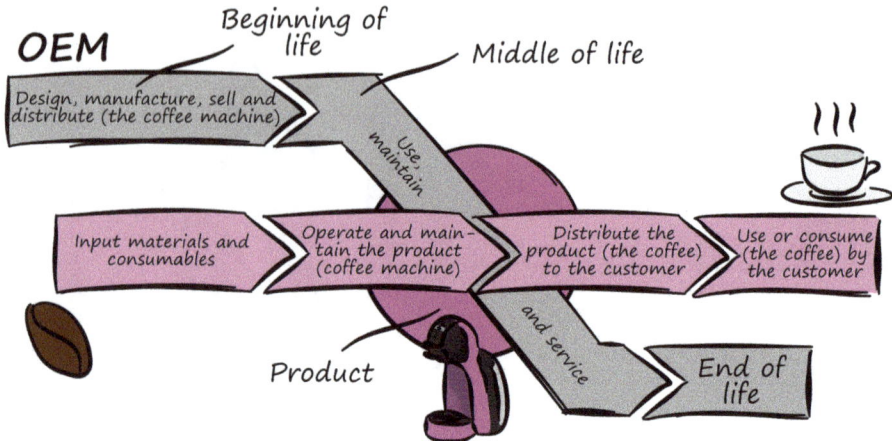

Fig. 1.9 Different perspectives: the operator's supply chain and the OEM's product silo (illustration by Annick Holland, authors' work)

1.3 The Journey to Services

The development of new services is not like new product development (NPD), and this is where the problem starts for many manufacturing firms. Indeed, service transformation creates a major disruptive change in a business, as it is really a journey that requires the implementation of a change management process. The barriers that firms face are both contextual (Dmitrijeva et al., 2020) and created from paradoxes (Brax, 2005; Kohtamäki et al., 2020) and involve both large and small firms (Confente et al., 2015). Strategically, senior management in a business likes the idea of services, because customers ask for them and because margins are usually higher than in traditional product sales. However, senior management generally makes this strategic decision without fully understanding how to overcome the barriers that could slow the journey into service. Strategy is often delivered through a set of loosely coordinated actions (Lütjen et al., 2017; Rabetino et al., 2017).

The journey to services is often bumpy. The Cambridge Service Alliance (Martinez et al., 2016) identified seven success factors that help improve the success of service transition for manufacturing firms:

1. Assess the market and internal readiness: making the shift to services means that all parties involved must be ready to change and understand the value of doing so.
2. Create the right strategic and cultural context: a service business is different to a product business and needs a completely new mindset to be instilled throughout the whole service ecosystem.
3. Build the structures and governance for services: firms need to make a clear commitment to services by creating properly empowered teams and the appropriate organizational structures.

4. Get the resources ready for service innovation and delivery: short- and long-term budgets need to acknowledge that services are very resource intensive and change over time.
5. Proactively manage engagement and trust: services are co-created and often co-delivered with customers who are active participants in the service journey.
6. Develop and embed service processes: firms delivering services must experiment and adapt, and they need processes that enable them to do that.
7. Optimize services and communicate best practices: services rely on continuous innovation and so require a "best-practice" mindset.

These are seven statements to assess the strategic aspirations of the firm, yet they do not necessarily address the barriers that delay, slow, or prevent a product-oriented firm from shifting to services.

1.4 Learning to Understand Complex Systems

Some terms we use in this book, such as "users, end-users, installers, distributors, owners, and manufacturers," come from the language that is used in many manufacturing firms (Fig. 1.10). This is because many manufacturers have complex relationships with the people who benefit from the products they make and the

Fig. 1.10 The community of users, end-users, customers, owners, and manufacturers (illustration by Annick Holland, authors' work)

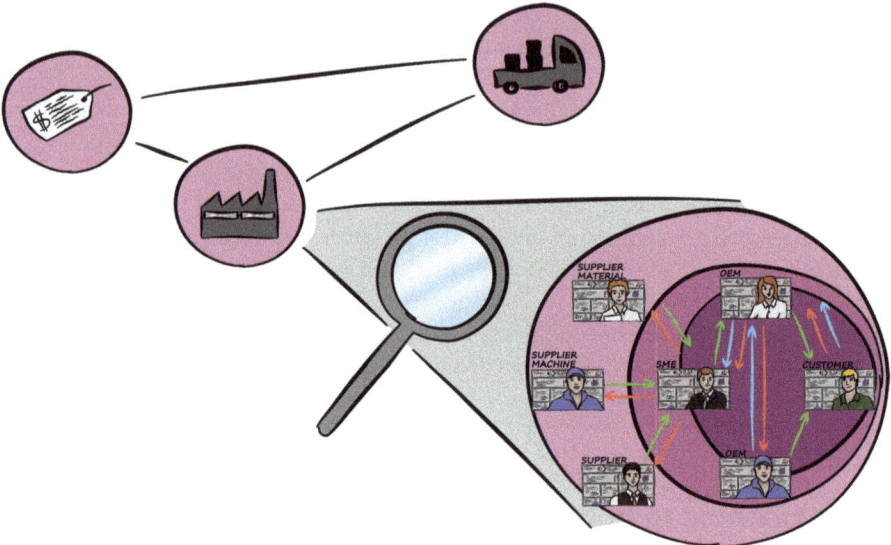

Fig. 1.11 Learning to understand complex B2B environments (illustration by Annick Holland, authors' work)

services they deliver. Therefore, we have tried to be clear with the language we have used to define the people involved (the actors) and their roles, to make our discussion and presentations unambiguous.

Using the terms and defining the roles that each actor takes will help you to gain better insights into the services and products you are delivering. We have shown this in Fig. 1.11 for a project where we were learning about the customer (the installer) and the end-user (the firms who own, operate or maintain the equipment or system). The language in business-to-business (B2B) environments is often challenging, so it is really important we are clear about the terms we use, to help avoid misunderstandings:

- **Ecosystem** – the whole environment around the company, its suppliers, its customers, its contractors, installers, etc.
- **Actors** – every person in the ecosystem (e.g., within supply chain or network, etc.)
- **Avatars** – personifications that represent all the machines in the ecosystem as people.
- **Stakeholders** (indirect and direct) – the people taking part in the interaction or process either directly or indirectly.
- **Beneficiaries** (indirect and direct) – the actors who benefit from the integration either directly or indirectly.
- **Users** – some of the stakeholders and some of the beneficiaries that may be direct users of the products and services.

1.5 Seven Barriers Stopping Firms from Moving to Services

Academic research (Hou & Neely, 2013) has identified seven types of barriers (or categories of barriers) that are important for manufacturing firms to overcome if they want to develop and deliver new services. Others (e.g., Alghisi & Saccani, 2015; Martinez et al., 2010; West et al., 2018) have provided more details about the barriers and how firms overcome them. The relative importance of each category is shown in Fig. 1.12. In this book, each of the categories has been broken down into its constituent barriers, detailing problems and difficulties that have been experienced by companies during their journeys. Then, the relative importance of each of these barriers has been defined by the business community we researched (West et al., 2019). Overcoming these barriers is a change management process that requires development of people, capabilities, and processes. It is important to pay close attention to the many potholes that can trip up the unwary. To deliver a strategy, individual managerial actions are necessary to overcome the barriers (Lenka et al., 2018; Lütjen et al., 2017). Therefore, for each of the barriers, case examples have been used to describe how managers have approached the problem. Quotes from managers add more depth to the cases and support the lessons learned. Where appropriate, we have suggested tools that can help you to analyze your situation.

Before considering each of the barriers individually and developing a service excellence roadmap, it is worth a short detour to look at some of the literature and research that have been published.

Customers – This relates to external servitization barriers that need to be overcome. The critical aspects here are linked to sales and gaining access to customers or end-users – both are closely associated with the sales process and the role of "sales" within a firm. This barrier can be experienced through heterogeneous demand (Vandermerwe & Rada, 1988), together with lack of customers' trust (White et al., 1999) and control over their behaviors (Heiskanen & Jalas, 2003), making it

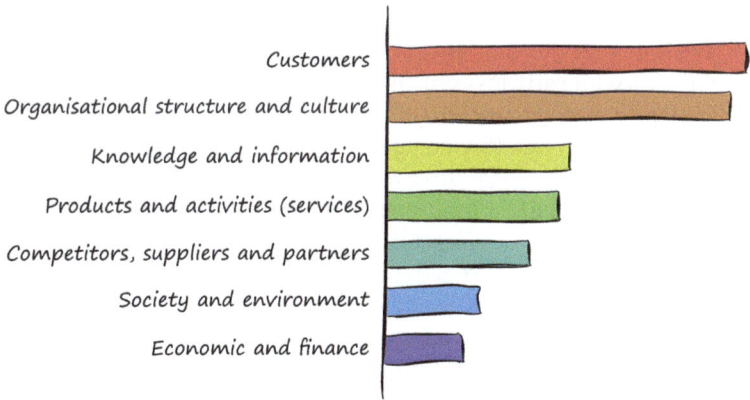

Fig. 1.12 Relative importance of the seven key barriers (illustration by Annick Holland, adapted from West et al., 2018)

difficult to get cooperation and acceptance from customers (Vandermerwe & Rada, 1988).

Organizational structure and culture – This barrier deals with internal themes, as servitization business models often face issues from "the management" as well as R&D or NPD. There are often preconceived thoughts and resistance to change (Vandermerwe and Rada 1988), which make a transition to services difficult. To these are added conflicts among different departments and different hierarchies in organizations. Frequently, the lack of service-based organizational structure (White et al., 1999) and service-oriented culture (Mont, 2002) hinders the transformation process.

Knowledge and information – These are both important in a service business, where much of the knowledge is tacit information (Alghisi & Saccani, 2014) that is, therefore, difficult to convert into written instructions. A lack of expertise (Brax, 2005) and innovation ability (Kindström et al., 2013), together with difficulties in knowledge and information management (Vandermerwe & Rada, 1988), complicates the understanding of customer demands and product-service properties (Cook et al., 2002; Mont, 2002).

Products and activities – These were considered less important than the way knowledge and information is shared. On one level, this was surprising, as firms often focus more on their products and activities. In the literature, the lack of competences (Cook et al. 2002) and infrastructures (Maxwell et al., 2006), together with difficulties in designing service packages (or scenarios) and in measuring them (White et al., 1999), makes service design and management more complex.

Competitors, suppliers, and partners – Consolidating the ecosystem is an obstacle for many firms as they discover they are active within complex and competitive environments, involving different actors. This complex multi-actor environment creates difficulties in coordination and cooperation among the increased number of players (Mont, 2002; Vandermerwe & Rada, 1988).

Economics and finance – Firms need to learn to share benefits and obligations from a win-win perspective. From the economic-financial viewpoint, management is often searching for new revenue models, or ways to report service sales and margins that link to the firm's servitization performance. Often, there is an associated lack of financial competence for early investments (DiPeso, 2000), high risks (Stremersch & Frambach, 2001), to manage new forms of product-services, unexpected costs, and difficulties in pricing services (Steinberger et al., 2009), leading to ineffective and unprofitable service solutions that drive companies to abandon the business.

Society and environment – Firms often found it hard to move forward from their prior position of delivering services for free. Also, the "think local, act global" approach that was pioneered by ABB in the 1990s remains an issue for firms as they work to both standardize and localize their services. Difficulties in achieving these benefits, which largely depend on circumstances (Mont, 2002), are often based on lack of policy, weak infrastructure support (DiPeso, 2000), and limited incentives (White et al., 1999). All of which undermine managers' confidence by encouraging them to leave the service transformation process.

1.6 Further Reading

For those who would like to go deeper into the subject, the book written by Tim Baines and Howard Lightfoot *Made to Serve: How Manufacturers can Compete Through Servitization and Product Service Systems* will give you more ideas about how and why manufacturing firms compete with services (Baines et al. 2009; Baines & Lightfood, 2013). *Practices and Tools for Servitization*, by Kohtamäki et al. (2018), also provides excellent reading on this topic with insights from many different academics and practitioners. *Service Strategy in Action: A Practical Guide for Growing Your B2B Service and Solution Business*, by Kowalkowski and Wolfgang (2017), is another useful industrial book written and complements this book, as it is a strategic book rather than an operational one.

Other useful books include *This Is Service Design (Thinking/Doing)* Stinkdorn et al. (2018), cowritten by Marc Stickdorn (https://www.thisisservicedesigndoing.com), which can help but initially can be a little remote from an industrial perspective. The same can be said about *An Introduction to Service Design* by Lara Penin (Penin, 2018). Nevertheless, we would recommend buying one or all of them as they support the tools. These are listed and explained in detail in the tools section at the end of this book with useful cases. The Service Design Tools website (https://servicedesigntools.org) is another good resource to visit.

The Service-Dominant Logic by Vargo and Lusch (2008) is a concept that has been developed from marketing theory over many years to describe or explain value creation, through exchange, among various configurations of actors. It has not been described in depth in this book; nevertheless, some readers may spot links to it in the cases and may wish to read more.

References

Alghisi, A., & Saccani, N. (2014). Development of a Knowledge Management framework to support installed base information management practices in a servitized context. In M. Toivonen (Ed.), *Proceedings of the 24th International Conference of RESER "Services and New Societal Challenges: Innovation for Sustainable Growth and Welfare"* (pp. 28–42). Helsinki, Finland.

Alghisi, A., & Saccani, N. (2015). Internal and external alignment in the servitization journey-overcoming the challenges. *Production Planning and Control*. https://doi.org/10.1080/09537287.2015.1033496.

Baines, T., & Lightfood, H. (2013). *Made to serve: How manufacturers can compete through servitization and product service systems*. London: Wiley.

Baines, T., Lightfoot, H., Peppard, J., Johnson, M., Tiwari, A., Shehab, E., & Swink, M. (2009). Towards an operations strategy for product-centric servitization. *International Journal of Operations and Production Management*. https://doi.org/10.1108/01443570910953603.

Brax, S. (2005). A manufacturer becoming service provider - Challenges and a paradox. *Managing Service Quality*. https://doi.org/10.1108/09604520510585334.

Confente, I., Buratti, A., & Russo, I. (2015). The role of servitization for small firms: Drivers versus barriers. *International Journal of Entrepreneurship and Small Business, 26*(3), 312–331. https://doi.org/10.1504/IJESB.2015.072394.

Cook, L. S., Bowen, D. E., Chase, R. B., Dasu, S., Stewart, D. M., & Tansik, D. A. (2002). Human issues in service design. *Journal of Operations Management*. https://doi.org/10.1016/S0272-6963(01)00094-8.

DiPeso, J. (2000). P2: Putting environmental issues in a new light. *Environmental Quality Management*. https://doi.org/10.1002/1520-6483(200023)10:1<13::AID-TQEM3>3.0.CO;2-C.

Dmitrijeva, J., Schroeder, A., Ziaee Bigdeli, A., & Baines, T. (2020). Context matters: How internal and external factors impact servitization. *Production Planning and Control*. https://doi.org/10.1080/09537287.2019.1699195.

Gebauer, H. (2007). The logic for increasing service revenue in product manufacturing companies. *International Journal of Services and Operations Management*. https://doi.org/10.1504/IJSOM.2007.013462.

Heiskanen, E., & Jalas, M. (2003). Can services lead to radical eco-efficiency improvements? - A review of the debate and evidence. *Corporate Social Responsibility and Environmental Management*. https://doi.org/10.1002/csr.46.

Hou, J., & Neely, A. (2013). Barriers of servitization: Results of a systematic literature review. In Baines, T., Clegg, B., & Harrison, D. (Eds.), *Spring Servitization Conference. Proceedings of the 2013 Spring Servitization conference "Servitization in the multi-organisation enterprise"* (pp. 189–195).

Kindström, D., Kowalkowski, C., & Sandberg, E. (2013). Enabling service innovation: A dynamic capabilities approach. *Journal of Business Research*. https://doi.org/10.1016/j.jbusres.2012.03.003.

Kohtamäki, M., Baines, T., Rabetino, R., & Bigdeli, A. Z. (2018). *Practices and tools for servitization: Managing service transition* (pp. 1–429). Springer International. https://doi.org/10.1007/978-3-319-76517-4.

Kohtamäki, M., Einola, S., & Rabetino, R. (2020). Exploring servitization through the paradox lens: Coping practices in servitization. *International Journal of Production Economics*. https://doi.org/10.1016/j.ijpe.2020.107619.

Kowalkowski, C., Gebauer, H., & Oliva, R. (2017). Service growth in product firms: Past, present, and future. *Industrial Marketing Management*. https://doi.org/10.1016/j.indmarman.2016.10.015.

Kowalkowski, C., & Ulaga, W. (2017). *Service strategy in action: A practical guide for growing your B2B service and solution*. Business: Service Strategy Press.

Kowalkowski, C., & Ulaga, W. (2017). *Service strategy in action: A practical guide for growing your B2B service and solution business*. Service Strategy Press. https://www.amazon.com/Service-Strategy-Action-Practical-Solution/dp/069281910X

Kowalkowski, C., & Witell, L. (2020). Typologies and frameworks in service innovation. In E. Bridges & K. Frowler (Eds.), *The Routledge handbook of service research insights and ideas*. Routledge.

Lenka, S., Parida, V., Sjödin, D. R., & Wincent, J. (2018). Exploring the microfoundations of servitization: How individual actions overcome organizational resistance. *Journal of Business Research*. https://doi.org/10.1016/j.jbusres.2017.11.021.

Lütjen, H., Tietze, F., & Schultz, C. (2017). Service transitions of product-centric firms: An explorative study of service transition stages and barriers in Germany's energy market. *International Journal of Production Economics*. https://doi.org/10.1016/j.ijpe.2017.03.021.

Martinez, V., Bastl, M., Kingston, J., & Evans, S. (2010). Challenges in transforming manufacturing organisations into product-service providers. *Journal of Manufacturing Technology Management*. https://doi.org/10.1108/17410381011046571.

References

Martinez, V., Neely, A., Urmetzer, F., Allison, N., Lund, M., Buckler, T., Leinster-Evans, S., Pennington G., & Smith, D. (2016). *Seven critical success factors in the shift to services*. University of Cambridge, Institute of manufacturing, Cambridge Service Alliance. Accessed January 6, 2020, from https://cambridgeservicealliance.eng.cam.ac.uk/resources/Downloads/Monthly%20Papers/SevenCriticalSuccessFactorsintheShifttoServices_ExecBriefing.pdf

Mathieu, V. (2001). Product services: From a service supporting the product to a service supporting the client. *Journal of Business and Industrial Marketing*. https://doi.org/10.1108/08858620110364873.

Maxwell, D., Sheate, W., & van der Vorst, R. (2006). Functional and systems aspects of the sustainable product and service development approach for industry. *Journal of Cleaner Production*. https://doi.org/10.1016/j.jclepro.2006.01.028.

Mont, O. K. (2002). Clarifying the concept of product-service system. *Journal of Cleaner Production*. https://doi.org/10.1016/S0959-6526(01)00039-7.

Penin, L. (2018). *An introduction to service design: Designing the invisible paperback*. London: Bloomsbury Arts.

Rabetino, R., Kohtamäki, M., & Gebauer, H. (2017). Strategy map of servitization. *International Journal of Production Economics*. https://doi.org/10.1016/j.ijpe.2016.11.004.

Schmiedeberg. A, Strähle, O., & Bendig, O. (2010). *Wachstumsmotor Service (Service as a growth motor)*. Bain & Company. Accessed January 6, 2021 from https://www.bain.com/insights/wachstumsmotor-service/

Schmitt, P., & Sipen, S. (2017). *Services for capital equipment*. Roland Berger. Private email.

Steinberger, J. K., van Niel, J., & Bourg, D. (2009). Profiting from megawatts: Reducing absolute consumption and emissions through a performance-based energy economy. *Energy Policy*. https://doi.org/10.1016/j.enpol.2008.08.030.

Stinkdorn, M., Edgar Hormess, M., Lawrence, A., & Schneider, J. (2018). *This is service design doing*. New York: O'Reilly.

Stremersch, S., & Frambach, R. T. (2001). The purchasing of full-service contracts: Maintenance market. *Industrial Marketing Management, 30*(1), 1–12.

Tukker, A. (2004). Eight types of product-service system: Eight ways to sustainability? Experiences from suspronet. *Business Strategy and the Environment*. https://doi.org/10.1002/bse.414.

Vandermerwe, S., & Rada, J. (1988). Servitization of business: Adding value by adding services. *European Management Journal*. https://doi.org/10.1016/0263-2373(88)90033-3.

Vargo, S. L., & Lusch, R. F. (2008). Service-dominant logic: Continuing the evolution. *Journal of the Academy of Marketing Science*. https://doi.org/10.1007/s11747-007-0069-6.

West, S., & Gaiardelli, P. (2016). Driving the servitization transformation through change management: lessons learnt from industrial cases. In T. Baines, J. Burton, D. Harrison, & J. Zolkiewski (Eds.), *Proceedings of the 2016 Spring Servitization Conference 2016 "Servitization: Shift, Transform, Grow"*. Manchester Business School.

West, S., Gaiardelli, P., Bigdeli, A., & Baines, T. (2018). Exploring operational challenges for servitization: An European survey. In A. Bigdeli, T. Frandsen, J. Raja, & T. Baines (Eds.), *Proceedings of 2018 Spring Servitization Conference "Driving Competitiveness through Servitization"* (pp. 9–17).

West, S. Gaiardelli, P., & Mathews, A. (2019). Overcoming the challenges of change management associated with servitization: Lessons from 20 practical cases. In Bigdeli, Kowalkowski, Kindström, and Baines (Eds.), *Proceedings of 2018 Spring Servitization Conference "The Spring Servitization Conference 2019: Delivering Services Growth in the Digital Era"* (pp. 9–17).

West, S., & Pascual, A. (2015). The use of equipment life-cycle analysis to identify new service opportunities. In T. Baines & D. Harrison (Eds.), *Proceedings of the 2015 Spring Servitization Conference 2016*. Aston, UK: Aston Business School.

West, S., Schmitt, P., & Siepen, S. A. (2014). A comparative assessment of the service cultures of industrial businesses in the DACH region of Europe and their impact on business performance. In *Proceedings of the 2014 EUROMA Conference "Operations Management in an Innovation Economy"*, Palermo June 2014.

West, S., Stoll, O., & Mueller-Csernetzky, P. (2020). 'Avatar journey mapping' for manufacturing firms to reveal smart-service opportunities over the product life-cycle. *International Journal of Business Environment*. https://doi.org/10.1504/IJBE.2020.110906.

White, A., Stoughton, M., & Feng, L. (1999). Servicizing: The quiet transition to extended product responsibility. *Table*, (May), 1–97.

Open Access This chapter is licensed under the terms of the Creative Commons Attribution 4.0 International License (http://creativecommons.org/licenses/by/4.0/), which permits use, sharing, adaptation, distribution and reproduction in any medium or format, as long as you give appropriate credit to the original author(s) and the source, provide a link to the Creative Commons license and indicate if changes were made.

The images or other third party material in this chapter are included in the chapter's Creative Commons license, unless indicated otherwise in a credit line to the material. If material is not included in the chapter's Creative Commons license and your intended use is not permitted by statutory regulation or exceeds the permitted use, you will need to obtain permission directly from the copyright holder.

Overcoming the Barriers to Service Excellence

2.1 Customers

Customers are essential in any business, but they become even more critical for service businesses because of service relationship. There are many different types of customers. This calls for the necessity to creating service business able to adapt to different needs through appropriate solution and flexible operations (Fig. 2.1).

To compound the problem, customers can change their behavior over time. As they become more familiar with the equipment, they may move from a situation where an inexperienced customer asks for "do-it-for-me" services to one closer to a more experienced customer asking to "do-it-with-me" or even a confident customer saying "I'll do it myself" with supplies of consumables or spare parts. Customers can also be cost-focused; some may demand long-term contracts, and others buy transactionally but always from the same supplier firm, while yet others shop around for the best deal. Essential differences from manufacturing are that it is vital to look for customer problems and find ways to improve performance for them and cooperate in the solution's delivery, to maximize value.

> ...we look for our customers' problems... we moved our target to offer service as a product, to what customers value...

Again, this can be very different from the standardized equipment sales approach to customers. Therefore, it emerges crucial to find the best way to connect with customer, which often requires a step-by-step and gradual approach.

> ...we are well aligned with key customers. We do co-creation ... to enter the unknown and test/pilot new offers before selling them more widely...

The main customer-related barriers from the survey are shown in Fig. 2.2. In general, the critical aspects here are linked to sales and gaining access to customers

Fig. 2.1 Learning to overcome the barriers on our journey is challenging (illustration by Annick Holland, authors' work)

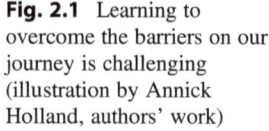

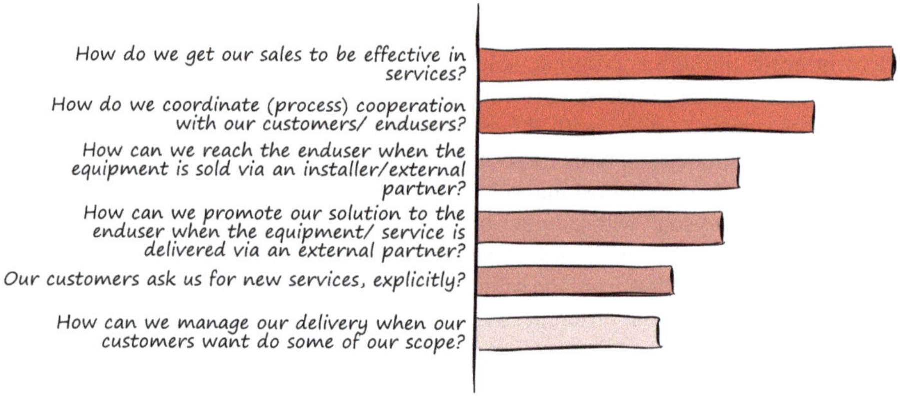

Fig. 2.2 Relative importance of the "customer"-related barriers (illustration by Annick Holland, adapted from West et al., 2018)

and end-users. In the first two instances, the barriers are closely associated with the sales process and the role of "sales" within a firm. This is also true for the third and fourth most critical aspects, which reflect the difficulties equipment suppliers encounter in developing their sales strategies when their end-user is served via an installer or a third party. Finally, it emerges that service companies face barriers when the customer is not aware of what is possible or is unable to give the right importance to the services and the related delivery process.

Problems with customer motivation, in all circumstances, may be due to the following: a lack of awareness of the importance of services, the need to bring out their role and weight in business decisions, or, simply, personal reasons. These are

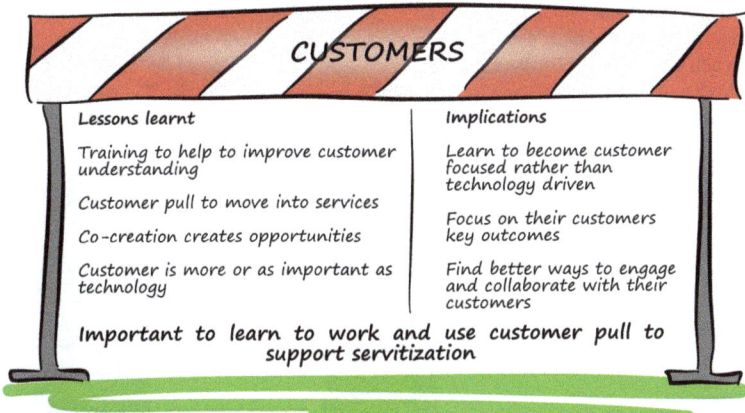

Fig. 2.3 The lessons and implications for overcoming customer barriers (illustration by Annick Holland, adapted from West et al., 2018)

difficulties that may affect the company internally, its partners or the customer/end-user.

One simple way to overcome these barriers was proposed by some service managers who suggested strengthening the service force at the expense of the sales force. On the other hand, some stimulated participation by introducing incentive systems that look at the joint results of sales and services. In other cases, the service process was activated from the moment of sale (the service contract is always linked to the sales contract). In other cases, to stimulate external partners, the winning strategy was to take away customers' risk by paying them directly if service is inefficient. In this way, the company demonstrates its willingness to create a win-win relationship based upon mutual trust and partnership, stimulating the partners to share information about customers and promote the product-service. Figure 2.3 describes some of the lessons learned and the implications from the interviews.

Cooperation with customers can enable new forms of service offers and, in some cases, this comes from direct customer demand or "pull." However, some firms are too slow to accept these requests, which highlights the cultural issues around customer co-creation and co-delivery. Sales training for all should be considered important, as it helps employees become more customer-centric and gives them a better understanding of customer values and outcomes. Training also creates a common language to help employees understand customers. What this means is that firms who want to make the switch to services should consider:

- Training staff to understand customers.
- Encouraging the sales force and service staff through incentives.

Fig. 2.4 Learning to deal with different perspectives is important when dealing with services (illustration by Annick Holland, authors' work)

- Listening to customer requests to move into services.
- Promoting co-creation to create new service opportunities.
- Thinking of the customer as equally or even more important than technology.

This can be a big leap for a product-focused firm as the firm has to consider the situation from different perspectives (Fig. 2.4). Part of the jump can be made by the firm considering itself a "solution" business rather than a traditional product business. This allows the firm to understand its customers better, enabling them to identify triggers for services and create better balance between the customer, product, and service aspects. To help you better understand how to overcome the barriers, we offer insights from cases. The barriers indicated by the service leaders are (in order of importance):

1. How do we get our sales to be effective in services?
2. How do we coordinate with our customers/end-users?
3. How can we reach the end-user when the equipment is sold via an installer/external partner?
4. How can we promote our solution to the end-user when the equipment/service is delivered via an external partner?
5. How do we react when our customers ask us for new services, explicitly?
6. How can we manage our delivery when our customers want to do some of our scope?

2.1.1 How Do We Get Our Sales Team to Be Effective in Services?

Sales managers and the sales processes for a service business are not the same as for an equipment business – there are different customers to sell to and various value propositions to offer. Why do many firms use the same sales managers and processes to sell services and are then surprised when they achieve poor results?

Often, sales managers who work from product lists find the move to sell solutions difficult. Leaders in services suggest that service sales is a complex process, yet it can become a great growth engine for the business (Fig. 2.5). The complexity comes from the context that is composed of the market structures, the customers, the OEMs, and the technologies. The sales have to be flexible and learn to operate in this environment and learn to offer advanced solutions the customers did not (directly) asked for! Managing this complexity effectively means living the customer experience together. Only in this way you can understand what your customer wants and build valuable solutions.

> ...we need salespeople to spend more time with our customers than in the office...

> ...our sales managers need to build solutions for our customers, we are no longer box movers...

GE Power services, for example, separate sales into three main groups: new equipment, contractual services, and transactional services. The system can work efficiently because each business group has different people and different processes to help close deals. This approach is not for every firm as it is resource intensive, yet it highlights the importance of separating the sales processes. To be effective, it is important to first understand what customers do (their job-to-be-done, pains, and

Fig. 2.5 Using service as a growth engine for sales is important for the transformation (illustration by Annick Holland, authors' work)

gains) and then understand what they value and what channels they prefer to use. Some channels may be self-service or automatic reordering; others may be via a local partner for some services and direct to the original supplier for more complex services. Other options to support service sales include separating sales of spares and field service sales and uncoupling the ordering process from relationship management and from new equipment sales. This is particularly important where sales do not go directly to the "end-user." Finally, a highly trained sales team with modern tools to help them track relationships is critical to effective sales.

The two cases that follow highlighted that managers' need to map out the sales process as a team so that they can identify and understand the actors who are involved in the buying process. This will help them to better understand the buying process, know when different actors are active stakeholders in the process, and know who to influence and when.

The tools that help to explore the barriers and to build actions to overcome them are:

- Customer jobs-to-be-done.
- Customer value proposition.
- Detailed empathy card.
- Job-to-be-done insights.
- Job-to-be-done outcomes.
- Keeping focused.
- Personas.
- Service blueprint.
- Visual journey map – high level.
- Visual journey map – detail level.

Details of the individual tools are given in Chap. 3.

> **Case 1 Learning to Capture Relevant Operational Information to Support Pro-active Sales**
>
> The original equipment manufacturer (OEM) had the advantage that premature failure of the equipment they supplied would cause significant operational problems due to reduced engine fuel efficiency. This meant the shipowners were careful about the procurement and servicing of the equipment and returned to the OEM for service time after time.
>
> The need was to ensure the OEM had a proactive sales team, always in contact with the owners and operators of the equipment and able to keep the end-users and owners up-to-date with current knowledge and information.
>
> Proactive sales mean keeping in contact with the owners and operators. Given the long operational life of the equipment, this means developing long-term relationships; however, the end-users or shipowners can change over the

(continued)

life of the ship. This means that to build a proactive sales program, the service supplier has to maintain many relationships as well as understanding the operational and maintenance strategies applied by the different parties over time. Additionally, the OEM has to keep on top of the installed base data, including the operational hours and the maintenance history of the machines.

An installed base database was created and maintained; this has become the repository for the operational and maintenance history of the machine. Alongside this, a customer relationship management (CRM) system was created. By linking the two systems, it was possible to create service sales triggers to sustain sales while supporting the customers to keep the machines in optimal condition. Sales were instructed to make a minimum number of sales visits each year to keep the owners and end-users up-to-date on the technology and on recommended maintenance regimens. Without having service contracts in place, these basic steps improved sales for the business by enabling the whole sales team to take a more proactive approach.

Case 2 Splitting Sales Teams to Focus on Either New Equipment or Service

The firm made high-value equipment used in the production of pharmaceuticals. The equipment was sold with a 2-year warranty, so the operator (the pharma firm/customer) of the equipment had to undertake only routine maintenance tasks – replacing consumable items and cleaning the equipment. The sales managers were responsible for sales of both the equipment and the services for an individual customer. "One point of contact" was the commercial approach that had been adopted.

Services, such as routine checks and maintenance, were often given away as part of the equipment sale for the warranty period. This left the customers with low-price expectations of the service business. It also reinforced the position of services as a team that limited the firm's warranty exposure.

After the warranty period, customers were asking for services; however, the sales managers saw their value as too low, and the effort involved was considered too high. Due to this, service opportunities were often lost, and customer expectations were left unfulfilled.

The sales of services were separated from the sales process for new equipment. Service sales teams were created, and they supported the new equipment sales by providing services during the warranty period and focusing on sales of services post-warranty, either via a service contract or as transactions, depending on the customer's preference. There was a risk of conflict between equipment sales and service sales, so senior management was

(continued)

> involved in agreeing on the rules that prevented equipment sales from providing spares bundled with the initial product sales.
>
> New equipment sales accused service of "ripping off customers" with their service prices. This was really due to the margins generated by the two halves of the business. They said that the customer would not pay the prices for the services. The customers were buying at the prices and the separation of sales responsibility lead to customers buying service contracts to cover the warranty period as well as the post warranty period.
>
> The post warranty period generated more value for the firm because the service sales responsibility led the sales manager for service to use the installed base of equipment to increase the sales opportunities.

2.1.2 How Do We Coordinate with Our Customers/End-users?

Service managers need to learn to understand their customers' (and customers' customers) businesses and employees to cooperate effectively with them. There are many different people who they need to coordinate with in both their own firm and the customer's firm, and this makes the process complex to orchestrate. Often, time is not made available for what can be considered project management tasks that are then poorly managed by the sales team. Customer relationship management (CRM) tools provide information on the contacts but do not often link them up so that it is impossible to understand the customer's process well enough. This is a particular problem where there are equipment installers between the OEM and the end-user's company (Fig. 2.6).

All firms have problems with coordination and most fail to view this activity as a core service role. When facing such barrier, it is important to understand both the internal and the external processes at the customer. Mapping out the whole business ecosystem makes more knowledge about people and their roles within the customer firm. This helps with service sales as much as with service execution and prevent errors (like spares being sent to the procurement office rather than the operational site).

> ...we need to understand our customers' process and work with theirs rather than ours...

> ...we need clarity with roles and responsibilities on both sides...

Having clearer views of the customer's process also helps with basic issues, like getting invoices paid on time.

What is interesting here is that the supplier has to provide service to the customer and vice versa. In effect, all parties support each other. Because of this, you can use customer journey mapping to understand the web of relationships much better. Working on a map of their journey together with a customer is really powerful, as

Fig. 2.6 Coordinating different actors is important to achieve the outcomes (illustration by Annick Holland, authors' work)

the customer is often unsure of their actual processes or the consequences of their actions. Approaches (e.g., responsibility assignment matrix or RACI matrix) can also be borrowed from project management. These can help define roles and responsibilities during the execution phase and also in sales.

The lessons from the two cases are that not all sales managers can make the transition to selling services, even with training. Training and coaching are needed to improve the effectiveness of the sales team and should be supported by sales tools that help keep the sales managers on track.

The tools that help to explore these barriers and build actions to overcome them are:

- Case/actor matrix.
- Customer jobs-to-be-done.
- Customer value proposition.
- Ecosystem mapping.
- Empathy maps.
- Personas.
- Service blueprint.
- Visual journey map – high level.
- Visual journey map – detail level.

Details of the individual tools are given in Chap. 3.

Case 3 Learning to Identify Customers' Service Trigger Points
The sales approach in this firm was reactive rather than proactive. The customer's site engineers wanted to understand the budget implications during their budgeting planning process, but the supplier was unwilling to provide budget figures due to the risk of competitors finding out their prices – which somehow always happened. Turning up too late to influence the service budgeting process resulted in the customer being unaware of the cost for the service or the upgrade. This meant that even if the work was tendered for, it may not be done. So, the firm lost sales at worst or margins at best. This was very frustrating as the firm could have won the work if they had known early enough in the process.

Several actions helped improve the proactivity of service support. The first was to provide an estimate of the annual maintenance spend on the equipment based on a set of clear and simple assumptions, which was not easy to achieve. The second step was to make better use of the installed base information to provide a forecast of maintenance requirements based on actual operational data. The third step was to provide benchmark budget costs for specific maintenance interventions (with a band of tolerance) based on the expected cost of maintenance. Finally, all service sales managers were expected to meet with their customers during the budgeting process and to support the early scoping of maintenance activities with each customer.

Creating a benchmark cost of ownership model was not easy and took time. Many customers argued about the actual costs and the frequency of the maintenance, others suggested that the costs were wrong. The conversion of the cost of ownership into a benchmarked cost was tough, as it required the development of benchmarks that a range of owners could use in their budgeting. One owner requested that the firm provide a service contract, based on the basis of the cost of ownership, that included all scheduled maintenance and component replacement.

Using the installed base to provide a market forecast plus the cost of ownership information, the sales managers could be given reliable sales targets based on real data. The more accurate the operational plan of the equipment, the more detail the firm knew about the maintenance triggers for the equipment. The accurate plan also helped with the identification of upgrade options.

Having a catalog for the interventions (with tolerances) provided budget support to customers, helping to ensure sufficient money was budgeted for the work and helping customers to see the value.

Case 4 Learning to Understand Its Customers' Buying Process

Often, this firm only entered the sales process with a potential customer when it was asked to bid for work. They had no idea who was involved in the buying process, only that the service purchase had to be bid for and that three to five other companies would be asked to provide a quote to service the equipment that the firm sold to the customer. This created some frustration as some in the firm considered that only they could maintain the equipment correctly.

Actually, the service sales manager had good contacts with the customers' maintenance teams, and the equipment sales teams generally had better contact with customers' procurement teams. The sales managers did not talk to each other, and the OEM firm did not understand the bidding process for service work or how the bids were assessed by the customer. There were processes and people that were not known or understood.

With the help of the researchers, the company journey-mapped the tendering process of several of the firm's customers. This mapping started with the initial trigger for the tendering process and identified who started it and why. The team then followed and mapped this journey along the customer's buying process until the tender was awarded at the start of the execution phase. The team identified all the direct and indirect contacts inside and outside the customer company and created personas for all these people, or actors, to better understand the actions behind the process. The team then started to identify new hidden actors in the buying process and to understand their impact on the decision-making process. LinkedIn helped with this as it provided insights to "who knew who," although it was rather like detective work.

The team actually created a new tool to help the sales mangers close deals. The existing CRM system did not provide the details on the buying process because this journey-mapping found that the customer's buying process started before they put it out for tender. The team identified new people in the buying process, what drove them and how to influence them. Using a set of templates, an updated toolbox was built for the sale managers to help them to follow the process and support them to close deals. This allowed the firm to match their sales processes to their customer's individual buying processes.

2.1.3 How Can We Reach the End-User When the Equipment Is Sold via an Installer/External Partner?

Many OEMs have limited contact with the final customer or end-user as they sell via intermediaries, such as installers or distributors. Problems then occur as the OEM

Fig. 2.7 It is important to deliver services to the end-users, owners, and operators (illustration by Annick Holland, authors' work)

has limited information on the final owner of the equipment and its operation (Fig. 2.7).

> ...how can we understand which customer pains to solve in order to create a value experience for our customers when we have no access to the end-user?...

The equipment business is often worried about breaking the relationship with their intermediary and so supports this activity poorly, leaving it up to the local service business to track down the end-user. In turn, the intermediary perceives the OEM's service center (third party) as a potential competitor who wants to steal the customer's business.

> ...The installer, who sold a product to an end customer or installed it, also wants to service the device. The manufacturer's service organization is therefore often seen as a competitor, which can adversely affect product sales...

The OEM's service team are then only called in when something goes wrong. Service managers and leaders find this situation difficult to deal with as the equipment could be half a world away.

It is important to understand where equipment is installed and how it operates as this installed base is the main asset on which the service business can feed. Knowing where the equipment is located means that decisions to set up local service centers can be justified with underlying data. In some cases, export regulations are a mechanism that justifies the OEM's need to know the equipment's final location. Improved relationships with installers and distributors can help show them that there is no threat – on the contrary, closer collaboration means that they and their customers are better supported. Knowing where competitors' equipment is also provides an additional service opportunity, as well as potential new equipment sales. Without knowing the actual data, internal benchmarking of new equipment sales against service sales can help to give an indication of expected regional service spend.

The lessons learned from the two cases show that it is important to identify all of the actors (hidden and visible) and understand their motivations. This is best done as a team so that everyone learns from each other.

The tools that help to explore these barriers and build actions to overcome them are:

- Case/actor matrix.
- Cradle-to-grave lifecycle visual mapping.
- Customer jobs-to-be-done.
- Customer value proposition.
- Detailed empathy card.
- Empathy maps.
- Personas.
- Visual journey map – high level.
- Visual journey map – detail level.

Details of the individual tools are given in Chap. 3.

> **Case 5 A Firm Sells to an Installer Yet Was Able to Develop a Relationship with the End-User**
>
> The equipment that the OEM firm manufactures is added into a system by a system integrator and then sold to the end-user. In effect, the firm had two sets of customers: the installer and the end-user. The end-users always phoned the OEM for support with the equipment during the operational phase. The installer always blamed the OEM for any equipment failure during the warranty period. The installers were only interested in completing the project, so their support to the end-user was often poor, their specification was cost-driven, and they did not necessarily select the best fit for the project. So, it was not a major surprise when the end result did not work as well as planned.
>
> The problem was that the installer created problems for new equipment sales by demanding compliance to their specification, while the end-user was expected to operate and maintain the equipment. The result has been that the
>
> (continued)

end-user often initially blamed the OEM for premature failures or poor performance of the equipment.

The firm needed to balance the needs of the installer and the end-user: the firm sold to the installer via their equipment sales channel and then sold the services and spares via the aftermarket sales channel.

The firm has little influence on the cost-driven project-based installer, despite previously having tried to influence some installers with limited success. Consequently, the decision has been simply to deliver what they specify. With the end-user, the firm discovered that much more action is possible, as it needs to build a longer-term relationship and educate the end-user to understand why a failure occurred and to work with them after the warranty phase to improve operational performance and implement the correct maintenance strategies. The OEM firm really had no choice as their nameplate remained on the equipment and was well-known, unlike the name of the installer.

From this, the OEM firm learned that the end-user of the equipment was "short-changed" by the cost-driven project team who oversaw the installation of their equipment. Effectively, they had some of the same problems the OEM firm faced. In response, the OEM firm became more disciplined with the operation of the two sales channels and started to build new solutions to adapt the initial installation to match the actual operational conditions. Pushing back on warranty claims from the installer and the project team was hard, and it took time to educate them about the real issues and for the equipment sales teams to become more commercial in their dealings with the installers. It was not easy.

Case 6 The Installer Wants to Provide Services to the OEM's Customers (the End-Users)
The OEM firm was unable to provide services to the users of the equipment that it manufactures. Management made a strategic decision to move into services, but the firm only provides components, and the system integrator holds the keys to access the customer.

The OEM firm does not get feedback on the equipment it sells to customers, most of whom integrate the equipment into machines. They have no idea of the operational performance or if their recommended maintenance schedule is correct for the job at hand. There is great confusion about who the real customer is and how to provide them with the services that they need.

The OEM firm looked for the customers with whom they had the best relationship and those who returned the largest number of products for repairs.

(continued)

The firm then offered a certification training plan for those customers' service technicians.

They found it was possible to train some of the system integrators (the direct customers) to do the level one maintenance on the equipment the OEM supplied. The firm even managed to charge them for the training, as it provided the technicians with a certification. The OEM found that their customers liked this, as did the service technicians that were trained. They also discovered that it improved the relationships and understanding between the two firms. Effectively, the OEM created a field service team without having to invest and hire the staff. They use the OEM's spares, return equipment to the factory when an overhaul is needed, and even share information on where the equipment is and how it is being installed. Their customers like this, as they consider they are getting a full OEM service.

Because of this, the OEM firm is now delivering service (a management wish) without major investments from the business.

2.1.4 How Can We Promote a Solution to the End-User When the Equipment/Service Is Delivered via an External Partner?

Many firms sell their products to an installer or distributor who sells directly to the end-user. This can mean that it is then hard to sell service, as there is limited information on where the equipment is installed and who owns it. The approach creates barriers that can be hard to overcome and can initially be considered impassable, but firms need to insert the idea into others' minds (Fig. 2.8).

> ...How do we really manage to get access to customer needs?...

Overcoming these barriers means that education on solutions must be pushed out to all partners and customers. Caterpillar manages this by treating their dealers as if they are part of the firm, while Uster (https://www.uster.com) do this by treating their local partners – no matter how large or small – as part of their family. Every year they bring all of their partners together for a summit to help transfer new know-how or develop a basis for their solutions. They also have user-group meetings, where they bring end-users together for two-way sharing of operational and maintenance issues as well as new solutions. The critical aspects are preparing the groundwork and being sure to provide value to all partners by providing proactive support based on the installed base. Sharing the benefits with partners can also encourage and reinforce the cooperation:

> ...Whoever is in contact with the customer must have benefits from the sale of the service. I leave a share of the profit to the sellers...

Fig. 2.8 It is important that there is a link back to the manufacturer via services (illustration by Annick Holland, authors' work)

The lessons learned from the two cases are threefold, focusing on the business partners, customers, and the installed base. All partners who support with service should be treated the same and all invited to partner meetings. Annual user-group meetings can provide important touchpoints with the customers and help improve understanding of their experience. The installed base data is as important as the customer data, and it should be used proactively to generate sales.

The tools that help to explore these barriers and build actions to overcome them are:

- Case/actor matrix.
- Cradle-to-grave lifecycle visual mapping.
- Customer jobs-to-be-done.
- Customer value proposition.
- Detailed empathy card.
- Empathy maps.
- Personas.
- Service blueprint.
- Visual journey map – high level.
- Visual journey map – detail level.

Details of the individual tools are given in Chap. 3.

2.1 Customers

Case 7 Learning to Understand Installers as Well as End-Users

Installers always reminded the manufacturing firm that their contract was with them and not with the end-user. The firm struggled to find information on which to base the development of new products and services and had no idea how the equipment it delivers really performed in the field.

The contract was to provide products to the installer on time and at an agreed price, because the installer was the customer. They blocked the manufacturer from asking the end-users about their requirements and getting feedback. How could the OEM develop new products or provide services in this situation?

The firm used a mix of databases to find out where the equipment they sold was installed and find out who was using it (this was in no way easy). They then went to visit some of the end-users (firms who were using the OEM's products) to ask them exactly how they used the equipment. The firm then created simple use cases from the feedback and listed the pains that the operators and the maintenance team faced. They also learned how the equipment is supported by the system integrator and how much the installer sells spare parts for.

It felt rather underhand to circumvent the system integrator that was the firm's main customer, making it important to do this research independently for a number of reasons. So, in investigating the use of their products, the OEM firm was careful not to use any information provided directly by the installer.

Through this exercise, the firm learned a lot about problems that end-users were having with the equipment and delays they were having in getting spares when ordering them via the system integrator. Some machines were being over-maintained, others under-maintained, and, generally, the intermediary company provided poor support documentation on the operations and maintenance requirements. The firm also learned that it was hard for the end-users to find the manufacturer's name on the equipment.

First, the firm made its name more visible on the equipment so that end-users could find them on the Internet easily. Putting a QR code on the equipment gave end-users access to an aftermarket portal that linked up directly with the equipment, so that they could order spares and services directly from the OEM firm. This was done on all of the firm's equipment so that they could not be accused of "going behind our customer's back." This was simpler than trying to connect all of the products to the Internet as it only needed a smartphone. Yet it allowed the firm to have direct contact with end-users and start to learn more about their operations and expectations.

Case 8 Sharing the Sales Leads and Getting Rewarded for It
Within the business, a proportion of the sales came from outside the service sales channel. Often this provided the firm with new service leads that they had not identified before. These suggestions could come from the equipment sales team, agents, direct customers, or third parties.

The biggest challenge was with the equipment sales teams, who felt that they were not being rewarded for the sales leads they were making. Agents complained that their effort was much larger than their reward, as the firm was using the equipment agent rates and the typical order size for equipment was over ten times larger than for services. However, customers were happy to provide referrals for service sales.

The firm developed a new approach where they would provide a commission to the equipment sales team for any service sales that they supported, insisting that this went two ways. They also agreed to add targets to the sales managers' annual review for supporting service sales (and did the same for equipment sales). The firm's annual sales meeting included both service sales and product sales.

By capturing and paying the commission between equipment and service sales, the sales teams were motivated to support each other. The aim was to have, in effect, zero net payments by correctly balancing the commission levels between the product and service business units. It was close after some adjustments.

Dealing with agents was not so easy and the level of commissions did not allow them to make money on small service orders. An easy solution could not be found. The most successful solution was a graduated annual payment to agents, based on total volume of sales rather than on individual sales.

Paying customers for referrals was not considered appropriate. Simply thanking the customer was the reward adopted.

2.1.5 How Do We React When Our Customers Ask Us Explicitly for New Services?

Direct customer pull is a feature of service business that is not seen as widely with manufacturing firms, and there is a clear difference between new product and service development (Fig. 2.9). Customers often ask, "can you do it for me?" which in service business is an open invitation and can lead to the direct innovation of a new service that may include the integration of technology. For equipment businesses, this question is much less common, and with the longer reaction times of manufacturing firms, it often means that the customer pull is not acted upon. More of the innovation in services is around the product, focusing on the wider business model or ecosystem.

2.1 Customers

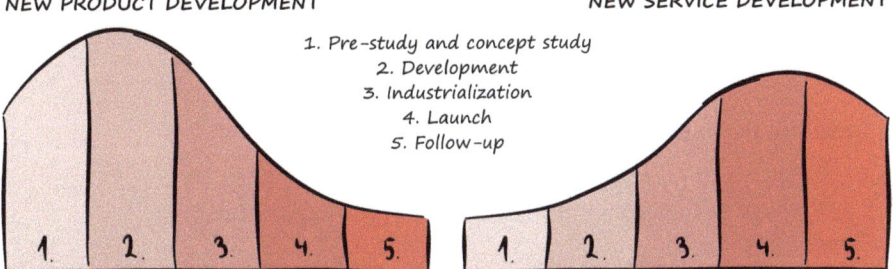

Fig. 2.9 There are significant differences in the required resources for new product development (NPD) and new service development (illustration by Annick Holland, adapted from Kowalkowski, 2016)

> ...we have a stage-gate process for controlling new product development – it does not work well for customer service requests...

Using direct pull from customers for new services requires an empowered service network that can take a risk. It needs to be based on lean and open innovation and provide confidence that there is space in the market for the new service. What is often overlooked is that there is a need to share innovations (technical or commercial) with the service network so that the services can be duplicated. Copying rather than reproducing the outcome reduces risks and increases the specification. Co-creation of new services should be welcomed.

Lessons from case studies confirm that new service development can be very different to new product development (NPD) and that firms should work with customers to jointly develop solutions. Solutions that are developed should be reusable in other locations for other customers – this can often be problematic.

> ...we say 'YES' and work with the customer to build a solution for the customer. They pay for it and we reproduce it in other locations...

Due to the differences between NPD and service development, the standard NPD process will require modifications to make it work for services.

The tools that help to explore the barriers and to build actions to overcome them are:

- Business model canvas.
- Cradle-to-grave lifecycle map.
- Cradle-to-grave lifecycle visual mapping.
- Customer jobs-to-be-done.
- Customer value proposition.
- Detailed empathy card.
- Job-to-be-done insights.
- Job-to-be-done outcomes.

- Keeping focused.
- Personas.
- Service blueprint.

Details of the individual tools are given in Chap. 3.

Case 9 New Service Development Is Different to New Product Development

In the past, the manufacturer provided basic services to support their products – spares, field services, and repairs. They did not consider additional services, expecting customers to come and request new services. The firm assumed (wrongly) that customers would remain faithful; however, they started to try competitors' services. The firm's reaction was to reduce prices, but they noticed that competitors were offering different services, which the customers liked and valued. So, the NPD team was asked to start to develop new services.

They discovered that the development of new services is very different to the development of new products, yet they were using processes that were designed for the development of new products, based on the full stage-gate process.

First, the firm moved service development to become a business development function. This allowed a much wider view of innovation: a major step as it enabled the firm to define innovation within the area of service experience and business models rather than having a narrow focus on "product configuration." With this wider perception of innovation, the customer's team was brought into the process, along with the field service technicians. The firm moved to an agile innovation process based on many lean principles and insisted that the customers had to be involved in the feedback loops. Finally, they separated innovation into "right here/right now" and "longer-term transformational" innovation.

The firm learned much more about how their customers used (and abused) the equipment that was sold to them. They learned more about where and when their services created value for customers. They discovered hidden services they were unaware that the customers value and other "unique" services that they did not value. To do this, the firm used a completely different set of innovation tools and involved a wider cross section of people than with a NPD.

Business development helped create different solutions that the firm could test with their customers, which provided focus on the intangible aspects that were important to the customers. They also supported the development of more advanced service concepts because they had the commercial, legal, and

(continued)

financial experience to be able to repackage base services into "pay-per-use" models. Business development also helped reduce time-to-market.

The separation of short-term and longer-term innovation and the different risk profiles provided the basis for sustainable development.

Case 10 A Firm Has Been Asked by Customers to Deliver New Services
Customers asked the firm time and again to deliver services in different ways. The firm felt this was because the customers were not happy with the services, for example, because they were saying they would like to do some of their basic field services. In other cases, customers were asking for a pay-per-use model. Others wanted the firm to repair other additional equipment. The firm had a problem from two sides: first, management within the firm said that the innovation process was out of control; second, the firm needed to learn to share innovations.

A new step was implemented in the bidding process that could identify if the work could be considered innovative. This was done so that the risks could be understood, and if need request help from other service centers (in case they had prior, undocumented, expertise) and allowing others to know that they could apply the solution in their region.

For higher risk requests, it provided a way to feed the innovation into the business development team who could support the bidding process. This was important for longer-term contracts or for new revenue models (e.g., pay-per-use).

The aim was not to create a complex process, and this was achieved, as the system was generally simple to use. The process also allowed new innovation to be shared. Importantly, sharing the information across a fragmented network of service centers by highlighting "what's new" provided a database of services sold and a contact name of who sold and delivered the work.

For higher risk jobs with value propositions or new revenue models, it provided support to the service centers with building offers and reducing any risk involved. There was some tension between the service centers and business development, often due to poor understanding of the embedded risks in the service offer.

On a strategic level, it supported understanding of the portfolio and the developments that should be shared around the business to improve sales. It also helped to identify innovation "hot spots" and "innovation leaders." Sales liked the process as it provides them with more services to sell.

2.1.6 How to Manage Delivery When Our Customers Want to Perform Some of the Tasks Themselves?

How often are manufacturers asked by the customers to share the scope of supply? Not often. As with customer pull for new services, there are many instances in service delivery when the service execution depends on the customer or another third party.

> …Some of our customers do all the field service themselves; this reduces our scope and sale volume…

Risk management is different than with manufacturing, as are the depth of the relationships that it can bring. This difference creates tension between the service and equipment businesses as the customer becomes a key partner.

Is it possible to use co-delivery of services positively? The answer is clearly yes, as Uber and others have created business models where this occurs. It is also possible in an industrial environment, as the equipment owners do on their own routine or operational maintenance on machines. Extending this further, allowing the customer to act as the local troubleshooter, means that with remote monitoring it is possible to diagnose problems and failures more quickly and accurately, far quicker and cheaper than dispatching a service engineer for what could be a 10-minute job. This makes the customer feel part of the team.

> …by making the customer part of the solution and part of the team, we deliver a higher customer experience and satisfaction…

Other opportunities exist to use customer employees to support inspection work under the supervision of the service company. This has many advantages; clearly it is cheaper for the customer, but more importantly the customer's employees understand the local working conditions and are able to support the service company to perform the work better, and at the same time this improves customer relationships. Over the operational life of the asset, customers' maintenance strategy may change from "do-it-for-me" to "do-it-with-me" to "do-it-myself" (Fig. 2.10).

Fig. 2.10 Being able to support different customer's preferences is important (illustration by Annick Holland, authors' work)

Lessons from the two cases confirm that services need to be developed based on a flexible modular approach that helps service firms adapt the scope of service, so allowing a range of different level of service engagements. Using customers to perform part of the solution, brings the customer staff closer to the service team and increases their service experience. The final lesson is that service firms should be ready to learn from their customers as they often can execute parts of the service scope better than the service provider.

The tools that help to explore these barriers and to build actions to overcome them are:

- Avatar map.
- Case/actor matrix.
- Cradle-to-grave lifecycle map.
- Cradle-to-grave lifecycle visual mapping.
- Customer value proposition.
- Job-to-be-done insights.
- Keeping focused.
- Personas.
- Service blueprint.

Details of the individual tools are given in Chap. 3.

> **Case 11 Building Field Services in Collaboration with Customers**
> Customers were insisting on doing the installation, commissioning, and removal of the equipment that a manufacturing firm had sold them. This meant the OEM firm's scope and sales volume were being eroded. At other times, the customers were asking for increased scope, as there were components within the machines that their technicians could easily remove and replace.
>
> Both losses of control and sales volume were considered the main problems with the work being done by the customers.
>
> The firm had to accept that their customers were able to install, commission, and remove the equipment faster than the manufacturer was able to. The customers also always shipped the equipment to the manufacturer for repair. Because of this, the firm was able to learn from its customers. They offered customers' technicians a week in their repair facility to learn about what the manufacturer actually did with their equipment. As well as sharing know-how in both directions, it also tightened the relationships between individuals in both firms on a personal level.
>
> In other cases, the firm created a flexible scope for routine and scheduled maintenance. When customers wanted to increase their in-house service, the
>
> (continued)

firm either had to first certify their competence or would scale back the warranty they were providing.

These approaches worked well. Unexpectedly, the OEM learned how to do jobs from their customers (not all customers). After some nervousness, the field service technicians quite enjoyed the process and found it improved relationships with customers. This was especially true after inviting the customers' service technicians to the OEM's workshops for a week.

In terms of providing a modular flexible service definition, the approach where different levels of customers did their own service and maintenance worked well. The firm was able to identify the competence level of each customer and consequently provide appropriate service levels with different responsibilities. The firm anticipates that this will increase customer retention. They now have a continuum of offers based on do-it-for-you, do-it-with-me, and do-it-yourself.

Case 12 Working with the Customer to Make Them Part of the Solution
A number of customers of this manufacturing company were having difficulties doing routine maintenance or would contact the firm for small-scale problems. With mobile phones and smart technology, the OEM firm wanted to move to a more direct way to support customers. Other companies offer online support, such as Caterpillar providing videos online to help people take on service and repair tasks such as changing oil filters.

The firm wanted to help support customers when they have a problem and, if possible, to do it remotely, so they do not have to send a service technician for a 2-minute job or help the customer to provide machine status information so that the failure can be correctly repaired first time.

Skype and FaceTime provided the inspiration for the remote support solution, but what was missing was the integration of the standard operator procedure for routine maintenance and a link to order consumables and spares. The solution was designed to allow direct contact, along with integrated billing, depending on the customer's service contract.

Using mobile phones and Bluetooth allowed the firm to collect information data from a machine to diagnose the failure and ensure that the field service technician had a better chance of fixing it first time. And the customer was part of the solution, so both parties saved on time and effort.

It became possible to make the customers feel like they were part of the service team and supporting the delivery of the service as it allowed the customer's staff to get their jobs done more effectively with the appropriate support of the OEM.

2.2 Organizational Structure and Culture

Preconceived thoughts and conflicts due to resistance to change among different departments and different hierarchies in organizations lead to poor service delivery. Manufacturers are fact-based and hierarchy-based, while effective service organizations have flat structures with empowered employees who demand results rather than endless analysis. The effective service firm needs to hire by attitude and behavior rather than only by a list of technical capabilities that can be improved (or even learned) later. Therefore, separating from the product business, although not easy, may be indispensable to better comply with customer distinctive needs and develop local staff accordingly. Indeed, service is, after all, a people business where many of the employees have direct customer contact – this is often different in the equipment business, where a single point of contact is maintained with customers. Building a service business will mean that a new service-minded culture is required.

> ... by being separate we are able to be effective for the customer...local empowerment is hard to achieve but it means effective and efficient service provision...

The relative importance of the barriers around "organizational structure and culture" are shown in Fig. 2.11 with the ranking based on the survey results.

"Organizational structure and culture" deals with internal themes. Here, three critical issues confirm that servitization business models face issues from "the management" as well as NPD/R&D. Some examples of initiatives introduced by companies to facilitate internal promotion and stimulate people's involvement include promoting services with presentations of success stories, the activation of simple service projects with high profitability, and the introduction of "ad hoc" training projects and incentive systems.

There are firms that hire by attitude and behavior and they tend to perform better than others, particularly where this is supported by human resources (HR) management and leadership.

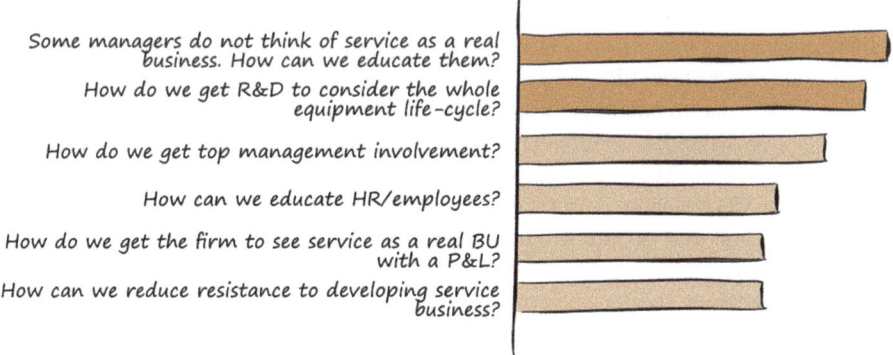

Fig. 2.11 The relative importance of the barriers around "organizational structure and culture" (illustration by Annick Holland, adapted from West et al., 2018)

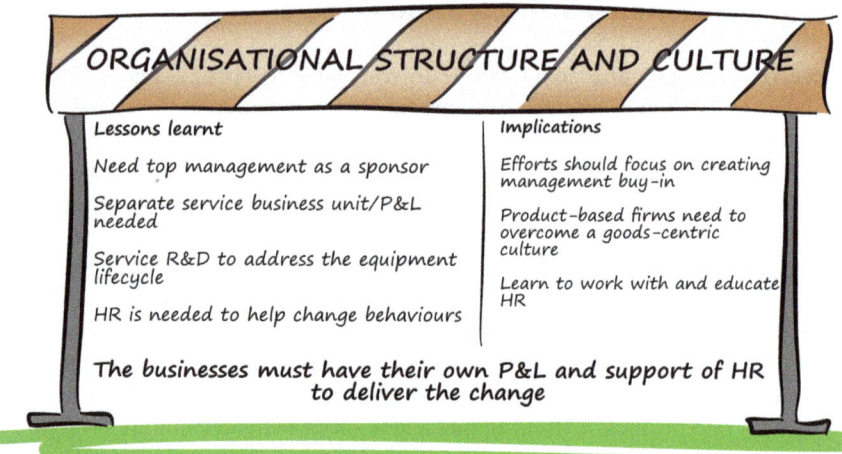

Fig. 2.12 The lessons and implications for the organizational structure and culture barriers (illustration by Annick Holland, adapted from West et al., 2018)

…Culture is everything, attitude and behavior… support from HR is needed to drive business thinking in a knowledge management rich environment…

The employees in such businesses share know-how openly and can safely be empowered to "do-the-right-thing." Empowerment comes with responsibility to share both the highlights and the lessons from what goes wrong. Underpinning successful service cultures is the freedom of being separated as a business with a profit and loss sheet (profit and loss) rather than simply being considered as a cost center, as this allows the service firm to operate through guidelines rather than regulations. Figure 2.12 describes some of the lessons learned and the implications from the interviews.

All of the firms we worked with told us that top management support was key to successful servitization. As in any change, the process needs a sponsor, and internal politics and organizational structures can act as inhibitors or enablers and integrate the different resources (Fig. 2.13). Accomplishing service successes required the firms to have separate business units (BU) or a clear management system to monitor the changes (a virtual BU). Human resources was considered a key change partner to support service behaviors, with the definition of roles and responsibilities within the service network considered critical for success. Human resources support was needed in hiring new workers with behavioral and technical capabilities and to provide rotations and create conditions to help the sharing of know-how, trust, and cooperation between the service centers. The lessons learned were:

- Need top management as a sponsor.
- Separate service business unit is needed.

Fig. 2.13 Bringing the organization together can be like completing a complex jigsaw (illustration by Annick Holland, authors' work)

- Service research and development (R&D) has to be involved to address the equipment lifecycle.
- Human resources is needed to help change behaviors.
- Promoting services with presentations of success stories.
- Activating simple service projects with high profitability.
- Introducing "ad hoc" training projects and incentive systems.

To help you to navigate the process, we offer detailed descriptions of the barriers faced by other companies and insights from cases explaining how others overcame the barriers. The barriers identified (in order of importance) were:

1. Some managers do not think of service as a real business, how can we educate them?
2. How do we get R&D to consider the whole equipment lifecycle?
3. How do we get top management involvement?
4. How do we get the firm to see service as a real business unit with a profit and loss?
5. How can we reduce resistance to developing service business?
6. How can we educate human resources and employees?

2.2.1 Some Managers Do Not Think of Service as a Real Business. How Can We Educate Them?

"Manufacturing and designing new products is a real business" is the mantra of many technology firms (Fig. 2.14). The focus of the business remains on new technologies and selling the next generation of products. Many new, disruptive businesses manage to balance design, manufacture, and service. A leading example is Apple, where the customer experience end-to-end is considered vital to their success. This should also be the case with industrial businesses, because service, even if related almost exclusively to spare parts, is their main cash generator.

Fig. 2.14 Service needs to be presented as a "real business" with its own profit and loss (illustration by Annick Holland, authors' work)

> ...The margins in service are much higher than in new equipment sales, the cash generation is also much better...

Nevertheless, in many engineering/technology firms, the product is dominant (because of its impact on sales volumes) and technical capabilities are rewarded rather than customer facing activities. In such firms, managers often confuse innovation and NPD – innovation in their mind is only about developing the next hot product.

> ...The sales volumes are too small in service; I could chase a 100k new equipment sale or a 1k service sale – it's a no brainer...

For the shareholders, the service business is a real business, as it creates the cash flows that are needed to support dividend payouts. The profit generated is used by the firm to fund future technology investments so that NPD can be maintained. Service requires different types of innovation, often away from the technical area and more in the customer experience area, which for the technical expert may not be perceived as "real" innovation. In today's world, many of the most disruptive innovations have been based around new business model configurations rather than in new technologies. Often, these new business models are supported by the application of new technologies – successful industry 4.0 applications are good examples of this. Creating service business solutions upon innovation technology can be a good way to reconcile a service perspective with a product-based technocentric view.

The lessons learned from the cases confirm the need to create a profit and loss for service that is separated from the manufacturing business. The separation of the profit and loss will lead to different sales channels for service. This makes sense as the equipment is often sold to an installer, and the service demands then come from the owner or operator of the equipment. Splitting the sales channels will highlight the margin delivered by services, and the aim should be to focus on quality of sales (i.e., contribution margin and cash flow) rather than just the volume.

The tools that help to explore the barriers and to build actions to overcome them are:

- Avatar map.
- Business model canvas.
- Cradle-to-grave lifecycle map.
- Cradle-to-grave lifecycle visual mapping.
- Job-to-be-done insights.
- Job-to-be-done outcomes.
- Service blueprint.
- Visual journey map – high level.
- Visual journey map – detail level.

Details of the individual tools are given in Chap. 3.

> **Case 13 Sales in Services Take So Much Effort and Yield Too Little Value**
> The firm sold products that cost hundreds of thousands of dollars, while service orders were much smaller in volume and often only spares were sold. Service orders were a real distraction from closing sales for new equipment. With such a disparity between the new equipment sales and aftermarket services, the firm focused on new equipment sales, where the sales team could ensure that they hit their sales targets.
>
> The firm had the same sales process for complex product orders as it did for selling spares and field services. For small orders, this tied up the sales managers in paperwork that created long lead times for quotes, while customers asked if the firm really wanted the spares orders. Sometimes, internally it was not clear if the firm wanted the aftermarket sales, as the management was unwilling to understand the challenges or make improvements.
>
> Internally, spares sales were moved to a young and ambitious team member within the supply chain. He had the oversight of the parts needed by production and had created a bill of materials (BoM) for many of the products they sold, allowing him to quickly identify the supplier, lead time, and the costs for
>
> (continued)

each part. This resulted in a simple quoting process for spares when a request was made. A senior sales manager was given the responsibility for field service sales to stress the importance of field services within the business and as a tool to capture spares sales.

Spare sales increased, and this improved the cash contribution of the aftermarket business to the firm's bottom line. Customers found that the service on spares was better than before and their experiences improved. Better visibility of spares sales helped to identify the real consumption of spares, which gave the firm new insights.

The senior sales manager leading field service provided a focus and he worked closely with the field service team and the spares sales to improve the aftermarket services. The growth in sales (spares and field services) in terms of quantity and quality helped to improve the positioning of service in the firm.

Case 14 With Clear Aftermarket Targets, the Firm Started to Grow Services

"All sales are important" was how the firm worked. However, the sales managers were rewarded only according to the volume of their sales rather than the quality of their sales. Initially, there was no separation of new equipment and service sales – all were measured in the same way and rewarded identically. Service was considered a cost and an area of low recognition as the "serious stuff" was done with the design of the new equipment; this is where the firm's culture perceived real innovation was done and where the big money was made.

However, the real problem was that sales were all mixed to hide the fact that product sales were losing money and that the firm actually made money on service aspects (e.g., installation, spares, field services, and upgrades), which they sold later. It was a classic razor/razor blade sale; in the past, things had been different with good margins on both the product and the service sales.

To overcome this challenge, service sales were given a separate profit and loss and were made responsible for it. The aim was to develop transparency with the cash contributions and to set up a real business around the services, which could build a stable cash contribution and provide valuable feedback to the product business. This was focused on product lifecycle, which was substantially shorter than the asset lifecycle from the perspective of the equipment owners. There was initially push back from the product side of the business as they felt they were losing control by losing the cash-generating service business.

(continued)

> The service centers were now given separated profit and loss to achieve and told that they had to provide positive cash contributions on spares sales, field service sales, and shop-based repairs. In effect, they were empowered to grow their local business and to support the growth of the new service business. The income from spares sales was not taken from the product division completely, as a "license" fee was paid to the product division on all spares sales. The separation of the two profit and loss allowed both halves of the business to focus on what they were good at; it allowed the service shop coverage to grow, as it was now profitable, and it provided financial transparency for the individual businesses.

2.2.2 How Do We Get R&D to Consider the Whole Equipment Lifecycle?

The manufacturing view of the equipment lifecycle is quite different to the view that the service business has. Typically, a product lifecycle is short from the manufacturing perspective, whereas the operational life of the equipment may be 10–20 times longer than the production phase (Fig. 2.15). This means that the short-term perspective typical of NPD, which considers only the latest products as valuable, does not work well in the services business.

> ...NPD only ever consider the latest technology...

The operational phase may include additional upgrades to overcome obsolescence brought about due to changes in technology or changes in operational requirements. In fact, rather than being a problem, these can provide opportunities for the service business.

In the operational phase, the service business will find ways to drip new technology into the equipment to ensure that it remains relevant to the end-user. This may extend its operational life beyond the original design life – there are many examples of equipment having its operational life extended more than twice its design life. This is because of the design margins built into the equipment, the operational environment, and repair and upgrade technologies have continued to improve.

The clear lessons from the cases are that NPD is fascinated with new technologies rather than existing problems. Nevertheless, service managers need to create opportunities to share operational experiences with NPD by providing real operational experiences from the installed based, so as to get the right information from the field and determine the most appropriate technologies to implement.

> ...we do not get enough feedback from the operational machines to understand if our technology worked...

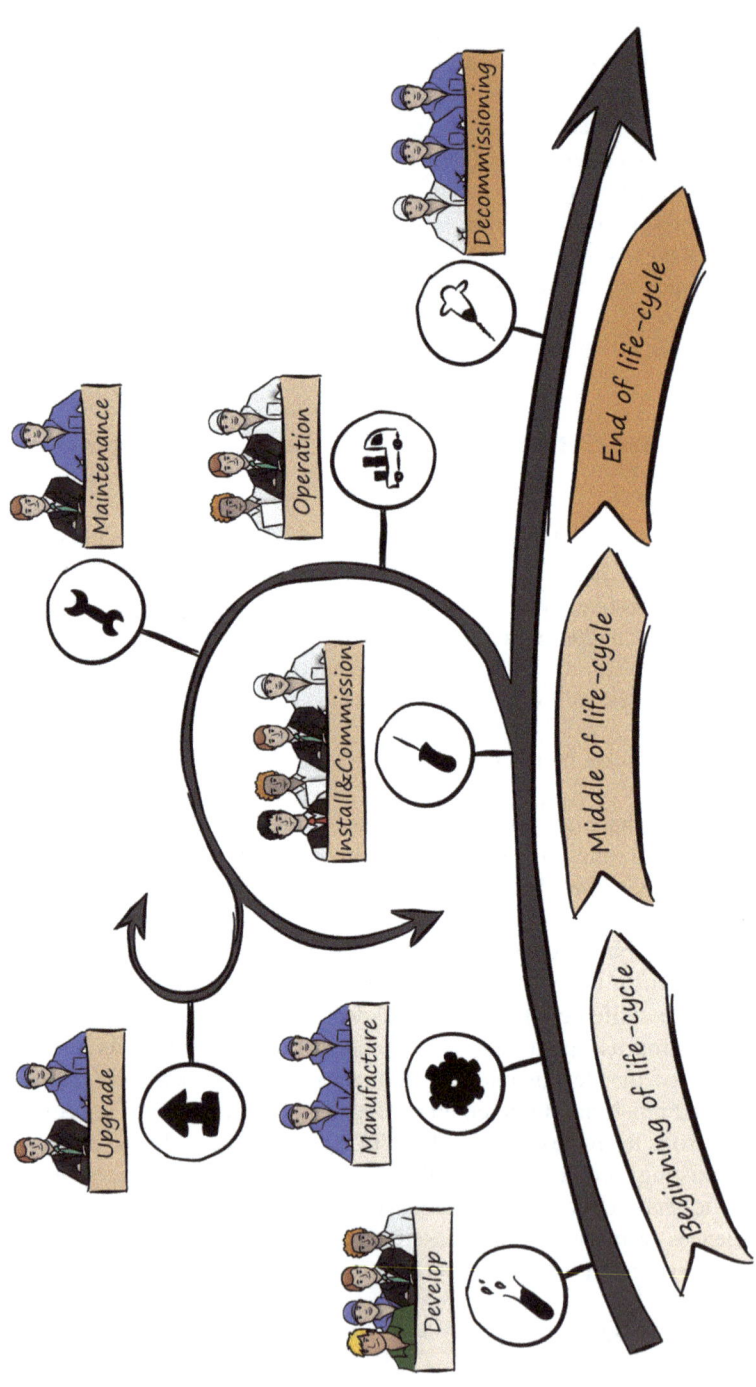

Fig. 2.15 NPD need to develop solutions for the installed base as well as for new products (illustration by Annick Holland, adapted from West et al., 2020)

2.2 Organizational Structure and Culture

To do this effectively, managers should map the lifecycle of the equipment to find new service and upgrade opportunities with their service teams and with NPD.

The tools that help to explore these barriers and build actions to overcome them are:

- Avatar map.
- Case/actor matrix.
- Cradle-to-grave lifecycle map.
- Cradle-to-grave lifecycle visual mapping.
- Customer jobs-to-be-done.
- Job-to-be-done insights.
- Job-to-be-done outcomes.
- Service blueprint.

Details of the individual tools are given in Chap. 3.

> **Case 15 NPD Only Ever Considers the Newest Technology**
> NPD clearly did not value making improvements for the service team on existing (or old/legacy) equipment. The field service team considered that small improvements to the equipment would improve its serviceability – making it easier or quicker to complete a planned inspection or making an unplanned breakdown less likely. Any change suggested was not considered innovative as it "only came from service," and because the improvements were not technology driven, they were not considered really valuable.
>
> For NPD, innovation started with a price tag of 100,000 euros or more, but the suggestions by the field service team generally only cost a fraction of this, and because of this, they were not considered to be "real" innovations. Product development also insisted that any modifications were channeled via their "product change management process," which actually stopped the improvements. Product development had a blind spot that they admitted but failed to address – they wanted more customer feedback on product performance to help with future product development.
>
> Lean management supported the change, as using standardized approaches the service engineers had new tools to assess and measure the effectiveness of changes. They started by only considering their area of control and focused on the delivery of field services at first. One change they made was to agree on standard inspections on the equipment and, in doing so, identify what was the same and what needed to be adjusted for each site.
>
> Within the inspection reports, a new section was added to provide product development with operational performance information. This was sent directly to the lead of product development with a formal meeting held twice a year.

(continued)

Local changes could be delivered within standard inspections; the changes were also documented and reviewed by the service team and with the product development. The analysis helped to ensure that risks were managed and, at the same time, the changes were shared (and the reason for the customization). The twice annual meeting helped product development get real feedback on performance and bought the two teams closer together, with the expectation that development engineers would spend time working with the field service teams on inspections.

Case 16 Using the Lifecycle of the Equipment to Discover New Services
In this firm, the NPD design team focused on the product's beginning of life and at best the middle of life, considering only the basic services needed to keep the equipment working. This meant they missed service opportunities both before the traditional sales process started and at the end of the product's life. To be fair, the products that they sold were installed by their customer, and the whole installation was then sold on at the end of the project to what they called "the end-user."

The firm was used to selling only to their customer and had limited understanding of the other actors involved with the equipment they sold. They were not proactive with service sales, because of their poor relationships with the operations and maintenance teams. When designing new products, they only focused on the needs of the people buying the equipment they sold rather than the operators of that equipment.

In a workshop, they mapped out the cradle-to-grave lifecycle of the equipment from before the initial sale to the end of life and identified new services (some of which they were already providing for free). To create the map, they brought in representatives of their customers and end-users and built-up personas for all the actors. This was very new for them, as they identified many people who were important for the operation and maintenance of the product that they had not considered. They started to understand the expected demand for spares and field services, as well as other critical events and opportunities to improve the customer experience.

New opportunities at the products' end of life were instantly discovered, such as the return of old units, which were then cleaned, overhauled, and rented out to a different market segment, with a credit note given against a new purchase. Adjustments to the value propositions were made to improve the

(continued)

customer experience at each of the crucial transactions. A move to supporting the end-user was made, as new and more detailed personas were created that helped to describe the value that was being missed – in effect, because only weak relationships existed in the past.

The total cost of ownership (TCO) was also built up based on the lifecycle analysis, providing, in a quantitative way, an assessment of expected spend per year in spares and field services over the operational life of the equipment. This had been missing in the past and could now be validated and described to potential customers.

2.2.3 How Do We Get Top Management Involvement?

Top management involvement is critical to allow a firm to start to transform into a successful service business as well as a manufacturing firm. Support and encouragement from top management helps to reduce resistance from the design and manufacturing areas of the business. The resistance is often because people feel threatened by the change rather than from rational arguments for (or against) the transition, and top management need to see the light on the value of service (Fig. 2.16).

> …Service is as important as new equipment, and the leadership needs to have top level representation of both parts to be successful in the long-term…

A top management sponsor is important (all change management texts state this) as they can help remove blocks as well as convince middle management about the

Fig. 2.16 Top management needs to be shown the value of services for the firm (illustration by Annick Holland, authors' work)

urgency of the change. The top management sponsor needs not only to be able to see beyond the basic financial benefits for the firm but also to understand the value it creates for the firm's customers as well as the value of the improved customer experience.

The lessons for service managers are to ensure that service is a profit center and is profitable. Service centers are not just a channel for the sale of spares but they also provide services that are profitable in their own right.

> ...You need to have profit and loss responsibility; without it the management will only ever see it as a cost...

The head of service must also have a seat on the board at the same level as the manufacturing head. This should be the case as they will both create around the same contribution margin. Finally, to improve visibility, the CEO needs to spend as much time with service as with new equipment.

The tools that help to explore these barriers and build actions to overcome them are:

- Business model canvas.
- Business process mapping.
- Customer value proposition.
- Metric cascades.
- Service blueprint.
- Understanding your business.
- Visual journey map – high level.
- Visual journey map – detail level.

Details of the individual tools are given in Chap. 3.

> **Case 17 A Cost Center is Always Under Pressure to Reduce Its Budget**
> The service business was run as a cost center that supported new equipment sales. The job was to support the installation of the equipment in the field, which was a cost in each new equipment sale. The technicians also got involved when there were warranty problems with the equipment, and this often extended to fault finding on the equipment when it was in the field. The customer was expected to return the unit to the manufacturing facility when it needed a major inspection. The service team's role was to keep the machine in the field and to defend warranty claims.
>
> The customers complained about the poor service they received from the company: the equipment was plumbed in, and then the firm walked away and did everything they could to limit warranty claims. The customers wanted to know how to operate the equipment better and undertake the routine

(continued)

maintenance, but either support from the manufacturer was not provided or responses were slow. Often, when service support was provided, it was done grudgingly.

The change made was to turn service into a business unit with its own profit and loss. This was challenging as it required a separation from production, and the manufacturing section of the company did not want to see cost increases or lose control. An agreement was made between the two departments for the installation of new equipment, based on annual volumes and costs. The service business was now expected to grow its turnover (and margins); it did this by selling services on the equipment: emergency callouts, planned inspections, providing operational support, and training. Initially this was provided on a time and materials basis.

The service business had two important customer groups: the production business within the firm and the owners and operators of the equipment; both had different needs and requirements. The internal agreement to provide installation services was often problematic and strained. However, customer relationships improved, the support services for the equipment were broadened, and the service team expanded to deliver the wider range of services. Unexpectedly, the purchase of spares increased, because the customers had regular direct contact with the service team.

Case 18 Service Is Now Headed by a Senior Manager
The aftermarket department of the firm had been embedded within the manufacturing business for years. It was not held in high esteem by the company or, in many cases, the customers. Each of the manufacturing centers held onto a number of local service teams and viewed them as a channel to sell spares to customers or as ways to keep the machines in the field. The service teams were managed as cost centers and operated within their budget.

The root cause of the problem was that the firm's aftermarket was viewed more as an afterthought rather than having a clear role within the business. The service centers were fragmented, viewed as a cost line of manufacturing, and used to push spares sales to the market. It was often where the least talented were sent before retirement or as a "last chance."

The approach taken was to create a central leadership position and put a senior manager into place. This was viewed as a brave move, given the poor performance of the aftermarket services. The major operational change that this provided was that the service centers gained their own profit and loss and became profit centers. The strategy for service was then driven by the new leader. The sale of spares was a separate problem, as the equipment business

(continued)

needed the cross subsidy from the spares to remain profitable. Here, a "license" fee was paid to the new equipment business to reward the design team for their original effort.

All of the service teams started to make money after getting the message: "we now have our own profit and loss, and I expect all of the service centers to make money on the services as well as the spares sales." This was both a strong strategic message from the new leader and one that gave focused, actionable direction. The visibility of the new service business unit with its own profit and loss under the leadership of senior manager helped to promote its contribution to the company in terms of cash and customer experiences. It was clear that service was a "real" business and one where people wanted to work rather than being sent to hide. A challenge nevertheless remained with the distribution of the spare parts sales and arguments over the "license." This was seen as a dilution of margins on one side and a distraction, as the service centers had the capability to reengineer the spares. The service centers experienced spares being delivered late, and this had a negative impact on their customer relationships.

2.2.4 How Do We Get the Firm to See Service as a Real Business Unit with a Profit and Loss?

Historically, many manufacturers considered service a cost, a protection against warranty rather than a business in its own right, which makes it subservient to the equipment business. This is seen in many firms as service is part of the sales organization as a cost to the business. Service business often, and rightly so, demands to be a separate business line with its own profit and loss ledger and shares the success with others in the business (Fig. 2.17).

> ...Every service shop needs to make a profit in addition to the margins it makes on selling spares...

With a separate profit and loss, the service business is able to make money. The workshop managers feel that they should generate a profit and sell services that their customers value. This creates better feedback to the business; it also makes service hungry for more investment and more employees. Moreover, a profit and loss make the service business responsive to its customers and more responsible to the parent firm. It increases the respect from the rest of the larger business.

> ...Service creates deep customer relationships, and from this we grow sales...

2.2 Organizational Structure and Culture

Fig. 2.17 Showing the results of the service activities to others confirms that service is a business (illustration by Annick Holland, authors' work)

The lessons from the cases confirm the need for a full profit and loss for the service business, and for it to be responsible for delivering a healthy contribution margin for the firm as the equipment business needs the support. The contribution of service to the customer relationship should be highlighted by the CEO to the whole organization. This will again support the position of the service business as a "real" business rather than an extension to the sales and marketing function.

The tools that help to explore these barriers and to build actions to overcome them are:

- Business model canvas.
- Business process mapping.
- Customer value proposition.
- Metric cascades.
- Service blueprint.
- Understanding your business.
- Visual journey map – high level.
- Visual journey map – detail level.

Details of the individual tools are given in Chap. 3.

Case 19 Service Helped to Deepen the Customer Relationships

The firm just sold products and pushed them into the market via distributors and integrators. The product was king as the firm was the leader in the market. The engineers developed more complex and better products and the market took them. They were unsure where the products were actually installed, but customers (or "end-users") returned to buy spares and services. One day, the firm found that customers started to buy from other manufacturers; then, the service business started to slip away.

What had happened was that the advantage on new products had been lost and competitors were providing better value for money. The price premium being charged did not equate to higher value. The firm had generally limited contact with the owners and operators of the equipment it sold. They had a limited installed base list, and this was out of date when it came to the names of the owners, operators, or maintenance managers.

The firm realized that they did not have real relationships with their customers. They also did not understand how to deal with the equipment owners; instead, they dealt with the installers of the equipment and occasionally directly with the maintenance teams. They were a technology-focused firm and needed to transform into a customer-focused firm.

Strengthening relationships with the installers helped the firm to learn what the installers valued. Tentatively, they also started to build relationships with the owners, operations, and maintenance teams of the installed equipment. As these relationships were built up, actions were developed in coordination with equipment sales, service sales, and field service so that they could broaden and deepen their relationships with all the direct stakeholders and beneficiaries. This took time and effort.

The firm learned that service relationships helped with both service sales and new equipment sales. The relationship management was overseen by a single person who supported the multiple touchpoints of the relationships between the firms. There was an investment in a CRM system, as the original CRM was not suitable because it focused on the new equipment sales to the installers rather than supporting the product-service system (PSS) and the many touchpoints that existed in reality. It took time to train the employees and to change the relationships with the installers, who initially felt threatened.

Case 20 Running a Business Means Every Service Shop Has to Make Money

The cause of the problem was that the OEM considered its service centers as shops: simply a channel to sell spares and to keep the equipment out of the

(continued)

production facility. There was limited investment by the OEM, as money was made on the spares sales and not on the local services, and the service centers could not make a case for more backing. This meant that the services that were delivered were often of poor quality; the equipment was often worse than the competition, and the staff were poorly trained. Any surprise that the business did not make money?

The target of every service shop was moved toward making money and margins on their service business as well as the spares they sold. This was a major change in the business model and created a cultural challenge for the whole firm. It required an investment plan for each service center and a training plan for the staff to upgrade both their managerial and technical skills.

All but two of the service centers ended up in profit at the end of the year. Most of the service center managers appreciated the opportunity to improve their working environment and to invest in both equipment and staff. The customers liked the improvements that they experienced. The upgrades to the service centers included spending on new customer suites where their customers could work and be productive when visiting the service centers. This led to improved relationships. Offering free tea and biscuits also encouraged customers to stay longer at the service centers and increased the informal interactions.

The empowerment provided though the profit and loss accounting gave the managers the motivation to build "their" business. They were able to retain some of the earnings to invest directly in local improvements. They were encouraged to work on other equipment (including competitor machines) and start to grow their local installed base. Not everything went as planned; however, the managers and the staff of the service centers considered that most of the changes were for the best.

2.2.5 How Can We Reduce Resistance to Developing Service Business?

There is often resistance to developing a service business, and a carrot can be as good as a stick in terms of overcoming this barrier (Fig. 2.18). The use of storytelling with simple cases designed for internal and external consumption has been shown to reduce the resistance to developing a service business. Human nature tells us that being told something is good for us or the firm is not sufficient to win over "hearts and minds."

The results from the profit and loss simply confirm that the assumptions that service is a cash generator are correct; however, understanding the motivation and what drives others within the firm is important when pushing messages. Stories that demonstrate the successes of individual service managers and integrate these with

Fig. 2.18 Getting the firm to value service may need a carrot rather than a stick approach (illustration by Annick Holland, authors' work)

the bigger picture of the service strategy help to reinforce the communication. The human side of the story coupled with the integration of new technology used in the field can capture the imagination of others in the firm and overcome prejudices that are often the root cause of the barriers to change. Describing the synergies between the product and service activities can be highly motivational and can foster earlier integration of service thinking into NPD activities.

> ...When we started to show how we made our customers successful our product colleagues started to get the message...

> ...Our profitability was only really interesting for our CFO, others were much more interested in hearing how we supported our customers...

The lessons from the cases show that positive service results need to be shared within the firm. The success stories should enjoy the support of senior management from the service business and elsewhere in the firm. When the focus is on the customer experience, more than the financial success for the firm, the stories are more engaging. Such messages can balance the technology use cases that are often used by equipment firms to push their new innovations.

The tools that help to explore these barriers and to build actions to overcome them are:

- Avatar map.
- Cradle-to-grave lifecycle map.
- Cradle-to-grave lifecycle visual mapping.
- Empathy maps.

- Personas.
- Understanding your business.
- Visual journey map – detail level.

Details of the individual tools are given in Chap. 3.

> **Case 21 The Firm Needs to Show Real Success: Not Just Financial Numbers**
> The business was highlighting large contract awards on the Internet as a way of showing success. This had the opposite effect on the service business, where the contracts were generally much smaller. The sales notices did not take into account the margin quality and often focused on the complex technical challenges the team faced. The real kudos was seen to come from a large order intake coupled with a technical challenge.
> This focus on top-line sales and technical challenges puts the service business at a disadvantage to the equipment business. The firm had developed providing engineered solutions and had always considered service as "nice to have" at best and a cost at worst. The equipment business did not consider the repairs that the service business developed as innovative, nor did they really appreciate the cash flows that the service business created, which subsidized the equipment business.
> Three different approaches were taken: (1) to highlight cool innovations, no matter how small or large, and to focus on the technology development; (2) to present regularly the positive cash flow that the service business was able to develop and show how this supported the equipment business, and (3) to show how the service business supported new equipment sales via insights from customer relationships. The proactive approach was to provide different types of information to the wider firm rather than focusing mostly on financially driven data.
> Within the company, the story of service providing the cash that subsidized the equipment business did not stick. In fact, it was reversed, to show that without new equipment, service would not have a business (the integrated idea of a product-service system (PSS) was totally overlooked). The innovation stories worked well and were well received by the new equipment engineers, who had not fully understood the technologies that the service business used and developed as part of their services. The linking of service insights to support the new equipment sales was also appreciated by the equipment sales managers. The service sales managers discovered that the service teams had a deeper customer relationship than they could have imagined.

Case 22 Creating a Protected Service Business as a Single Unit
Service was spread out without a clear focus within the firm. Rather than being a separate business unit, it was expected to deliver services under the control of manufacturing centers where it was generally co-located. Service reported its financial numbers with the local legal entity, which used the cash service generated to hide its operational performance. This led to demotivation of the service employees.

Senior management did not appreciate the value that service brought them, and this meant that they did not see it as a real business rather as a cash cow to be controlled by the manufacturing business. Employees were parked in the service business, which had to operate within business processes designed for the design, sale, and manufacture of large capital equipment rather than for services and spares sales.

Leadership was brought in, to guide service with performance metrics that looked over the whole service business. In effect, a full profit and loss was developed, although often it was a compromise with the local reporting systems of the manufacturing center. The leadership demanded that service was "set free" of the manufacturing business, although they were happy to be co-located and to share some resources. They must be in charge of their hiring and firing policy and have business processes that were designed for service business rather than the manufacturing business.

The challenge initially was with the local manufacturing centers, which were not at all happy showing their real financial performance to the leadership of the firm.

The first success was the reporting of the consolidated service profit and loss across the business and within regions. There were discrepancies, and these suggested that it could be possible to grow the top and bottom lines in services in different regions. Seeing the differences started to encourage the local managers to want to improve performance as no one wanted to be at the bottom of the pile.

The second success came from the new focus on the customer's experience with the service business. This was put down to the fact that the service shop managers viewed their customers as the owners and operators of the equipment rather than their customer being the local manufacturing center. They discovered that providing more services, which they charged for, allowed them to deliver more services that their customers wanted.

2.2.6 How Can We Educate HR/Employees?

In a firm that focuses on equipment, employees are often hired on the basis of their technical competencies. This works well in a design and manufacturing firm, but it

Fig. 2.19 Service leaders need to spend time with human resources to help them understand their business (illustration by Annick Holland, authors' work)

can bring some conflicts when it comes to services, because services are based on people – interpersonal skills here become as important as technical competence. The approaches of the two parts of the business are quite different, the equipment firm being more rational and the service firm being more emotional in outlook. For these reasons, it is important to spend time to educate human resources and the wider employees (Fig. 2.19).

> ...you have to spend time with HR to make them understand...

The clear recommendation is to hire by behavior. Service technicians are best hired for having excellent customer facing behaviors, and they can then learn the necessary technical skills. This is likely to be new for human resources in a technological firm and will lead to a change in culture in the business. Service managers themselves need to be entrepreneurial and to take personal responsibility for their actions rather than hide behind the processes. Sometimes, it may be good to move people within different departments in order to deepen relations as well as exchange expertise and points of view.

> ...Moving staff between locations has been really successful in creating new relationships and a shared culture...

The lessons from the cases are that the service team must spend time to educate human resources so that they understand what you are looking for in terms of new hires and development. Also, when new hires are taken on, people are chosen as much because of their soft skills and entrepreneurial approaches as their technical qualifications. Finally, to help with developing a shared culture and improving competencies, it is important to work with human resources to gain a budget to support relocations and short-term assignments.

The tools that help to explore the barriers and to build actions to overcome them are:

- Avatar map.
- Cradle-to-grave lifecycle map.
- Cradle-to-grave lifecycle visual mapping.
- Service blueprint.
- Understanding your business.
- Visual journey map – high level.
- Visual journey map – detail level.

Details of the individual tools are given in Chap. 3.

> **Case 23 Taking Time to Work with Human Resources Pays Off**
> Every time the firm wanted to hire someone new for the service department, human resources produced a list of people who would not fit. They all seemed to be overqualified and under experienced with the type of work the firm did: project managers with PhDs who had never worked on-site or assembly specialists who had no experience with disassembly of machines. The firm was looking for people who enjoyed the challenge of taking a machine apart and then rebuilding it, often working with the engineers so that they could build a strip-and-rebuild scope of work and bill of materials together. The company did not want or need design engineers.
>
> Looking at the root cause it appeared that human resources was used to hiring engineers and technicians for the design and manufacturing departments. They had well-defined competencies for those departments, but they were missing many of the service profiles. For example, they had no idea what was really needed of a field service technician where they needed a profile based on problem-solving, customer focus, technical capabilities, and the desire to travel.
>
> Human resources processes had to be integrated into the service business. Where the service center was too small to support a human resources manager, the firm hired a service human resources manager to oversee the business and had them spend time at each of the service centers and on-site with field service and the customers. They also started a "recruit a friend" program.
>
> Job adverts started going out with the right profiles and being placed in the right newspapers and websites. The firm started to hire new apprentices for some jobs directly from school. They looked for people who wanted to travel

(continued)

rather than telling people that they had to travel. In effect, they turned the whole system upside down, as many people who succeeded in the manufacturing business were quickly underwater in the less structured service business, where being agile could make the difference between success or failure.

Case 24 Moving People Between Locations Can Be Disruptive in the Short-Term but Pays Off in the Longer Term
There was a general reluctance on the side of management and the employees to move between different locations. At the senior management level, there was a view that the service business needed more mobility and collaborative working, as many of the service workshops were parochial and only considering their own local colleagues and so were missing out on the advantages that a larger service business could offer. The business had local cultures – there was only limited bonding across the whole business. A project was put in place to try to overcome that limitation and build a more open and inclusive culture in the service business.

There were barriers that caused problems with mobility, collaboration, and building a common culture. Other than field service engineers, short-term placements to other service centers were considered disruptive to personal life – they were generally 3 to 6 months in duration and focused on a specific project. When a longer-term assignment was proposed, all of the additional costs were carried by the local service center, as these costs could be substantial, and this had a negative impact on the local financial performance. All of this meant that skills and lessons were not shared effectively, and there was no common service culture within the business.

The approaches taken were twofold: (1) a development fund was included in the management fees to pay for the additional costs of longer-term assignments; and (2) short-term project placements were reduced in duration. For management progression, it was expected that candidates for senior positions would have spent time on at least one long-term assignment. Within the workshop technicians and engineers, it became part of the annual approval system to review the time spent working with other workshops on joint projects.

There were complaints initially about the "holiday tax" that was being applied to pay for the longer-term assignments. This argument soon disappeared as each region became a recipient of the fund and when the incoming manager did not have a negative impact on the local performance. The management of cooperative projects was initially harder to deliver, and

(continued)

> some projects had to be created to help show the value locally. Once a project assignment had been completed, it created a lasting bond on a personal level. Building a common service culture took time; the basis was the mixing of employees at all levels of the business.

2.3 Knowledge and Information

Difficulties in knowledge and information management exist within most (perhaps all) service businesses. Manufacturing firms are concentrated, with most employees based at the manufacturing facility – this is not the case for service businesses, where resources are often spread out and physically distant from each other. The geographic spread of service centers to be close to the customer creates problems that are much easier to correct in a manufacturing firm. Know-how is also often concentrated in the heads (and hands) of blue-collar service workers, while in manufacturing firms, it is vice versa with much more know-how in the heads and computer systems of the white-collar workers.

To overcome these problems in a distributed service network that may also include key partners requires more active management than would be the case if the teams were all in one location. Technology can connect teams and individuals at all levels in the firm. Capturing experience from field service engineers also needs active management, as report writing is not necessarily one of their strengths.

> ...technology and service skills are the main areas we are likely to invest in the next 18 months...

The integration of service, operation, and the equipment into a product-service system (or PSS) with knowledge management and sharing of experience at its core is important when a firm really wants to use all the knowledge at its disposal to improve both the products and the services it delivers to customers.

> ...How do we move to 'service as a product' rather than just customer services? Through a product-service system based on knowledge management developed around cross learning...

The firms recognize that more advanced and complex service solutions require a change from a product focus to a customer process view. This requires a high level of intimacy (hence the importance of sales training) and understanding of each individual customer's business model. This implies a knowledge-rich organization, based on project management and founded on centralized coordination managed in back-office, and decentralizing front-office key processes. Effective communication is also needed between all parties in the service network, as effective knowledge sharing reduces risks. Based on the survey results, the relative importance of the barriers "knowledge and information" are shown in Fig. 2.20.

2.3 Knowledge and Information

Fig. 2.20 The relative importance of the barriers around "knowledge and information" (illustration by Annick Holland, adapted from West et al., 2018)

Knowledge and information are important in a service business, where much of the knowledge is tacit and difficult to convert into written instructions. The top two issues here dealt with sharing of know-how, both within the service teams and back to NPD. As the data suggest, it is often difficult to know how to share information between parties, especially with the research and development area, which generally has a product-centric vision. These two aspects provide barriers to service and service excellence. The data also indicate that it is very often difficult to transform the knowledge that is spread across the company into skills. Adopting open platforms that support the sharing of data, information, and ideas among the various departments, and also with partners, on products, services, and processes allows a greater circulation of knowledge in the service chain.

Project management skills are also important for successful service businesses. These are perhaps different to the project management skills that exist in manufacturing firms, as the service team delivers directly to the customer and must have a commercial aspect that is not present in the more traditional firm. The final two points consider how best to capture information from operational aspects of the equipment and from other parts of the ecosystem. These are important facets but not as critical as the first three issues. The implications for this barrier were:

- Project management skills are needed for delivery.
- Understanding of customer processes/value creation is needed.
- Understanding the product-service system is essential.
- Adopting open platforms that support the sharing of data, information, and ideas among internal functions and partners is key.
- Introducing standard and common processes enables the sharing of data.

Figure 2.21 describes some of the lessons learned and the implications from the interviews.

The barriers the managers identified (in order of importance) were:

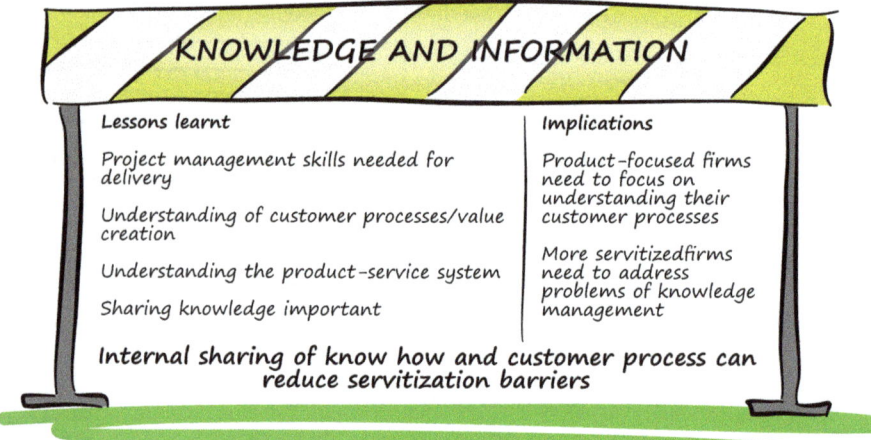

Fig. 2.21 The lessons and implications for the knowledge and information barriers (illustration by Annick Holland, adapted from West et al., 2018)

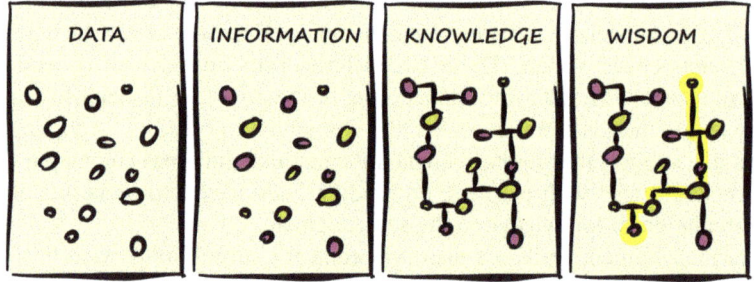

Fig. 2.22 Effort is needed within the firm to grow knowledge and create wisdom (illustration by Annick Holland, authors' work)

1. How do we better share know-how?
2. How can we better share service feedback with the equipment designers?
3. What new project management skills are needed for services?
4. How can we learn more about the equipment operation?
5. How can we mix know-how from installers and customers?

Knowledge and information need to be converted into wisdom within the firm. This is a complex internal process, which needs to start with data and then to integrate cause and causality insights with contextual knowledge (Fig. 2.22). The transformation is a complex process and often difficult in a distributed system.

2.3.1 How Do We Share Know-How?

Know-how exists within the whole business ecosystem – in the manufacturing department, in the service department, with installers, and with the end-users (Fig. 2.23). The equipment manufacturer has design know-how and often overvalues this information, considering it their (OEM) intellectual property and becoming unwilling to share it with others. Within the service network, different levels and types of know-how also exist, both customer-specific and technical.

The best way to share know-how is for people to work together. This way, they learn to trust each other and appreciate differences in experiences. With a complex service network, effort is needed to share both customer information and technical lessons widely, as without effort being invested each service shop will not consider passing know-how on to others. Moving staff between service centers and the manufacturing facilities on rotation is another way to share know-how and increase trust by developing personal networks.

> ...We need to collaborate on projects – if we do not work together, we will not share...

> ...Field Service and Engineering need to spend more time together to value what each does...

The lessons from the two cases are that service managers need to encourage collaboration within and between their service centers. Performance metrics should be set up to support this. On an individual basis, it may reduce project margins, but overall, it reduces risk and increases sales. A more formal approach to sharing and learning from each other needs to be created, on a monthly basis as well as an annual basis to ensure that service technicians share know-how among themselves and with the new product engineers (not always easy).

Fig. 2.23 Sharing know-how effectively between service centers can be tough (illustration by Annick Holland, authors' work)

The tools that help to explore these barriers and build actions to overcome them are:

- Avatar map.
- Business model canvas.
- Business process mapping.
- Case/actor matrix.
- Cradle-to-grave lifecycle visual mapping.
- Detailed empathy card.
- Ecosystem mapping.
- Service blueprint.
- Understanding your business.
- Visual journey map – high level.
- Visual journey map – detail level.

Details of the individual tools are given in Chap. 3.

> **Case 25 Sharing of Know-How Comes from Collaboration**
> For a number of years, there had been attempts to improve the sharing and know-how between the firm's service centers. Workshops and annual meetings were social events that supported connections between people, but they did not create the real depth that supports collaborative working and sharing of know-how. Websites such as SharePoint were viewed as extra work rather than tools for collaboration. Some workshops were understood to be innovative centers that were always pushing the limits, while others wanted to have new information shared with them so they could take advantage of the know-how.
>
> The main points of contact were through the technical teams, while the sales department had a limited idea of what sites were doing. Every site was working locally and only considering its own region. Individual sales teams were incentivized to sell their own local services and working with other service centers could reduce their bonus, even when cooperation was best for the firm. Therefore, the operations teams worked locally, there were few shared projects, and generally engineers did not talk or mix widely outside their region.
>
> There were three issues to focus on. The first action was taken on sales and this was relatively easy to fix. Sales information was stored in a CRM system, and new reports that were shared within the firm (new services, new customers for a service center) focused the high-level solutions on a single page with the name of the service center and the team leader. Second, an open monthly "engineering" call was set up for the engineers to share technical lessons.

(continued)

Thirdly, workshop managers were required to have collaborative projects and intercompany cooperation.

Sharing customer stories with the sales teams worked well, and it gave them a resource of case studies to help sell more solutions to more customers. The monthly open engineering call required a fixed agenda, facilitation, and some simple rules – it then become an open forum to share "what does work and what does not work." This was a success in that it created an "engineering excellence club"; interestingly, no formal meeting notes were kept, and it provided a bridge for experienced and new engineers to discuss engineering challenges. The collaborative working only succeeded with the support of the finance department, which was forced to simplify the requirements for intra-company trading, that had become very complex and did not represent a fair sharing of the margins between workshops.

Case 26 Developing Field Service Behavior in Product Development Engineers

The product development engineers started to ask for more product performance information from the field service engineers and technicians, but they complained about the quality of the information that they received. The field service engineer would take a development engineer to a customer but generally only after a warranty claim. A lot of the feedback from the customers was that they found the development engineers arrogant and lacking empathy – often customers were told that "they had used the product incorrectly."

The operations and maintenance (O&M) teams on the operational sites were in many cases staffed with similar people to the field service engineers. Generally, the operations, maintenance, and field service staff were closer in experience and background than the development engineers. Most of the development engineers had spent little or no time working on an operational site. They were driven by requirements lists and facts that did not change with context and would "correct" the O&M teams when they did something that they considered incorrect. The development engineers wanted to enforce compliance and assumed that the customer was wrong and poorly informed if they used the equipment differently.

There was a radical change in the approach taken by the development engineers – it became a requirement that they spend a month each year on a customer site, with at least half of this time working buddied-up with a field service engineer. The goal was to force collaboration and appreciation of each other's skills and capabilities and to gain a wider understanding of the customer.

(continued)

> The initial result was grumbling that it was a waste of time and money to send a highly qualified engineer to work with a field-tech as "what could they teach me?" was generally the view. Putting the goal into the product development engineers' annual targets made it a requirement, and if engineers did not achieve it for 2 years, they would not gain advancement. In the longer term, it build up a buddy system not only between the field-techs and the engineers but also between the engineers and the O&M staff of the customer's firm. This had not been expected but improved the customer relationship and supported new equipment and spares sales.

2.3.2 How Can We Better Share Service Feedback with the Equipment Designers?

Designers in a NPD team are focused on the development of new technologies and are trained to a high technical standard. This can make them very narrow in outlook and cause a focus on the new technologies rather than addressing existing problems that operators and asset owners are facing. Getting field service technicians to meet with the designers can work, but there is a risk because of the difference in the two personality types. This makes communication between the parties particularly difficult and misleading. Figure 2.24 shows the feedback from different actors.

> ...Knowledge is too little or not shared. Information must be collected by good networking...

Fig. 2.24 Feedback loops must be built between the equipment and service businesses (illustration by Annick Holland, authors' work)

2.3 Knowledge and Information

The application of new technology into older equipment can help to broaden the focus of the equipment designers, as it provides a new route-to-market for technologies developed for new products. It also means that designers have to visit operational sites and meet operators to learn about their problems with existing equipment. Often, designers need to learn that the equipment installed or bought was not the best fit for the operation and that this leads to operational problems or means the equipment does not perform as anticipated.

> ...Engineering is often under pressure because the information is not flowing. The customer watches the equipment for a long time. In case of problems the cause is usually unclear...

When visiting an operational site, it is always good to pair a field service technician with a designer, as both can learn from each other and collaboration helps break down some of the cultural barriers and build personal relationships.

The lessons from the two cases are based on sharing information between technicians and engineers and, to some degree, personal motivations. Designers are driven by new technology, so provide options for them to develop solutions to tough customer problems. Consider developing a program to upgrade operational equipment. Buddy field service technicians with designers to visit operational sites together. Sharing know-how is not easy and it requires management effort to make it happen.

The tools that help to explore the barriers and to build actions to overcome them are:

- Avatar map.
- Cradle-to-grave lifecycle map.
- Detailed empathy card.
- Ecosystem mapping.
- Empathy maps.
- Service blueprint.
- Understanding your business.
- Visual journey map – high level.
- Visual journey map – detail level.

Details of the individual tools are given in Chap. 3.

Case 27 Information Can Only Be Shared Effectively Through Trusting Relationships

In this firm, ineffective information flows meant the design department were talking about failures and grumbling that customers and service should have to provide more technical feedback on the operation of the equipment. The customers did not trust the designers not to use the data and information

(continued)

against them – part of this came from the experience of warranty claim "discussions" and lack of feedback when they did supply data to support operational fault finding. Some customers complained that data had been shared with their competitors, while others said that they did not want product improvements to be made that their competitors could gain from.

The customers were right: yes, the information was generally not going to support them; yes, in the past data provided had been used in warranty claims; and, yes, there was almost no feedback on information when it was actually handed over. The cause of this was that the OEM's service engineers did not often get the information the design department needed and did not follow up directly and in a timely way with their contacts, so the flow was almost always one way with no value being created for the person who handed it over.

To address these issues, an agreement that defined how and what information would and would not be used was drafted, for instance, it could not be used for warranty claim management without both sides agreeing; also, feedback on the use and findings would always be sent directly to the person who handed it in. This approach was initially rejected by the manufacturer's lawyers; however, management pushed it through as they felt trust could not have a price placed upon it.

Direct contact between the customer's staff and the design team was also initially rejected. But case-by-case, the use of the "information disclaimer" allowed open sharing of data, information, and experience. Moreover, the requirement for feedback helped to build and nurture relationships between all the actors, allowing information to be shared more openly. To help with building trust, an unwritten rule was developed, where an engineer with direct contact with a customer would not be used in a warranty claim.

Case 28 Learning to Share Long-Term Equipment Operational Information

Operational information on the long-term performance of products can be used to improve the next generation of equipment or to identify upgrades that can benefit the owner/operator. The challenge for this firm was getting the right people to meet and learn to understand what information was useful and how it would or would not be used. The benefits of sharing equipment's operational performance were well-known, as Rolls-Royce do this exceptionally well, enabled in part by their "power-by-the-hour" service contracts.

Collecting operational data was often not easy, as many of the old machines were not equipped for remote or digital data collection and customers often did not want to share their data. Contextual information was even more difficult to

(continued)

collect, with or without a direct data collection system on the machine. The result at best was "ad hoc" information and data flows and at worst no information other than that collected during a planned or unplanned inspection – hardly enough to identify a suitable mid-life upgrade, recommend new operations and maintenance (or O&M) practices, or provide validated product feedback to the product development teams.

The changes undertaken were as follows: Firstly, all sales managers had to collect basic operational data at every customer visit. They were unable to close a visit report without entering this data. Secondly, lead customers were identified, and field technicians were given a goal to visit their site with a design engineer once each year. Thirdly, a "box" was developed that could be used to collect operational performance data directly off the machine and then suggest upgrades.

Sales mangers did not want to have to collect the data until it was pointed out that it could help them plan their sales targets. Combined field techs and engineering visits were a hit with some customers and developed into a routine event for many customers, generating additional sales. Attaching a data collection box generally failed, as the firm wanted the customer to pay for the "box" even though the value and benefits were mostly for the manufacturer. Only where the "box" was associated with an upgrade did it become possible – although even here discounts were provided.

2.3.3 What New Project Management Skills Are Needed for Services?

An equipment business needs project management skills to develop new products as well as operational management skills to ensure that equipment comes off the production line. Often, what is missing is commercial project management that is needed to deal directly with customers – for a service business, this is also a critical skill to possess (Fig. 2.25).

> ...The service team need to be coached and their project management abilities should move from technical to commercial...
>
> ...Commercial project management is just different to project management for new product development...

Project management skills are important to manage the expectations of the customer in a service business – in actual fact, they are "commercial project management" skills. These skills also provide a risk management process, as some industrial end-users prefer to reduce maintenance activities, and this can often lead to a claims process. Good commercial project management skills help to reduce the risk

Fig. 2.25 Service businesses need effective project management skills to succeed (illustration by Annick Holland, authors' work)

of this behavior. Others may prefer to be at arm's length, and the project management needs to be responsive, with the capability and flexibility to deal with these different situations.

The lessons from the two cases are based around commercial project management; this is different to the type of project management required for new product development. Project managers must be empowered to deliver the project: we must not forget that they are responsible for service execution. Training and coaching are needed to help them to make the move to commercial project management from technical project management. Finally, risk management must be managed in a proactive way.

The tools that help to explore the barriers and to build actions to overcome them are:

- Case/actor matrix.
- Customer value proposition.
- Detailed empathy card.
- Ecosystem mapping.
- Metric cascades.
- Personas.
- Service blueprint.

Details of the individual tools are given in Chap. 3.

Case 29 Commercial Project Management Is Just Different to Project Management for Product Development

The firm has proven project management systems and competencies for product development, but they just do not seem to work for service. Many projects have been late or over budget, and the firm has not charged the customers for out-of-scope work. The project managers keep asking the steering committee for guidance and for requests rather than asking the customer. This is slowing down the whole process and causes the firm to be repeatedly late with delivery.

Their traditional project management processes were based on the NPD compared with service projects. The processes were also designed around centralized project control rather than local empowerment within guidelines. This meant that the firm was slow to respond to requests and projects often looked to the management for solutions rather than discussing changes to scope with the customer. When waiting for the central "OK," the customer often thought that the firm was trying to hide issues from them, and this reflected on their experience with the service team.

The firm moved to commercial project management, initially needing to hire in new staff. They were amazed at the potential revenue the firm was missing out on and created a structured and controlled approach to manage project issues. The project managers were empowered to act and given guidelines to help them know where the limits were. They also always had an open line for coaching and support when on a customer's site for an inspection. The firm became proactive with their "extra works" management and used it to get additional (justifiable) work – their customers actually liked being chased.

The change was not easy as it was a culture shift. Contracts had to change so the firm could become more proactive with extra work and waiting time. They also used the change to get closer to the customer by issuing daily status reports to base discussions on and drive them through. Previously, things had been hidden and so the firm had to have some tough commercial discussions. However, these changes drove up project sales, margins, and customer satisfaction.

Case 30 The Service Team Needs to Be Coached in Project Management

All of the service project managers had attended (and achieved) the Project Management Institute (PMI) certification, but something was just not working. There were late projects, blaming the customer for being late, and projects with

(continued)

cost overruns, yet the service team thought they were following the process. It felt like the team was just trying to do the right thing without really knowing what the right thing was.

In fact, it was about a lack of a proactive approach to work, doing the right things in the right way rather than following processes written (often badly) by others. The cause of this was the lack of experience of the newly appointed project team, coupled with the fact that they worked differently within a workshop than on a customer's site.

The firm took the opportunity to hire an experienced project manager who was used to working on customers' sites and delivering projects on time, to budget and quality. Their task was to coach the other project managers how to do the right things in the right way. The coach visited sites and learned about the problems the project managers were having first hand. A workshop was held to bring them together to confirm the problems – very much like a lean workshop. All of the projects were given the management coach's phone number and encouraged to use it. Post project, lessons learned meetings were held – for the first time – to try to break down the work process and allow for peer-to-peer reflections on performance and to share ideas on what to improve next.

An open door to a coach had built up the team's confidence and skills and led to a coming together and maturing of the project management team within field service. Encouraging the service teams to learn from each other and to question the processes they were following gave them purpose. Before this innovation, it felt to the service group that they had to just follow the rules and perform the work rather than leading the development of the processes to make their lives better and to improve the outcomes for the customers.

The transition took twice as long as expected and cost many airline tickets. However, the result was a more professional project management approach in the repair workshops.

2.3.4 How Can We Learn More About the Equipment Operation?

There is nothing better than knowing where the equipment you make is, who is operating it, how it is being operated and maintained, and how it is performing (Fig. 2.26). The Internet of things promises to provide answers to all of these questions and more. Yet, many operators are unwilling to share the data automatically, while on the other side, many manufacturers have not put in place systems to track the location of their installed base. Therefore, information sharing between the service provider and the product developer is often impossible. Without a basic

Fig. 2.26 Learning from the operators can help improve equipment performance (illustration by Annick Holland, authors' work)

nameplate with an address, the chance of learning about operations is low. Worse, there is chance that you will miss the opportunity to sell basic services such as spares and planned inspections.

> ...With the IoT in place we should know much more about the operation of the equipment...

> ...We need to share service feedback with the equipment designers in a more effective way...

Assuming that owners and operators do not allow their machines to be hooked up to the Internet, what could you do to improve your understanding of the equipment performance and operation? Every new equipment sale must be shared with the service team – every service sales manager or field service technician then needs to confirm basic data on the equipment during a site visit. More can be archived later; however, the basic data should quickly become the core tool for proactive services.

The lessons from the two cases that follow are in many ways quite technical, in that firms should build and maintain an installed base database and integrate it into the CRM system. On top of this, they should collect basic operational and maintenance data on the equipment, as the sensor data is not sufficient as it misses the essential contextual information. Importantly, the manufacturer needs to ensure that all machines are connected to the IoT and that any monitoring is paid for by the customer.

The tools that help to explore the barriers and to build actions to overcome them are:

- Avatar map.
- Business process mapping.
- Case/actor matrix.

- Cradle-to-grave lifecycle map.
- Cradle-to-grave lifecycle visual mapping.
- Customer jobs-to-be-done.
- Customer value proposition.
- Detailed empathy card.
- Job-to-be-done insights.
- Job-to-be-done outcomes.
- Metric cascades.
- Personas.
- Service blueprint.
- Understanding your business.
- Visual journey map – high level.
- Visual journey map – detail level.

Details of the individual tools are given in Chap. 3.

Case 31 Using the IoT Provided Insights into the Performance of the Equipment

Apple knows everything about the use of their phones; a phone only costs a few hundred euros. This engineering firm knew very little about the use of the products it provided, even though they cost tens of thousands of euros. There was no installed base of equipment, and, where they did have data, it was only partially correct. The firm asked the sales team to keep the database up-to-date, but they did not do it; they asked customers to register their equipment, but they did not. Customers did not want to connect their equipment to the Internet. No one feels responsible for tracking the equipment, but it should be a core asset for the service business unit.

On the service front, there was no apparent value for the customer; too many customers were worried that the firm would use service calls to police their warranty obligations. The service team's basic needs were to know where the equipment was actually installed and its operational hours. This really helped to understand the demand for aftermarket parts and services; it also made sure that sales representatives visited each customer at least once a year.

The firm started to track all sales and created an installed base database from the enterprise resource planning data they had. This was initially problematic as there was often confusion between the invoice address and the installation address. The firm made it a requirement (due to export controls) for the customer to provide the end destination of the equipment. This approach was not perfect, but it helped, and sales and field services could then use the information to support the customer better.

(continued)

Connecting the equipment to the Internet via the customer's WLAN was not as simple as anticipated. IT, changed passwords, and weak signals all caused problems, so the firm moved to 4G technology and GPS and, for under 100 euros per unit, they had a workable solution. It also allowed them to read basic machine operational data so they could start to build up some operational insights. To achieve all this, the firm had to be very open and transparent with customers when the machines were first connected to their systems.

Starting with new machines, the firm made connection a requirement for a warranty extension. The data collected was shared openly with the customer, including if there was a warranty claim, as it was considered that the data should be "neutral."

The firm also integrated the connection system with their service contracts, allowing remote troubleshooting with the customer. This was a very positive aspect, as it started the process of designing new value propositions based around the customer rather than providing standardized solutions.

Case 32 Learning to Share Knowledge About Equipment Performance Within the Firm

Very few people in the firm had hard facts on how the equipment really performed in operation after the end of the warranty period. Sales pretended to have information, but it was generally not usable and poorly structured. Field service visited the customers to fix broken machines or to inspect them, but again they did not structure their findings in a way that was really useful. Customers generally only contacted the firm when something was wrong. Product development wanted to know how their products were performing so that they could develop new generations, but service provided almost no customer feedback on existing products and so did not offer value their development team.

Generally, the machines were not connected to the cloud, and so the machine performance information was all unreliable. The problem came from the firm creating "silos" of disconnected data and limited information, coupled with everyone having and needing something different. There was also a view within the firm that "we know best" and that the "customer expects us to know everything," while often the opposite was true. So, a new approach was needed.

The firm set up a user group and held an annual meeting each of their four major segments. The product development team was forced to attend, along with the product sales team, the service sales team, and the field service

(continued)

technicians. The purpose was not to have a sales push but rather a listening session, which needed careful management.

Buddying product development engineers with service technicians and customers was also done, in order to break down barriers. Every development engineer had it in their personal goals to spend 1 week each year with customers and field services.

Where machines were connected to the cloud, the firm ran joint workshops with customers, field service, and development engineers.

The user group showed that the customer was not the enemy and that they could support technical understanding of the machines the firm had designed. The meetings were a two-way street.

Buddying also allowed development engineers to get first hand insights of the jobs field service and the customers' technicians were doing and gain understanding from simple direct observations. Barriers were broken on all sides, and customers, designers, and technicians learned who to contact for the information they needed to improve performance.

Joint workshops with customers helped them to get more from their connected services, and the firm was able to develop the online system to offer better support for existing customers as well as new sales. This started to provide real value to the aftermarket customers.

2.3.5 How Can We Mix Know-How from Installers and Customers?

Installers and customers often have a better understanding of a product than the design engineers from the OEM. They may not appreciate the sophistication of the machinery as well as the engineers from the OEM who created it; however, they have a greater knowledge of the ecosystem around the equipment and of the many commissioning and operational issues. This know-how is often discounted by the OEM business' engineers, but it has direct value for the service business and indirect value for product design and the OEM, so it needs to be captured and integrated into that knowledge pool (Fig. 2.27).

> ...Our customers, installers and agents have real know-how, yet we fail to take advantage of it...

Customers and installers may well be able to teach the OEM's service engineers new and better ways to install or remove their products. They may also have more know-how on operating the equipment away from its design point, and they may have changed the maintenance schedule over time. This know-how should be collected, analyzed, used, and integrated by the OEM's service business. This can support the continued improvement process; it can also bind field service technicians with the end-user in a far more intimate way and again improve the customer experience.

2.3 Knowledge and Information

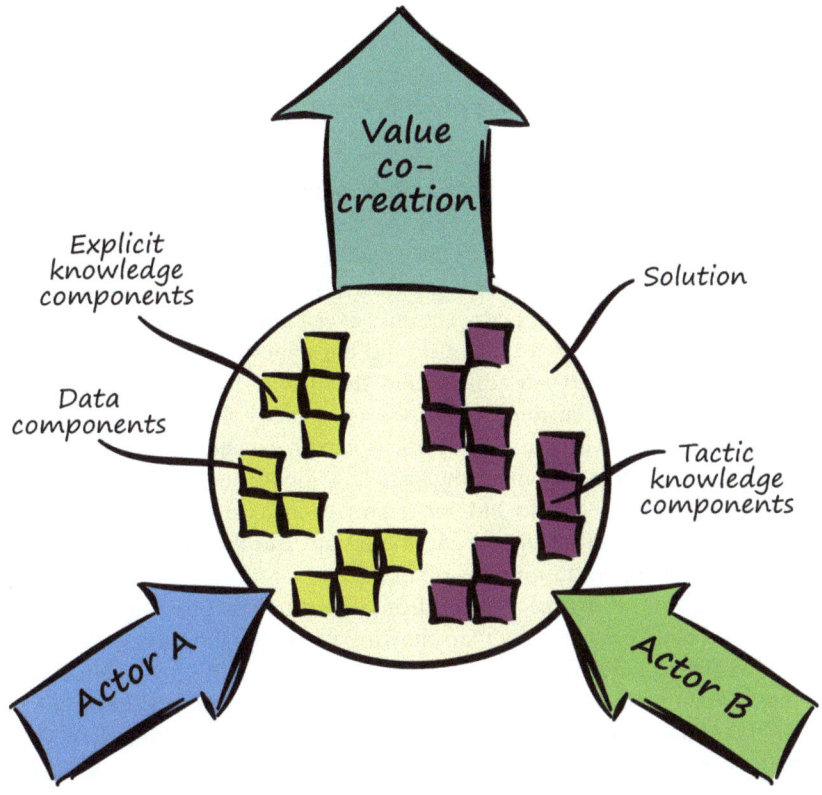

Fig. 2.27 Value co-creation means we need to bring together different actors and combine their explicit, tacit knowledge and data (illustration by Annick Holland, adapted from Valtakoski, 2017)

> ...We need to work harder to integrate know-how from our agents, installers and our customers...

The lessons here are that all actors can (and should) contribute to the value co-creation process. The service business should learn from the installers and the customers, and the manufacturer does not have all of the answers – this is the case for new equipment and even more so for older machines that have been in operation for many years.

The tools that help to explore the barriers and to build actions to overcome them are:

- Avatar map.
- Cradle-to-grave lifecycle map.
- Cradle-to-grave lifecycle visual mapping.
- Customer jobs-to-be-done.
- Metric cascades.

- Personas.
- Service blueprint.

Details of the individual tools are given in Chap. 3.

Case 33 The OEM Needed to Learn from Its Installers
The firm ignored their installers and always considered the end-users, viewing the installers only as a channel to the "real" customers. So, what could be learned from the installers? They were always complaining about prices and deliveries of new equipment and were only ever thinking of the new job.

The main problem was that the firm did not understand the installers and what motivated them. It was discovered that the installers had a difficult relationship with their customer who was not exactly the end-user but was normally a team set up to deal with CAPEX (capital expenditure) projects. The firm also found out that they made the installers' job harder by not giving them the materials they needed to bid for a project in a structured way. Then, materials would be delivered late and mixed up, and the installers were not very well supported with fitting instructions.

The OEM firm took time to learn from the installers, observed how they worked, and build up a journey map showing where the firm needed to learn. The OEM started to realize that the installers were in effect a franchise service business. The manufacturer had simply been providing products to installers rather than supporting them to sell those products to end-users. The firm needed to provide the installers with real service and integrate their know-how so that they did a better job for their customer and pulled through the firm's products.

Installers were given budget/benchmark figures to help them outline their projects in the primary phase. A tool was developed that allowed them to build and organize a bid using the firm's products, including allowing them to schedule deliveries and place orders. There was additional training for installation, and a post-installation review was offered, to confirm the quality and validity of the warranty from handover to the customer rather than from delivery.

The firm's relationship with the installers improved as it learned what they needed, when, and why. They found the whole process easier from bidding to closing out the installation. This changed the sales relationship with the installers and provided them with different levels of certification. It also gave them a direct feedback route to product development with their installation problems.

Case 34 Learning to Use Customer Know-how
The customer was very loyal, always working only with this firm. This was a real relationship business. But the customer never let the firm do the field service work – they always did the removal, installation, and commissioning of its equipment. This was rather frustrating, as they were reducing field service sales, and in any case, as manufacturers, the firm were meant to be the experts, so why was the customer maintenance team doing the work?

The problem was not really a problem. The customer had competent technicians available on-site who were able to quickly and efficiently remove the equipment and put it on a truck to the firm's repair facility. They always phoned once the machine was on the truck, so the workshop knew it was coming. Once repaired, the customer took delivery and installed it during a scheduled inspection. They always had a spare machine available.

The firm eventually asked the customer why they did not use the field service team. Their answer was simple; they confirmed that they could do the field work themselves faster, as there was no traveling time. They did say that if they were short of labor, they would call the field service team to come and help them.

After a lot of thought about the situation, the firm asked to come to their site and watch them working, to compare approaches, and offered their technicians the opportunity to visit the firm's repair center and watch the equipment being repaired. What was achieved was that the firm learned from the customer how to remove and reinstall the equipment faster, and since then, they have used the new know-how on other sites.

Having their customer's technicians visit the firm's repair center for a week as the machines are repaired has increased the personal bonding between the staff. The people really are very similar, and they were going out together in the evening on social events. The customer now knows the team who is taking care of their repairs and they understand who to contact.

2.4 Products and Activities

Designing service packages is, and is likely to remain, difficult for many firms, due to customers' demands. Standardization in services is not the same as for products, and this does create issues with the new equipment business. The workforce is likely to be mainly "blue-collar," which often also creates difficulties with the development of new services due to a lack of formal management skills. Therefore, design of modular – hence flexible – customer value propositions that include technical and commercial aspects is very complicated. When the customer value propositions also have to support an installed base of mixed age and operation, this is further compounded – creating a problem that the new equipment business does not want.

Fig. 2.28 The relative importance of the barriers around "products and activities" (illustration by Annick Holland, adapted from West et al., 2018)

Often overlooked by the new equipment business is that the service technicians get first hand feedback on any operational problems with the equipment in the field.

> ...new products drive our world, and we need to overcome design problems and provide service/upgrades that are of value to our customers...

Usually, this omission is as much due to cultural differences between the service and manufacturing teams as the difference in the business models. It leads to poor focus on product improvements that could be implemented both in the field and in new equipment models, to the detriment of the firm.

It is possible to get it right and create opportunities so that service and product businesses can support each other. The installed base is a critical asset and is often not considered as such.

> ...keep working on the installed base and improving market data, this is key...

Using online systems and field service engineers, it is possible to learn from operational problems that end-users have, potentially with root causes that are not associated directly with the equipment originally supplied. This can then lead to new ideas for solutions, providing opportunities to reapply new technologies as conversions, modifications, or upgrades.

> ...adding service to create a product-service system that has a positive feedback loop to new product development has been our biggest challenge in our service transformation journey...

The relative importance of the barriers around "products and activities" from the survey is shown in Fig. 2.28.

"Products and activities (services)" were considered less important by the businesses we talked to than the way that knowledge and information are shared.

2.4 Products and Activities

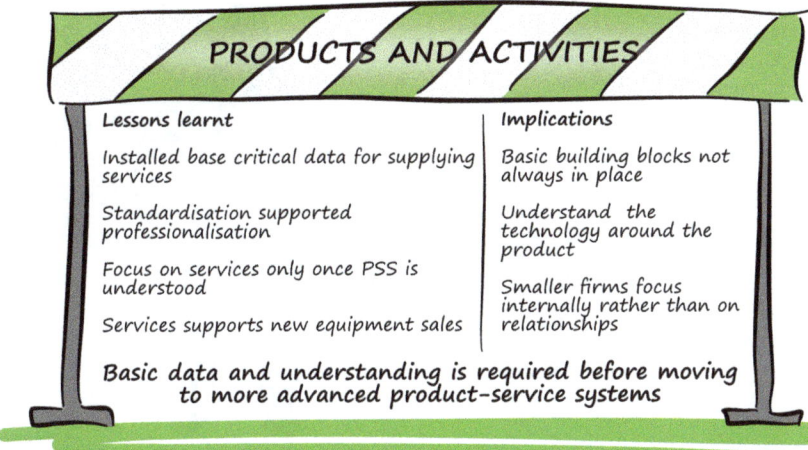

Fig. 2.29 The lessons and implications for the products and activities barriers (illustration by Annick Holland, adapted from West et al., 2018)

This surprised us, as it could have been expected to be the core of the service delivery. The top two issues were different and not related: professionalization of service delivery and understanding the installed base. The first issue is related to the firm's structure and processes, whereas the second is related to better understanding of the customer via the installed base. Hence, they are both outward-looking. Creating opportunities for the exchange and sharing of information and data with customers means a firm knows more about how the asset is used and based on the customer's gains and pains and assesses what the strengths and weaknesses are of the services offered. This makes it easier to segment customers and configure customized offer plans that meet customer expectations better, offering advanced services only to those who actually need them. At the same time, the introduction of training plans aimed at improving technical and relational skills helps overcome barriers related to competences.

The other three issues are clustered closely together. The design and delivery of advanced services shows that firms want to move to a new level in services. Supporting new equipment sales is an aspect that is important for service, as there are many more service touch points with the end-user than for new equipment sales. The least important issue was associated with the customer-driven demand for digital services – the results suggest that the firms questioned had limited market pull. Figure 2.29 describes some of the lessons learned and the implications from the interviews.

Results confirm what we had found in the literature: that the installed base data is critical for service delivery and combining the CRM data with the installed base simplifies the implementation of new product-service solutions. For manufacturing firms, such long-term data was not considered important, but for services, it is essential. Service standardization and modularization become a must for the firms

Fig. 2.30 Firms need to learn to understand both the product and the service aspects (illustration by Annick Holland, authors' work)

to continuously improve and diversify product-service offerings and react to market demands: this needs integration of product and service know-how (Fig. 2.30). In particular, modularization allows firms to focus on delivering services on other manufacturers' products. The integration of customer experience into NPD was considered critical to the development of new product-service solutions and changes to the standard product development processes. Internet of things-enabled technologies were often the enabler for advanced product-service solutions based on use. They also provided opportunities for cost saving via remote services and could also help build trust between the different parties. Implications for this barrier were that:

- Installed base data is critical for supplying services.
- Standardization supported professionalization.
- Focus on services once the product-service system is understood.
- Services support new equipment sales.
- Create opportunities to exchange and share asset information and data with customers.
- Segmenting customers and configuring customized offer plans meet customer expectations more effectively.
- Introducing training plans aimed at improving technical and relational skills helps overcome competence barriers.

To help you better understand how to navigate the barriers, we will provide insights from cases to help you understand how others overcame them. The barriers we identified were (in order of importance):

1. How do we understand the installed base?
2. How can we professionalize service delivery?
3. When can we start to design and deliver advanced services?

4. If a customer asks for digital service, where do we start?
5. How can services support new equipment sales?

2.4.1 How Do We Understand the Installed Base?

The concept of the installed base does not fit into the business model of an equipment business: they consider opportunities to sell new equipment. The installed base is the major asset for the service business and is where they make the easiest sales and help firms to understand where to locate service centers (Fig. 2.31). By not having the address of every machine sold, the service business may be missing sales opportunities. Even if the installed base is not fully documented, it may be possible to form proxies to confirm if the level of service sales is as it should be.

...Set up an installed base database which ensures a constant traceability of your own fleet...

Having the address for every piece of equipment in a database, along with its operational hours per year and the expected service spend, allows detailed service market analysis to be done and provides real targets for the sales managers. For some equipment, it is also possible to estimate the consumption of spares, consumables, and field services as well as evaluate the machine availability metrics. In other cases, it may not be possible to have a full address for the equipment, so the installed base is

Fig. 2.31 Service centers should be placed close to customers and the equipment (illustration by Annick Holland, authors' work)

not complete. Here, the basic ratios of service sales to a new equipment for a region may be enough to understand the level of sales and the faithfulness of customers to the OEM.

> ...The analysis of the installed base clarified how many plants are not yet under service or how many contracts were no longer active...

The lessons from the two cases are that it is critically important to create and maintain an installed equipment database as this is the basis of the service income. The installed base should be integrated with the CRM system and a market model. Once this has been done, the installed base can be used to proactively support the sales process.

The tools that help to explore the barriers and to build actions to overcome them are:

- Avatar map.
- Business process mapping.
- Case/actor matrix.
- Cradle-to-grave lifecycle map.
- Cradle-to-grave lifecycle visual mapping.
- Customer jobs-to-be-done.
- Job-to-be-done insights.
- Job-to-be-done outcomes.
- Service blueprint.

Details of the individual tools are given in Chap. 3.

Case 35 The Installed Base Is a Key Asset for Service Business

The firm had no idea where the equipment it sold was going and would be rather surprised when they were phoned up and asked for service or spares. Service was only provided on a reactive basis, and there was limited marketing support to keep track of where the equipment was. They felt something was wrong but did not really understand the problem or how to build a solution. Having seen ship and aircraft tracking systems, they thought that building an installed base tracking system was too complex to achieve.

The firm found that that data in the enterprise resource planning system contained both the "ship to" and the invoice addresses. However, this did not always connect to the final owner/operator of the equipment, because of intermediaries: installers or distributors. They also had a separate CRM system that contained all of the active service customers, but it was orphaned from the enterprise resource planning data.

(continued)

The firm used "export rules" to require installers and distributors to tell them where the equipment actually was. This required one additional field in the enterprise resource planning data, which was then exported monthly to the CRM system, and a sales manager from service was allocated each account. Over the life of the machine, touchpoints were identified: end of warranty, scheduled maintenance, and obsolescence events. The firm required their sales team to have an annual contact session with each customer. This was all done openly so that business partners such as installers and distributors were not annoyed. To help the customer keep in direct contact with the firm, they started to put QR codes onto the equipment, linked to their CRM system.

Building an installed base database does not happen overnight; a lot of cleaning was needed on the data, and as new data flowed into the system, it needed checking. The integration of the installed base with the service sales managers' normal day-to-day tasks was critical for the change management, driving customer contacts and sales targets. QR codes on the equipment helped continue to track off-line equipment. The firm even started to build up a logbook for each piece of equipment. It was not a perfect solution, and they keep finding new insights from the installed base database, but it is now their key asset for driving service sales.

Case 36 Learning to Understand the Market from the Installed Base
A firm found that it had a problem with its installed base when tracking aircraft online. They had a basic installed base (IB) system integrated into their CRM system that reminded sales to contact the customer. It was proactive but did not provide the type of information that could allow them to drive customer experience and sales. The world had moved on since they first developed the IB tool.

The problem was simple: the firm only had machines' serial numbers, customer, and location in the IB. They did not track or link orders or warranty claims against a machine, and they had no idea how the equipment was being used, or even if it had been decommissioned.

It was going to be impossible to put all of the machines online and track their operational life. Nevertheless, the firm built a basic operations tracker and linked it back to the CRM system to provide a simple phone app for customers. It only tracked basic operational data, but that allowed the service team to support the product more effectively, including uptime and unplanned downtime.

Where it was not possible to connect the equipment to the web, the firm instructed sales and field services to input basic data when they visited the

(continued)

customer. Again, this allowed sales to become more proactive in supporting the equipment.

In both cases, they linked up other data (e.g., inspections, spares shipments, warranty, etc.) with the machine to make the IB the focal point for the machine history.

Knowing the number of hours of operation supported the firm understand the condition of the machine and anticipate the need for maintenance. It helped offer better support for the customer and insights to product development. The firm could be proactive and provide early warning for maintenance events, allowing them to ensure that the maintenance team understood the needs and for sales to contact them before the event, also improving resource allocation.

Managing the machine history was not as easy as expected, and it took a number of iterations to get it right. There were arguments about the level of integration, especially with inspection reports. Product development argued that all inspection reports should be written in the online tool. The field service team pushed back strongly at this suggestion, and a pragmatic solution was built.

2.4.2 How Can We Professionalize Service Delivery?

When service is only a cost, it cannot be a professional activity, as it will be run under the control of the equipment business. When service has its own profit and loss sheet (profit and loss), it can take control of the way it delivers services to its customers (most often the end-users). When its role is only to prevent or limit warranty claims, this cannot be the case, which has been confirmed by leaders in the field. So, it is important that service teams are provided with the technology to help them deliver services professionally (Fig. 2.32).

It is only after being given full responsibility for all service work that the professionalization of the service business really begins. New service-focused processes are developed with core focus on the customer experience and satisfaction.

> ...We do not understand our customer's processes so how we can claim to understand how they create value?...

Prior to the change, the "customer" is often considered the internal customer (e.g., within the equipment business) rather than the final end-user. Once services take control of their own work and customer contacts, new services and improvements to the project management processes can be developed and deployed.

> ...We were able to convert a warranty event into extra work for the project at the request of the customer...

2.4 Products and Activities

Fig. 2.32 Service must be given modern tools to allow them to perform effectively (illustration by Annick Holland, authors' work)

The lessons here link with other barriers. Key to professionalization is providing service with full profit and loss responsibility. This is only the initial step, as the service managers then need to focus on customer experience and satisfaction. A part of focusing on the customer experience is to develop a commercial project management capability as this will help the service managers to provide increasingly high levels of service quality to their customers.

The tools that help to explore the barriers and to build actions to overcome them are:

- Avatar map.
- Case/actor matrix.
- Cradle-to-grave lifecycle map.
- Cradle-to-grave lifecycle visual mapping.
- Customer jobs-to-be-done.
- Customer value proposition.
- Empathy maps.
- Job-to-be-done insights.
- Job-to-be-done outcomes.
- Metric cascades.
- Service blueprint.

- Visual journey map – high level.
- Visual journey map – detail level.

Details of the individual tools are given in Chap. 3.

> **Case 37 Learning About Customer Value**
> The firm always spoke proudly about its "unique selling proposition" (USP) but did not understand how each of its customers created value in their individual businesses. The firm focused on the technology and not the segments. The engineers loved their innovations and often blamed customers for not using "their" equipment properly.
> The service teams also focused on the equipment and how to keep it operational, by following the OEM's maintenance recommendations, and did not really understand what was important for their customers' businesses.
> There was a technology focus in the firm in both the equipment and the service business. The firm weakly segmented customers without understanding in-depth which outcomes were important or how and why they operated the equipment in the way they did. They did not understand how maintenance worked around the customer's production schedule or how the equipment that they sold fitted in with other machinery within each customer's machine park.
> Segmentation was extended and made more actionable rather than the basic marketing profiles that they had used before. The sales managers were encouraged to segment their customers to help them understand how, where, and when their customers created value and when they did not. They were told to ask how their customer's businesses worked and to "walk through" each firm's processes. Field service technicians, who had the closest customer interactions, were supported to ask their contacts how their business worked. This built understanding of what was important for the customer and how the firm could help their client's business become more successful by understanding its purpose.
> It took a long time to move from a basic approach based on "quality, price, and delivery" to one that sought to understand the customers' value outcomes and processes. Process thinking does not come overnight when a firm has a long tradition of selling technology rather than solutions. Where it did work, lessons were shared within the sales and field service teams. Examples outside the industry were used to help demonstrate the need for change. Using Value Proposition Design became embedded within the business and helped the team to understand customers' problems and how to build solutions.

Case 38 Improving Warranty and Creating Extra Work

The firm was regularly called back following a service repair, because the machine did not work, and an exasperated customer was claiming this had to be rectified under warranty. It's a common challenge that is faced in service business. The problem was most often caused by incorrect reassembly or recommissioning of the machine, which was not often part of the firm's scope and was generally executed by the customer's maintenance and operations team. Usually, the firm's sales manager would visit the site and then agree to sharing the cost, a solution that was completely outside of the contract, but it worked.

The firm was not working commercially with its customers and was allowing them to dictate actions because of local practices. The equipment sales departments were often the cause of the problem, as they were always worried about the next order and wanted to make their business partners look good. Sales thought they were looking after ongoing business relationships.

The firm took the sales department out of direct customer interaction when dealing with warranty claims. Warranty was based within project execution, so a (service) commercial manager dealt with warranty issues, calling on the collaboration of sales where needed. A commercial approach was built based on the facts, and a face-saving solution was offered that was in-line with the claim and the signed contract.

Some customers confirmed that their own technicians were the reason for the supposed warranty claim when faced with the facts and then asked for training or field service support to correct the work. This led in many cases to extra works being created from the initial claim rather than losing margin. In other cases, more creative solutions were built, with more advanced service models based on long-term relationships.

These changes made the firm more commercial while at the same time assessing each failure with the customer as if it were a noncompliance of performance. The aim was to work collaboratively with the root cause – this was not possible in all cases – so that they could help the customer work out where things had gone wrong rather than just saying it could not have been their fault. The firm found that this approach built more trust with their customers, particularly when they conceded the warranty based on the joint root cause analysis. It helped to stabilize project margins and reduced the provisions made for warranty work.

2.4.3 When Can We Start to Design and Deliver Advanced Services?

You should first be able to deliver basic services in a professional way before moving to advanced services (Fig. 2.33). For some firms, the transition to advanced

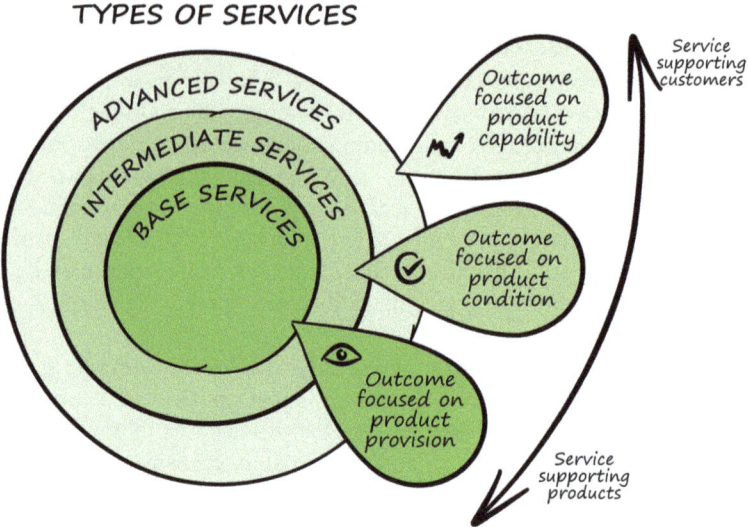

Fig. 2.33 Firms need to provide an excellent basic service before moving to advanced or intermediate services (illustration by Annick Holland, adapted from Baines & Lightfood, 2013)

services will be complicated, as it will require market acceptance. For others, the move is less complex. Often, this process may be necessary to satisfy specific needs coming from the market.

> ...We moved from repairing trucks to ensuring the operational outcomes for the fleet owners and operators...

Introducing advanced services requires the service supplier to be more commercially aware of the risks that they are taking, as many of those risks are embedded within the contract, with the supplier becoming liable for them. In many cases, the customer will provide the push for advanced services and in effect become the test case for the supplier. The design of new advanced services can lead, for example, a coffee machine manufacturer to take responsibility for the quality of the coffee produced by those machines and the ordering of coffee, cups, sugar, etc. to fill the machine.

There is no single route for moving to advanced services. All solutions are different and often customized for an individual client. However, there are some firms who have managed to standardize and create modules for advanced service delivery (often from building blocks of basic services). Importantly, the design of new advanced services is different from traditional services and requires business development to better understand the customer job-to-be-done, pains, and gains as well as the requirements of the equipment. Skills in contract design, financial modeling, and commercial project management are also key. That is why it is

2.4 Products and Activities

important to develop a separate working group, dedicated to manage advanced services.

> ...We built up a separate team to contract advanced service agreements. It was a big step in terms of contract management for us...

The first lesson for moving to advanced services is that the service centers need to deliver the basic services reliably. This is the foundation to advanced services, and without it, the service business may be able to sell new advanced services; however, they will face delivery issues. To provide advanced (or intermediate) services, a team who focus on commercial operation of the project is needed, and they are needed for both the sales and the delivery phases.

The tools that help to explore the barriers and to build actions to overcome them are:

- Avatar map.
- Case/actor matrix.
- Cradle-to-grave lifecycle map.
- Cradle-to-grave lifecycle visual mapping.
- Customer jobs-to-be-done.
- Customer value proposition.
- Empathy maps.
- Metric cascades.
- Personas.
- Service blueprint.
- Understanding your business.
- Visual journey map – high level.
- Visual journey map – detail level.

Details of the individual tools are given in Chap. 3.

> **Case 39 Being Pulled into Advanced Services by Customers**
> Customers liked this firm's trucks and service but disliked the initial investment costs. Their trucks were in fact more expensive than those of other manufacturers, but the TCO based on medium-to-high mileage was lower. Coupled with higher availability, fewer days of maintenance per year, and higher reliability, the value proposition was sound.
>
> Customers asked why they could not have an inclusive operational cost – it happens with company cars, trains, and aircraft – so why not for trucks? The firm was being pulled into advanced services.
>
> There really was no problem other than that the firm had no idea what they needed to do. The customer was saying they wanted to consume the product
>
> (continued)

and services in a different way and that they might prefer to rent the truck and pay per mile driven. The problem was really how to convert the costs into a completely different form within the new revenue model. Because this firm had a technical focus, not a financial one, this was new to them.

They spoke to a bank who could provide the leasing of the lorries, in much the same way as with cars. They dug into inspections and costs on trucks in order to understand the TCO. There were benchmark data that the firm could get access to, so they could understand the assumptions and make sure nothing was missed. The toughest part was the variability of fuel costs, so it was excluded, as it's easier and cheaper to allow the lorry fleet owner to pay directly for this.

A new revenue model was created where they charged the lorry fleet owner for the maintenance on a per mile basis. Very similar to Rolls-Royce with power-by-the-hour, this model included the planned and unplanned maintenance and consumables like tires. Inspections on the trucks were jointly planned so that delivery schedules could be integrated with the required maintenance. The firm provided risk-and-reward schedules based on fuel efficiencies (their main costs) and on availability – this required a minimum fleet size. They also offered driver training as an option, as they knew that this would improve the ability to hit some of the performance targets. The hardest aspect was the requirement to have a fixed cost or a minimum number of miles per year in the contract. This was needed to ensure the firm covered their (expanding) workshop network. The most successful approach was to agree an average truck minimum mileage per year for the fleet. Now with the new advanced service agreements in place, the firms are virtually guaranteed the work.

Case 40 Delivering Advanced Services
A firm found that executing advanced services was very different to delivering basic services. In effect, advanced services are a project with many project-like attributes, and they are different in many ways to the basic services the firm had been delivering for many years. After losing one contract early on, they wanted to understand what they were doing wrong and then adjust, so they could improve the value the customers were getting and help stop the time wasting they faced with the early failure and learn from it.

The firm did not have the commercial and project management skills that it needed to execute the contracts. They were using sales managers to deal with contract management and field services for project management. They did not have a routine approach to contract margin and risk reviews. And they were

(continued)

2.4 Products and Activities

> not necessarily delivering what was in the contract. The firm was too used to listening to the customer rather than reading the contract and discussing matters with the customer.
>
> A leader for commercial project management was hired with the aim of leading and coaching people who were responsible for project execution. Selected people were trained on commercial project management, because the skills were different to the firm's traditional product development project management. Processes and procedures were put in place to support the team.
>
> Monthly project margin reviews with all project managers were used to help coach the team and learn from each other. This helped to instill the commercial management processes into the normal work rhythm.
>
> Commercially, the projects improved with the emphasis on execution. The business struggled initially with the degree of empowerment that the project managers needed in order to be effective in their roles. In effect, this was a major change in operational culture. The team learned to be more commercially minded and to understand the consequences of their actions. Formalization of processes helped: from contract negotiation and contract signature right through to delivery. Other commercial and legal aspects were important to document and initially were overlooked (e.g., exchange rates and escalation). It was also found that customer experience needed to be measured (and acted upon) in additional to the contract performance.

2.4.4 If Customers Ask for Digital Service, Where Do We Start?

Digitalization, IoT, and Industry 4.0 are today being embedded in new technology, and manufacturing firms are starting to learn how to connect machines up, allowing monitoring and diagnostics to be put in place (Fig. 2.34). Specifically, service firms

Fig. 2.34 Using digital can improve the support your service teams provide to your customers (illustration by Annick Holland, authors' work)

are starting to work out how to monitor their machines and discover what can be learned from that monitoring and how to use it to accelerate servitization journey.

...Digitally enabled services allowed us to move more quickly to advanced services...

In many cases, today the starting points are quite basic, often limited to warranty protection – which can be a negative starting point.

Digitalized service means that the owner or operator of the machine shares data with their monitoring and diagnostics provider and perhaps others. Equipment does not exist in isolation; it is often from a mixture of manufacturers and is of mixed generations – this makes it significantly harder to create a solution that is appealing to the end-user. Value can also be for the OEM as well as for the end-user – you will not know what you will find until you start to look. This is why it is important to examine the options from every angle. It is recommended that any service firm starts with a pilot scheme to collect data, which should be shared openly with the end-user. The data should not be used to protect against warranty claims; rather, it should be openly shared to learn new insights; otherwise, trust would be eroded. Servitization therefore brings not only many advantages but also many efforts in terms of resources and skills

...The design of digital services is complex, and we do not have the skill set...

The lessons from the two cases are that customers have an expectation today of "something digital" from their service providers. Digital can help create contacts and new touch points with customers and with IoT technologies; firms can redesign your service offering. Digital can allow reconfiguration of the value propositions that let you find ways to build trust with your customer and support their operations.

The tools that help to explore the barriers and to build actions to overcome them are:

- Avatar map.
- Business process mapping.
- Case/actor matrix.
- Cradle-to-grave lifecycle map.
- Cradle-to-grave lifecycle visual mapping.
- Customer jobs-to-be-done.
- Customer value proposition.
- Job-to-be-done insights.
- Job-to-be-done outcomes.
- Metric cascades.
- Personas.
- Service blueprint.
- Visual journey map – high level.
- Visual journey map – detail level.

Details of the individual tools are given in Chap. 3.

Case 41 Digitally Enabled PSS Is Really Complex

The management decided the firm needed to "do something digital." The middle management team had no idea what was needed or how to develop it, so they asked product development to create "something digital" to support the service business.

Product development created a "black box" that could be attached to new machines and would offer warranty protection. They explained this would add value by reducing "unreasonable" warranty claims that customers made, and this would reduce the overall cost of poor quality.

Many of the firm's customers considered the box to be a spy that was looking for them to operate the equipment incorrectly in order to defend a warranty claim. In truth, it was exactly that, and it was being sold as a product that would protect the firm's position. Quickly the firm lost their customers' trust when they tried to sell it. Really there was not a value proposition for the customer in the offer – so the firm was naïve to expect to be able to sell it. They would have to integrate the box into their existing service offering and switch it from being a spy to expanding the firm's opportunities and supporting their customers.

The black box was opened up so that customers could see the data and the trend lines. Alerts were added to help customers know when they were getting close to their equipment's operational limits. Following warranty claims, the data was shared, so that the firm and customer could do a full root cause analysis, either together or separately. The firm also offered to extend the warranty on the equipment and provide longer performance commitments on the equipment where customers were willing to use the black box. In effect they redesigned the value proposition and tried to create a win-win solution.

It worked. The firm offered extended warranties on the equipment based on the inclusion of the black box on new installations. For the installed base, it allowed them to give performance commitments for the operation of the equipment – this was most successful where they provided an upgrade on the equipment rather than a basic inspection.

Joint root cause analysis was interesting. In some cases, it worked, as the engineers were talking together and jointly agreeing on the cause of the failure, so everyone learned something. It worked less well when both did root cause analysis separately and then argued the case in a confrontational way.

Case 42 Using Digital to Transform a Business
Monthly cleaning of the product was always a problem for customers. Daily routine maintenance was not an issue, but the tasks that were done infrequently tended to be more problematic for the operators. They did not repeat them sufficiently to become truly competent in completing them fully.

Customers would call the help desk and spent time talking with the service techs to complete their routine maintenance. The firm tried to improve the customer training and the documentation, but everything seemed to fail.

Digging into the roots of the problem, it became clear that the cause of the failure was that the task was done by someone different each time. The customer had four shifts working and each time a new shift worker did the task, so perhaps the same person did the job twice in one year. No one really learned how to do the job well – every time the task was done, it was that employee's first time. Was it any wonder that it created problems?

Given that the obvious things had all been done before and that the firm wanted to try something new, they decided to create a digital solution. They developed a standard operating practice on an iPad, allowing each step to be checked off, and videos to show how each step should be done augmented the written text and the figures. The task checks were logged within an auditable quality system. The iPad was provided with a big help button to connect directly with the service help desk – the service tech could see who the person was, make a video call, and talk them through the problem.

The paybacks were many. The firm saved time on the helpdesk, and when they did speak with the customer's staff, the help desk knew exactly where they were stuck and could quickly provide a solution. The saving in time paid for the equipment provided, although some firms downloaded the app onto their own iPads and iPhones. This saved more money.

The new solution also allowed the firm to start to charge for troubleshooting: customers had an allowance of free help per year and above that they would be charged for the service. Sales said it was not possible to charge for the service, but in fact, customers actually wanted to pay when they received good service. Providing the app to customers made the service more tangible for them and provided the firm with an additional channel as well as providing information on the installed base.

2.4.5 How Can Services Support New Equipment Sales?

On one side, we've heard new equipment sales teams saying that services cannibalize their sales opportunities. This can be true in a few cases but not in general. Both parts of the business should support each other by improving the relationships with the customers. Better relationships mean that the supplier should have a better

2.4 Products and Activities

Fig. 2.35 Service provides opportunities to improve customer experience and the chance of further purchases (illustration by Annick Holland)

understanding of the needs of the buyer as well as understanding the customer's buying process more clearly than the competition. In fact, there is evidence that confirms the chance of rebuy being higher where there is good service delivery coupled with good products (Fig. 2.35).

> ...The core business is the product supply and not the service, although it is acknowledged that it is thanks to the competent and timely service that the company I represent is a market leader...

For this to work, both parts of the business need to understand and respect each other. If that happens, the service business will have more contact with the customer here, but the one-time sales value of the new equipment will be higher than the maintenance fees on the equipment. Moreover, it is possible that service may have more insights and be able to recommend an upgrade option and identify the likely sales price – an opportunity that may create more value for both the supplier and the customer than a traditional equipment sale.

> ...New equipment sales are an enabler for services as they create the Installed Base, a base to build long-term relationships on. This feeds back to the new equipment sales...

The lessons from the two cases are based on customer experience and how it supports both the service and the product business. It is important for service managers to remember that service is predicated on selling new equipment and servicing the installed base. Also, services build strong relationships, and these can support new equipment sales, leading again to more service sales.

The tools that help to explore the barriers and to build actions to overcome them are:

- Case/actor matrix.
- Cradle-to-grave lifecycle map.
- Cradle-to-grave lifecycle visual mapping.
- Customer jobs-to-be-done.
- Customer value proposition.
- Detailed empathy card.
- Ecosystem mapping.
- Empathy maps.
- Job-to-be-done insights.
- Job-to-be-done outcomes.
- Metric cascades.
- Personas.
- Service blueprint.

Details of the individual tools are given in Chap. 3.

Case 43 Using Service to Support Product Sales
Two separate business units with different bosses and different drivers meant poor coordination between product and service sales. Often, product sales considered service the enemy for repairing the equipment – they'd rather it was replaced. At the same time, equipment sales would bundle parts and services with the new machine sale and expect the service team to deliver what they sold. It was almost like the right and left hands really did not see any reason to work together. Strange, as they had regular contact with the customer, and most of the time, they had great feedback from the customer.

Neither business unit saw any benefit in collaboration, so there was no collaboration. When the service team had helped product sales in the past, there had been no thanks offered, although service had more direct customer contact and insights. Often, the customer would ask the service team for advice on replacement equipment, which means that they trusted the team perhaps more than their own product business did. But because of the lack of collaboration, the firm was not getting the volume of new sales that it should have, and in the longer run, this would mean that the service market would be smaller than it should be.

The firm created a test case where product sales and service had to work together on a new equipment sale. They did this three times with three different teams and customers. The sales closed and the good news spread. The sales teams learned quickly that the service techs had new insights about the customers. More than just the technical elements, the service techs understood the important undocumented aspects that the customers valued.

After the trial, the news was shared with the equipment sales teams using direct feedback from the people who were involved in the trial. The firm also

(continued)

changed the accounting processes to ensure that where service supported sales a commission went to the team, which was helpful for motivation.

The firm has started to look more like a joined-up business, providing a full product-service system (PSS) rather than two different teams fighting between themselves. This builds additional trust with customers. The commission payment helped as well; the service team now get a reward for doing the right thing rather than what felt like a penalty. Both teams have now started to share the CRM data so that everyone can see the customer information. It could still be improved, but it is already better than it was in the past.

Case 44 Working in a Razor/Razor-Blade Market
The new equipment market has been getting tougher and tougher for this firm. It used to make good margins, but today they are lucky to break even on a sale. The real cash contribution to the firm was from selling spares; in effect, they had a razor/razor blade market where the product had become a "loss leader." The aftermarket business has become the cash cow, and the customers really value the service provided. Their net promoter score (NPS) on service really was in a different league and confirmed that their customers consider that the firm performed well.

The problem stems from low-cost imports that took the price and the value out of the market, according to the firm. The competition was coming from overseas and provided poor service. Service was the point at which the firm excelled, as they also had regular contact with their service customers, and they listened to the service techs, but customers' procurement teams always had the final say on a new equipment purchase.

The firm started to compare the cost of ownership of their machines with those of the competitor. They found many points of difference where their machines and the service they provided resulted in higher productivity than those from other manufacturers. This helped the firm to understand their business and their cost drivers; it also allowed them to demonstrate the higher total life value of the whole system they were providing.

The firm learned more about the customer's company, their people and their processes during the discussions.

They were able to manage the razor/razor-blade product-service system (PSS) that they were providing to the customer. They showed and quantified the points of difference between the offers, allowing them (as the buyer) to better understand their costs.

The firm could now see they could also change their business model and migrate to one where they have a relationship with their customers, moving to

(continued)

> a model more like Xerox, where customers pay for the outcomes rather than the input. This meant that they had to accept more operational risk for the service; however, the firm considered that this allowed them to push out some of the low-cost competitors. They are now also considering providing service on the competitor's machines, as they think they can improve their machines and in doing so make the installed base theirs.

2.5 Competitors, Suppliers, and Partners

In the service arena, where co-creation and co-delivery are normal, customers can quickly become key partners in some area. Partners such as installers, which already provide important channels to market for new equipment, can be either competitors or conversely be considered as key partners in your service delivery. In services, it is important to reassess your view of competitors, suppliers, and partners.

The understanding of ecosystems is important for service firms, and this represents a change for manufacturing firms, where they may have a simpler view of a linear supply chain. Therefore, cultural behaviors have to change as firms move to work differently with partners and former competitors.

> ...we must use an ecosystem view to help us work together better, but this is a mind-set change!...

There is no single best way – for some firms, it may be best to give up most of their service activities to their product installers. The integration of the installers in the product-service design process lets you identify the main barriers and difficulties that may arise in service delivery.

> ...we prefer to encourage our partners to do it directly! Actually, such a strategy involves losing part of our service profits, but it's the best way...

The loss of control has here to be "repaid" in another form, due to the reciprocity of the interactions. The relative importance from the survey of the barriers around "competitors, suppliers, and partners" is shown in Fig. 2.36.

Within the theme of "competitors, suppliers, and partners," the most important issue identified is how to expand capabilities. This suggests that many of the firms are finding it hard to identify new resources rather than expand the skills and capacity of their partners and align them with those of the company. Indeed, many people we interviewed told us that very often the service provider appears to customers as a separate entity, whereas it should be exactly the opposite. This is confirmed with the second, third, and fifth issues that have been identified, which are concerned with the service supply chain in different forms. An ecosystem/alliance approach based on co-creation and co-delivery of services is perhaps a solution here.

2.5 Competitors, Suppliers, and Partners

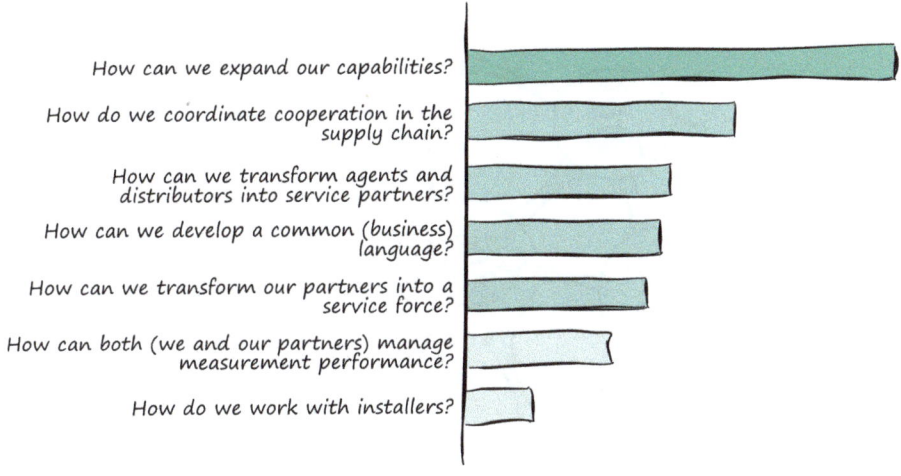

Fig. 2.36 The relative importance of the barriers around "competitors, suppliers, and partners" (illustration by Annick Holland, adapted from West et al., 2018)

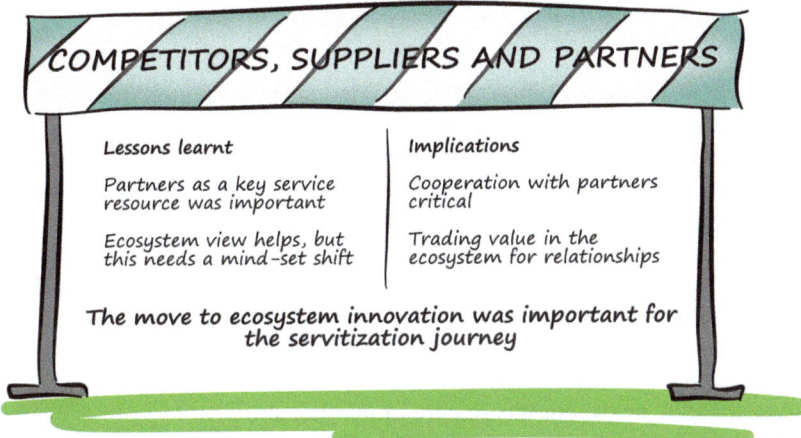

Fig. 2.37 The lessons and implications for the competitors, suppliers, and partners barriers (illustration by Annick Holland, adapted from West et al., 2018)

The fourth issue considers the organization and how to create a common language to support the business. To address these problems, in some cases companies have acted by selecting only partners with the same business approach. In other cases, common processes have been adopted based upon modularized structures, together with transparent and shared monitoring, and control and incentive systems. Figure 2.37 describes some of the lessons learned and the implications from the interviews.

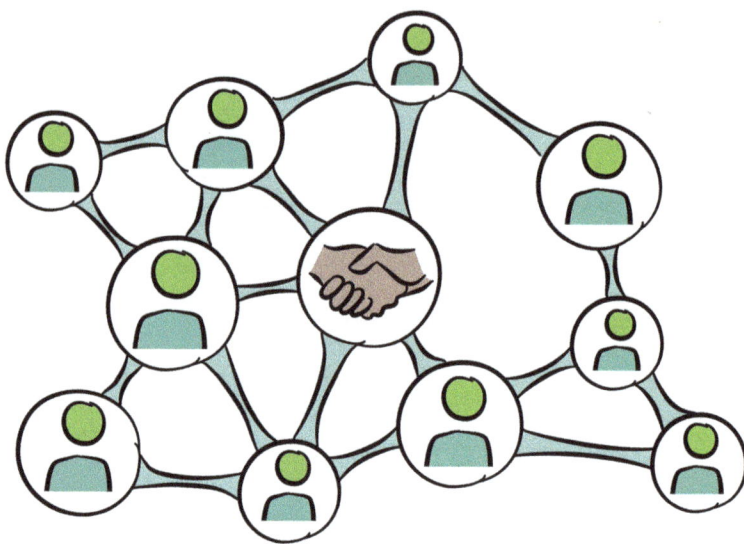

Fig. 2.38 Learning to engage with ecosystem actors can improve service delivery and customer experience (illustration by Annick Holland, authors' work)

The move to ecosystem innovation is important for the service journey. It provides a new approach to look at the full range of resources that are available, allowing services to be delivered close to the customer in a way that is attractive for them. This may create some new alliances for firms, which is particularly relevant, where firms manufacture locally yet sell products globally. It is neither effective nor efficient to be able to give all "end-users" the same level of services without a new approach, and it is possible to learn and share lessons between actors (Fig. 2.38). The implications for this barrier are:

- Partners are a key service resource.
- Ecosystem view helps, but this requires a mindset shift.
- Create an ecosystem/alliance approach based on co-creation and co-delivery of services.
- Select only partners with the same business approach.
- Adopt common processes based upon modularized structures, together with transparent and shared monitoring, control and incentive systems.
- Share benefits and obligations among the partners.

To help you better understand how to navigate the barriers, we will provide insights from cases to help you understand how others overcame the barriers, the barriers we identified (in order of importance):

1. How can we expand our capabilities?
2. How do we coordinate cooperation in the supply chain?

3. How can we transform agents and distributors into service partners?
4. How can we transform our partners into a service force?
5. How can we develop a common business language?
6. How can both we and our partners manage performance measurement?
7. How do we work with installers?

2.5.1 How Can We Expand Our Capabilities?

As services are developed (often by direct request from the customer), there are limitations in capabilities. A manufacturing firm can accurately plan its capabilities in advance, whereas a service business is normally more entrepreneurial in behavior, often grasping an opportunity that is offered before having built up the necessary capabilities. This creates problems with the more formal manufacturing business approaches and can lead to accusations of being "out of control." So how can you build up capabilities when you are not sure what is needed to support your customers? (Fig. 2.39).

The approach to growing a business that is normal for lean/agile startup or service innovation, where customer pull and market testing are ordinary activities, is in essence, 180° apart from the manufacturing development process, where actual market testing is the final stage and often leads to targets being missed. The approach of using the ecosystem to support capability expansion is deeply embedded within the business model canvas as "key partners." These not only agree with your firm's strategy and vision but are also better at supplying some parts of the services than

Fig. 2.39 Bring new actors into the service network to change the offer for your customers (illustration by Annick Holland, authors' work)

you and are, in effect, cheaper as you 'rent' their services as and when needed. AirBnB and Uber are both examples of such approaches.

> ...Project firms are able to use resources from the ecosystem, we need to learn to do it better, too...

> ...To address the situation, you need to identify partners who share the company's business vision...

The lesson learned from the two cases are that working with partners with common values can be fulfilling, whereas trying to work with partners with different values can be difficult or impossible. The best way to find out if you can work with a partner is to work together on a project before formalizing the relationship – no quantity of analysis can replace the experience of working together. As much as the "chemistry" of a business relationship, it is important to understand the payoffs between insourcing and using partners.

The tools that help to explore the barriers and to build actions to overcome them are:

- Avatar map.
- Case/actor matrix.
- Cradle-to-grave lifecycle map.
- Cradle-to-grave lifecycle visual mapping.
- Customer jobs-to-be-done.
- Job-to-be-done insights.
- Metric cascades.
- Service blueprint.
- Visual journey map – high level.
- Visual journey map – detail level.

Details of the individual tools are given in Chap. 3.

> **Case 45 Broadening Capabilities Through the Ecosystem**
> There were only limited resources within the firm, both in terms of numbers of people and the skills and competences that they possessed. This meant that in effect they had to ration the services they could offer. In periods of peak demand, they were fully booked, while in off-season periods, they were spending cash. This was all less than ideal as it was leading to a loss of customers and a reduction in their experience. The firm had seen other project-based firms being able to flex their skill base when they pulled a project together. When this firm tried it, they somehow got stuck with human resources or procurement policies or management telling them to use "in-house skills."

(continued)

On two projects, they tried to follow the approach of some of the firms that they often worked for, having in effect been told to go and use their networks rather than internal resources. The problem was that this broke many of the human resources and procurement rules, but by being allowed to try a new approach out, the team learned what it needed to do to make this work. The firm needed to move from being a relatively slow manufacturing firm that did most of the work in-house to one that worked with partners to fill resource and competency gaps. To do this, the team identified that the firm would need to change processes for outsourcing to speed things up.

The firm redesigned its processes with human resources and procurement as they were not at all used to project working. It put in place cooperation agreements with some firms that allowed them to work together directly without going through a complex tendering process. With labor agencies, they recognize a minimum based on prior years as well as agreeing to use their staff on a project when bidding while selectively hiring in specialist skills. When working with partners, the firm always considered "what's in it for me" from both perspectives.

They learned to use the ecosystem to provide a wider range of resources and companies than they ever had in-house. They did not always get the "best price" but were able to win and deliver projects effectively and efficiently this way. The real effort was with the design of new processes to help ensure compliance with internal risk management rules. The team learned not to use some actors in the ecosystem and discovered that a fit based around "can these people work together" was much more powerful than any other selection criteria. They still hear "oh we could have done that..." arguments, but now they are able to focus on what they're really good at doing. The ecosystem partners even bring in work now, showing that it is not a one-way approach.

Case 46 Working with Partners to Get a Win-Win Solution
The firm knew it needed partners to complete a job but felt disappointed every time; however successful the project was, the team would have done a better job on their own, which would lead to conflict between the partners that sometimes leaked out to customers. This was not good for anyone, and when it happened, it made everyone look bad. The firm always worked on the basis of "winner takes all."

Some people started to question this approach. The culture and mentality that this developed was in fact unhealthy. It failed to deliver the outcomes that customers wanted and made development and management of partnerships complex. It was actually everywhere in how the firm dealt with partners; for

(continued)

> instance, procurement teams using "best practice" required partners to accept 90-day terms and then paid late. Many of the firms were small businesses with no liquidity who would work hard, because of personal relationships to help the firm out, and were rewarded with poor rates and long payment terms. This is no way to deal with key partners.
>
> From the best cases, the firm learned that it achieved the best outcomes internally and externally by building a "win-win" relationship built on trust and understanding of "what's in it for me...." This needed to be reflected in how everyone dealt with each other at all levels and included payments. The cultural problems were hard-wired into the firm's processes, so they identified key partners with whom they needed to develop deeper partnerships. In some cases, these partners almost looked like commodity suppliers, but the firm knew that they provided a competitive benefit beyond a simple cost advantage.
>
> Procurement and finance hated this, as it had a negative impact on their free cash flow generation. Some key partners were paid after 30 days, even though on certain projects this was before the firm was being paid. From the start, they found that getting paid on time was important for their relationships. When building a partnership, they found it helped to understand what the different partners wanted on both the single project and as a longer-term relationship. The firm started to write these key objectives down so that they could clearly state the aim of the relationship with key partners and then build a "win-win" partnership.

2.5.2 How Do We Coordinate Cooperation in the Supply Chain?

A manufacturing firm has a complex supply chain with many suppliers and is typically optimized for cost. Optimization of costs is a good thing, as to remain in the game, a firm must remain competitive with new equipment sales. The professionalization of the supply chain has been an important aspect in allowing firms to achieve this. With service delivery, the existing supply chain is likely to have major weaknesses, leading to reduced levels of customer satisfaction, long lead times, and higher costs (Fig. 2.40). It can also create tensions between a service business and a manufacturing business, mostly due to misunderstandings of the underlying business models. Successful supply chain collaboration brings higher customer satisfaction, better partner relationships, and lower costs.

> ...In relation to supply chain, collaboration (both upstream and downstream) can be constructed with win-win processes, analyzing how it can create value for the partner and implement those solutions...

This means leading the supply chain to deliver spare parts in short times and having known inventories in known places. To achieve this, firms have to separate

2.5 Competitors, Suppliers, and Partners

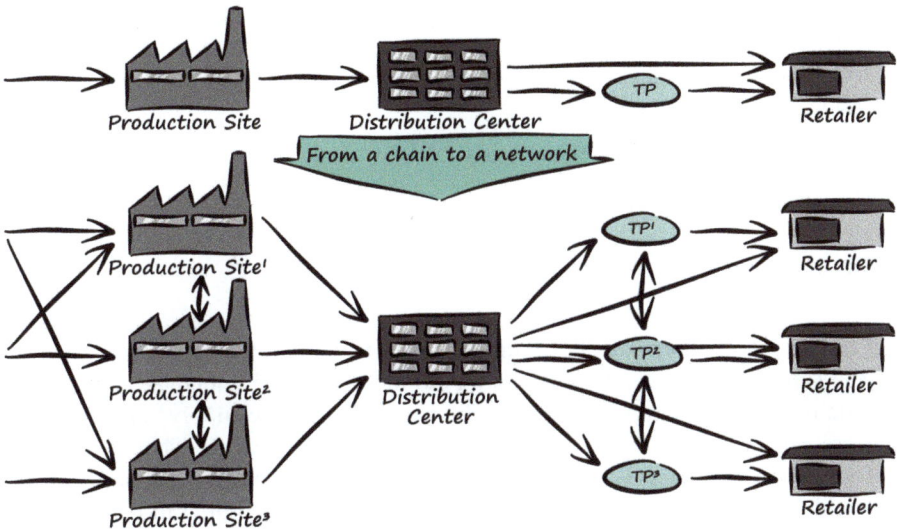

Fig. 2.40 Moving from a simple supply chain to managing a network improves the customer experience and can reduce costs (illustration by Annick Holland, adapted from Anderson et al., 2008)

the manufacturing supply chain from the service supply chain, which highlights that service and manufacturing have different business models with different processes and demands. At the supply chain level, this may mean that the equipment supplier no long supplies spares directly to the end-users. Separating service from new equipment sales business models empowers both to focus on their customers and to deliver the required value propositions while maintaining support of new equipment business.

> ...our supply chain is designed to support our new equipment business...

The most important lesson is that there will always be competition between service and new equipment due to the different business models and that you need to learn to deal with it. A complication comes from the fact that the spares supply chain must support both service and equipment businesses. This is compounded with the challenge that the supply chain must support customer experience and contract requirements as well as often being the driver for margins. Finally, a service business without spares (e.g., consumables or capital spares) cannot deliver service.

The tools that help to explore the barriers and to build actions to overcome them are:

- Avatar map.
- Business process mapping.
- Cradle-to-grave lifecycle map.
- Cradle-to-grave lifecycle visual mapping.

- Ecosystem mapping.
- Empathy maps.
- Job-to-be-done insights.
- Job-to-be-done outcomes.
- Service blueprint.
- Visual journey map – high level.
- Visual journey map – detail level.

Details of the individual tools are given in Chap. 3.

> **Case 47 Enhancing Supply Chain Learning to Support Service**
> The supply chain team complained all the time about the unbudgeted spares requirements that popped up during the year. In effect the supply chain team were asking the service team to budget for unplanned work. They wanted forecasts, much like production did, which was not something the service team could do, as machines break when they want and not according to a budget, plan, or forecast. In the end, the firm told the supply chain to adjust to a different environment.
>
> The problem was that the service team was budgeting and forecasting just like the manufacturing part of the business where they had longer time horizons. This does not work in a service environment, yet there was a large installed base to work with, and the service team saw similar events every year: with the planned inspections, they could estimate when they'd take place from the operational hours, with spares they could look at monthly operational trends. Service and sales managers could help improve this, and for customers with long-term agreements, they could closely estimate the requirements.
>
> Instead, they took a mixed approach, firstly looking at each planned inspection to build up the forecast from the installed base to create a bottom-up view. The team then did the same using data to understand the demand-driven materials resource planning requirements. Having both provided a solid foundation, but what was missing were the unplanned tasks that are needed following a failure, and here the past three years' data gave some statistics that could help to shape the forecasts. The team then combined and segmented the data to be input into the supply chain.
>
> From all of this data, the firm learned that incidents tend to bunch up together and now they had the data to provide the supply chain with the insight to understand what was happening and why it was not possible to provide 12 months' notice. On the planned materials requirements, the team jointly developed a rolling 3- and 12-month planning horizon based on the hybrid bottom-up and DDMRP models. This gave better consistency with the numbers and helped the team to understand the materials (as well as the repairs and field services) demands from the market. The end result was reductions in both lead times and stock levels.

Case 48 Build Supply Chain Collaboration

The business had started as a workshop and field service business that worked hand in hand with the customer and, at the time, an OEM. Over time that changed, and the business competed for the same job, sometimes working with, sometimes against, the OEM. The OEM thought that they had an advantage as they had the spares, but the owners of the firm worked carefully to ensure that this was not the case. Nevertheless, spares became a bigger issue, and although the firm learned how to reengineer them, they still needed access to the parts and to develop a mature supply chain to source parts. Integration with the customers (downstream) was of as much importance as upstream (suppliers).

The service team needed to get hold of spares that could be reengineered or procured directly from vendors. Repairing the OEM's machines was not an issue, neither was overhauling them, but the problem was getting hold of spares. Consumables were generally supplied by the customer when the service team did an overhaul on a machine. This was easier for the firm, but the customers would rather not supply the consumables, given that the firm were supposed to be the experts. Replacement systems, especially old PLC-based systems, were more of an issue, given that many of those OEMs were no longer in business. Access to capital spares was needed for some repairs, and of course the firm did not have access to OEM's upgrades before they hit the market.

Building the supply chain required close collaboration with customers who wanted to create competition in the market. The firm identified key technologies and customers who had these target technologies. They also identified regional hot spots where similar materials were manufactured and searched for partner repair centers for the electronic components needed. This took time and effort and required a different approach to commodity procurement, as the suppliers became core to the business model – and this included, in some cases, the customers. The team also had to build up a supply chain mindset, which is very different to that needed when you are making your own spares or consumables for a repair project.

They identified firms and regional hot spots for the supply or reengineering of some consumable parts. Many spares, even those used on complex engineered machines, are in effect standard parts. The firm got access to spares to scan them, make 3D CAD drawings, and then create the manufacturing instructions. With the electronic parts, the firm needed to start from scratch, but they found a number of partners who could support them with, what were mostly, obsolescence-related events when either the OEM had gone out of business or had stopped manufacturing the subcomponent.

2.5.3 How Can We Transform Agents and Distributors into Service Partners?

Consider a small-medium enterprise (SME) manufacturing products that are used throughout the world; to sell their products, it is normal to use agents and distributors. Agents are absolutely crucial in some parts of the world, as it is impossible to sell without their assistance. The downside can be that direct customer contact is lost, causing a loss in feedback to the NPD team as well as a barrier for service. As with installers, agents can offer and provide effective service channels for service businesses; however, this means a change in the approach to agents and distributors (Fig. 2.41).

> ...You need a clear legal framework. From the point of view of business, this must be redefined and made more flexible to support this transformation...

If you are developing channels for service delivery, consider how you can use your agents and distributors. On the most basic level, they can support the service team in the same way as new product sales. On a more advanced level, they can provide services directly to the end-user with the backup of the OEM's brand and expertise. The level of performance may be limited to more basic inspections and maintenance or, in other cases, offer more advanced installation and repair services using OEM parts. What is critical is engagement: it is important to understand what

Fig. 2.41 Widening the group and treating the members as a team can help create win-win-win (illustration by Annick Holland, authors' work)

drives them and how a relationship can be mutually beneficial for the end-user, the agent/distributor, and the OEM.

> ...What does the value creation and value capture look like when it comes to network relationships?...

An important lesson from the cases is that service businesses should consider their agents, and to some extent distributors, as local service resources. The service business needs to see them as complementary rather than cannibalistic. It is therefore important to find jobs that the local agents and distributors could do better because of their location and regional know-how. Caterpillar do this very well, and it is worth looking at the way that they integrate agents and distributors into their business processes.

The tools that help to explore the barriers and to build actions to overcome them are:

- Business model canvas.
- Business process mapping.
- Case/actor matrix.
- Ecosystem mapping.
- Empathy maps.
- Metric cascades.
- Personas.
- Service blueprint.
- Visual journey map – high level.
- Visual journey map – detail level.

Details of the individual tools are given in Chap. 3.

Case 49 Building a Framework to Get More Value from Agents and Distributors

The firm needed to consolidate the number of agents and distributors used in the business. As the process was being led by equipment sales rather than service sales, they needed a different type of local partner. Moreover, many of the agents preferred the size of new equipment orders, as they took a simple percentage of the sales value, regardless of the margin the firm made. What was needed was a change of approach to focus on customer experience over the operational life of the equipment and, at the same time, find better ways to use the skills of the agents and distributors.

The firm found that it really needed agents and distributors to collaborate with, so that they could become a local service force. This was different to what the equipment sales team wanted. With an extended service force and

(continued)

sales team, the service team could grow the business and provide localized customer experience. The firm played with the idea of doing this themselves but quickly realized that it would cost too much and break existing relationships. The team also knew that there might be political risks with the change as they needed to question some of the selections that the new equipment sales team had made.

The firm looked into the technical capabilities and the business vision of their agents. They did not just want agents who were "letter boxes," so they shared their vision with the agents to help to build their business within set guidelines. The firm also moved to treat agents and distributors as franchises, selling this to them on the basis of the success that McDonalds has experienced. As part of this, they were sold a training program to educate them on doing the basics locally to a good standard, with remote support when needed. An annual "partner event," where the firm could share new ideas with them and harvest the problems and ideas that they had, was organized. Once this system was in place in key markets, the firm started to question the new equipment sales team's approach to agents.

Dealing with the internal politics was tough, because equipment sales wanted to take the lead, so the service team tried this approach initially in a handful of markets, selected on the basis of growth or overall volume of sales. The team decided not to charge for the first training sessions but then charge for additional training. The annual partner conference was the first time they bought everyone together, and it helped to share more lessons with the partners and get insights into local problems. It was not free, but although the firm charged delegates to attend, the fees did not cover the costs and were more to ensure the partners valued the event. Trying to balance between small and large partners was difficult, and creating an agreement internally was tough, but the firm agreed to split the approach taken in each market, depending on direct or indirect equipment sales.

Case 50 Learning to Share Value and Risk with Service Partners
Treating service partners as simple subcontractors forced this firm to push on the price button all the time. They would always ask for the day rate and generally take the lowest rate. Procurement liked it, because it was easy for them to show value. For the operations team, it was rather more complex, as they had to live with the consequences of the lowest price. Often, it included hidden costs, which really did not help with costing or delivering services. Being told that they have the best value from procurement and then finding that the costs escalated ended up with the operations team being told they

(continued)

needed to project manage their contractors better. Something was wrong and it was eating at the margins.

Indeed, the margin loss was only the symptom of the underlying problem. In essence, this firm had a complex rate sheet, and using the rates, it was impossible to estimate the final price. Therefore, the suppliers were clawing back the rate reductions that had been forced onto them through extras, so at the end of the project there would always be an argument over the additional work. The firm also released that its drivers were out of alignment – if the job was finished faster, they would make more money, but their partner would make less revenue. So, partners tended to work slowly and finish late to make more revenue, to the detriment of the firm and their customers.

The big change was to move to a revenue sharing approach on a project, based on an agreement on the scope and the split of the scope between OEM and partners. In effect, together they produced a fixed price offer for the customer. This was designed to cover all the "normal" work. It also benefited the partner, because if they completed the work early, they would make more money on the project. If the project ran late, they had to absorb the first 10% of the cost overruns; afterwards, the OEM firms were fully responsible. Together they designed a revenue model that shared appropriate risks with the service partners.

It worked well. It did need trust between the bid teams; otherwise, there was a risk of "sandbagging," but then they soon learned that sandbagging meant they would lose the project as they would not be competitive. On-time completion of projects improved; everyone made more money when they completed the project early, and this was also transferred to the workforce, who gained a bonus for early completion. A claims book was used to list out all "extra works" for both parties and was used to drive justified additional income from the customer. This was hard to get used to, initially. The objective was to describe the claim in a neutral manner, but it became a "blame game" tool until senior management from both companies stepped in and forced a different approach.

2.5.4 How Can We Transform Our Partners into a Service Force?

The ability to transform partners into an effective service force is not easy. It is tough enough to transform your own business; it is harder to support the transformation of a partner. There are opportunities for misunderstandings between the parties, and it takes time to come to a common understanding with common expectations. It also requires a change in the mindset of the firms and changes the current status quo, which can be troubling for managers (Fig. 2.42).

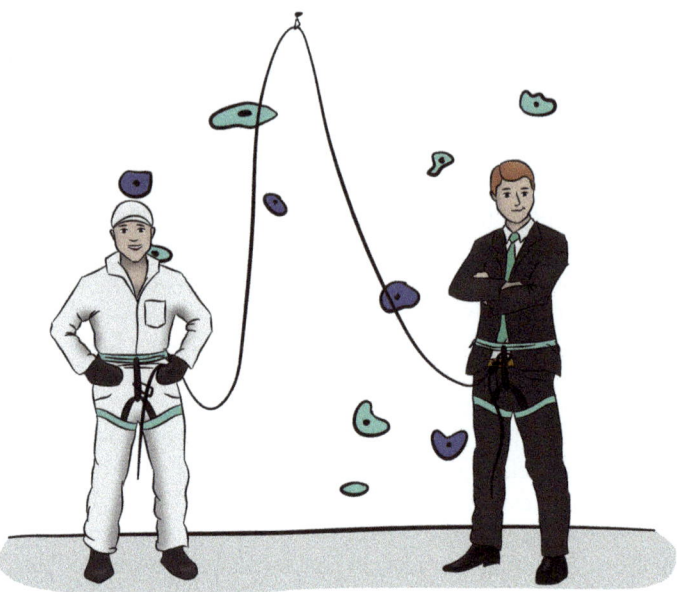

Fig. 2.42 Using all of the available resources means that you need to transform business outside your firm (illustration by Annick Holland, authors' work)

> ...Expanding the ability to serve involves a change of mindset that requires a personal and professional maturity that often contrasts with the propensity to change...

Holding joint workshops at multiple levels can help create a common mission and build a common understanding of services.

> ...Misunderstanding the scope of an offer between partners led to gaps in the services and increased risk. The solution was to have in depth discussions in a multi-workshop environment and come up with definition agreed by all...

The relationship needs governing, as locally old behaviors may return. A win-win relationship has to be built and maintained. This is tough, as both businesses need to have the maturity to accept the change: it requires flexibility and the ability and willingness to learn on both sides.

The most important lesson with the transformation of partners is that there will be failures. Not everything will go to plan, and you can help increase the likelihood of success by having a common vision for the service. As with any relationship, it is important to monitor and govern the business relationship, so that it can adapt on both sides as you will need to improve the upside for both parties and reduce friction between the parties.

2.5 Competitors, Suppliers, and Partners

The tools that help to explore the barriers and to build actions to overcome them are:

- Business model canvas.
- Business process mapping.
- Case/actor matrix.
- Ecosystem mapping.
- Empathy maps.
- Metric cascades.
- Personas.
- Service blueprint.
- Visual journey map – high level.
- Visual journey map – detail level.

Details of the individual tools are given in Chap. 3.

> **Case 51 Developing Agents to Become The Extended Service Force**
> The firm realized that its agents did not "do as they were told." They were thought of as part of the firm's sales network and not part of the local service delivery mechanisms. When the agents did some unauthorized service work and it went wrong, the problems always came back to the firm. It was essential to fix the problem of the agents taking on service work that was beyond their capability and outside their contract. However, much the firm told the agents not to deliver services; they would continue to do so. They did it to keep the customer happy, and as they had direct customer contact, how could they be blamed? It showed that a different approach to the agents was needed, one where both they and the OEM could shine in front of the customer.
>
> The firm assessed its relationships with five agents to find why it was happening. In all of the cases, it found that the agents had the capabilities to provide some level of technical support locally – something that the firm could not do with the same speed. They were also cheaper, as there were no mobilization costs. The firm just needed to get to an agreement of what it should do and what the agents should do. This was not clearly stated in the agency agreements, as they worked under the assumption that they were sales channels. This approach was based on the equipment division's needs rather than the firm's overall requirements.
>
> The firm held a workshop with each of the agents to understand and build a detailed service plan for their region. This started by describing the service needs of customers in the region and then considering how those customers preferred to have services delivered. From this, they developed a "current state" scope split and a "future state" scope split. The gap between the two
>
> (continued)

showed a training need for the agent's own service technicians – something the firm had never done, or thought of, before.

They started to look at what the agents could do for the firm and its customers beyond being a "letter box." This had never been done before, and the firm discovered that the agents already had many of the basic skills that were needed to support the customers; they also spoke the local languages and knew the local culture and customs. The firm found that, by helping the agents to develop a local service business, they were able to grow their business and indirectly become more dependent on the OEM. The customers preferred it too – it was often much faster and cheaper for them to get a problem fixed. The firm lost some work from cannibalizing its service business, but overall, it was worth it as the whole business grew and the pressure on the agency fees reduced.

Case 52 Transforming the Business to a Service Business

Being told to grow the service business without investment is challenging. How can you grow a business without any money? Senior management had great ideas but then failed to put the tools in place to allow middle management to deliver the new strategy. This team needed a disruptive approach to service provision, one that was customer-focused and built on its strengths and those of its partners, given that the team could no longer invest in service centers.

The team started to look at what it was really good at and what they could get others to do for them. It was clear that they enjoyed good margins associated with spares sales but were not always profitable on the associated field services. They looked at other models: ABB Turbo System in-house service, the Rolls-Royce hybrid model where customers provide much of the service in the field, and how CAT uses dealers to provide local services to the customers, much like a car dealership.

The firm pulled back to providing only spares and gave the responsibility for service to local partners. In effect, they developed a franchise model, and while it did cost money to set up, this was offset by the franchise fees. Essentially, this was a net zero cost. They used new technologies to help track the operational units and to keep an inventory of the installed base and provided the service partners (they never called them franchisees) with technical support and documentation to perform the inspections and workshop repairs – all backed up with certification training.

From the new business model, the firm was able to deliver at arm's length faster and cheaper service for customers. They discovered that other firms, such as Microsoft, operate similar models. The change allowed the firm to

(continued)

focus on its spares and consumables business and to gain predictable pull through for them from their service partners. There were even times when two or more partners bid for the same work – the firm could not lose in such a situation. A few service partners left the program, but noncompete clauses in their agreements made sure that they could not hurt the OEM, and it orchestrated the network to fill in the gaps. In the end, there were some costs associated with the change, but it was a good deal for the firm and was transformational.

2.5.5 How Can We Develop a Common (Business) Language?

A common business language is essential to bind partners together and help to limit misunderstandings though poor communication.

> ...I have been required on several occasions to involve service partners and service providers in delivering customer/end-user services, and [companies] do not always talk about transmitting the importance of customer loyalty through efficient services... To address the situation, you need to identify partners who share the company's business vision and language...

Developing a common language even within a single firm is hard, as it addresses many cultural aspects, so developing one with newly acquired service firms or partners is much harder (Fig. 2.43).

It is important to have feedback in a common language, with common terms, including names, descriptions, and acronyms, so that communication is clear and unambiguous. This helps to ensure that customer problems are quickly addressed before they escalate. A filter in communication does not help the situation and leads to politics.

> ...To be honest it was not managed very well. We tried to acquire and integrate service companies, but this did not work...

The lesson with developing a common language within a business is that it takes time and does not happen overnight. This common business language also requires localization. A tension between the center and the regions requires the ability to manage it, acting as a filter to mediate the differences and the misunderstandings. Remember that the differences between two native English speakers can be as great as between others, where English is their common language.

The tools that help to explore the barriers and to build actions to overcome them are:

- Avatar map.
- Business model canvas.

Fig. 2.43 Developing a common service language prevents misunderstandings (illustration by Annick Holland, authors' work)

- Cradle-to-grave lifecycle map.
- Cradle-to-grave lifecycle visual mapping.
- Customer value proposition.
- Metric cascades.
- Service blueprint.
- Visual journey map – high level.
- Visual journey map – detail level.

Details of the individual tools are given in Chap. 3.

> **Case 53 Three Acquisitions Later: We Have Four Different Languages**
> The service business was built on the back of several acquisitions. They had created a global platform, but somehow, they had not created a coherent business with a common culture and language. Misunderstandings created management challenges, which meant that the firm ended up firefighting internal issues rather than working with the customers. This lost them the benefit of being a single firm, and they risked looking ramshackle and unprofessional.

(continued)

2.5 Competitors, Suppliers, and Partners

After having a workshop with all of the key managers, the business owners came to the conclusion that everyone needed to work together to create a common language within the firm. This, they thought, would help start to build a shared vision. Part of the problem came from the fact that some of the firms competed with each other prior to being acquired. Nothing was really straightforward here.

The firm had ended up with different technical and managerial terms for the same things. This really hindered understanding within the business, but strangely it also made the staff approach problems differently. They released this when they all came together to discuss technical issues.

Understanding that there was less difference than similarity between the staff was a big step. Using it, the team worked to create a common terminology that described its competencies and capabilities. They also started to share one-page case studies based on projects. This helped to build up respect for each other, overcome the language challenge, and start to agree on common terms. They used the common language to improve the enterprise resource planning and CRM systems so that they could capture the same information and share it. It was very much a bottom-up approach within a management framework and vision.

The technical team coming together with the building of a common language worked, perhaps better than in the management area. Not surprising in some ways, as engineers and technicians, the world over get a kick out of fixing problems. And this is what started to happen. The grassroots approach made it work and stopped it feeling like management imposing a common language on the business. Different local cultures continued to exist, more because the management had not taken the time to understand their differences. The process broke down the local information silos and left everyone feeling it was the right thing to do to pick up the phone and ask one of their colleagues for help.

Case 54 Developing a Common Approach to Customer Feedback
There were many arguments about how to gauge customer feedback. In the firm, they ranged from "well, they paid" to "they keep coming back" and "warranty claims are low." None of which really gave insights into the customers' experiences. There was nothing quantitative to confirm what the team were doing was right, why people like it, and where they needed to improve. Internal metrics were from manufacturing and based on on-time delivery and lead time and a number of other internal activity-based key

(continued)

performance indictors or KPIs. Because of this, the service team decided that they needed to take a new approach to obtaining effective feedback.

Manufacturing had some customer KPIs that were output-based but none of them really fitted what service wanted. A quick and simple qualitative feedback system was needed. There was more than enough feedback from sales that said service was "too expensive," but these insights really did not help the service team to understand or change to improve their delivery to customers. Too many of the comments reinforced the firm's "unique selling proposition," rather than considering what delighted or upset customers.

The service quality metric was looked at for quantitative measurement of performance, but the team considered that it was too complex to use and settled on the net promoter score (NPS). For each job, they identified 3–5 stakeholders who were important for the project on the customer side. They did this to get a wider picture and to improve their range of contacts within the firm. For small jobs, they only check a random 10% for a rating of their satisfaction. For new customers and for large projects, they always asked for a full breakdown of their opinions. The data collection was outsourced to an agency, because the service team did not want to distract the sales team and they really did want a neutral approach. The second step was to treat all 1–5 and 8–10 scores as noncompliance reports (or NCR). One to five required senior management to contact the customer within a week, 8–10 within the month.

The firm learned where it annoyed customers and where it delighted them. Low-scoring customers could be turned into supporters once the team built an action plan out of their NCR. From the high scores, they learned where they really created value for customers – in many cases, they really had no idea, and sharing the one-page reports within the business allowed it to focus more on what customers really wanted from the firm.

2.5.6 How Can Both We and Our Partners Manage Performance Measurement?

Measuring service performance (Fig. 2.44) is more complex than just measuring the sales volume and the margin. And it becomes more complex when you combine this with measuring partners' performance. Too often, the method of measurement remains at the financial level, especially if there is a simple revenue share model being applied.

> ...We need to develop revenue (sharing) models (related to measuring performance), there were some legal issues (liability etc.) that then emerged...

2.5 Competitors, Suppliers, and Partners

Fig. 2.44 Look to improve service though direct customer feedback (illustration by Annick Holland, authors' work)

When considering joint liabilities with service performance, legal issues can become more problematic, unless there is a joint risk for the partners.

Benchmarking against other performance indictors is important for the performance measurement: inspection duration (planned and actual), safety, service quality, and net promoter score (or NPS) all should also be made part of that measurement. The soft measures should be taken from at least three people in the customer's firm.

> ...Non-financial KPIs (e.g., NPS) are as important when measuring performance as financial KPIs...

Performance can, in the end, only be defined by the customer, and key performance indicators only represent a proxy for the actual performance. That said, internal measures ensure a quality of service delivery and allow the business to identify areas for improvement. It is worth also considering that service-level agreements (or SLA) often provide a minimal service requirement and do not usually take into account specific situations but rather deal with a hypothetical situation. This can lead to behaviors that lead to what the customer sees as poor service performance.

The lessons from the cases confirm the need to create simple models that measure performance and that the metrics may be different to those for the manufacturing business. It is advisable to start with measuring customer experience and take it seriously even though it is subjective. Find other external metrics that help you assess your performance based on how you make your customers successful (align outcomes!). You also need to measure internal performance and benchmark this between service centers to allow you to learn from each other.

The tools that help to explore the barriers and to build actions to overcome them are:

- Avatar map.
- Customer jobs-to-be-done.
- Customer value proposition.
- Detailed empathy card.
- Ecosystem mapping.
- Empathy maps.
- Metric cascades.
- Service blueprint.
- Visual journey map – high level.
- Visual journey map – detail level.

Details of the individual tools are given in Chap. 3.

Case 55 Legal Team Was the Barrier to New Value Propositions that Aligned with Outcomes

The legal language this firm used was focused on drafting product-based contacts. The legal team had basic service contracts based on time and materials but did not have more advanced service contacts where risks were shared, other than with damages. This was creating problems for the service team, as customers wanted more complex arrangements, where the firm not only took more risk but also had the opportunity for an upside. The legal department always talked about liabilities and risks that the firm would take but did not provide any alternatives to their traditional approaches. Yet, other approaches existed, such as power-by-the-hour, subscription, and other outcome-based approaches. The service team needed something new, as they needed to align their performance with the customer's drivers.

The legal team did not understand how to structure outcome-based contacts even though the firm was used to buying service agreements in many different areas of the business. On closer examination, many of the service agreements were based on nothing more than service levels, where the firm expected problems to be investigated (not corrected) within a set number of hours. As such, they were close to product contracts. There were some that provided "availability" targets with gain/pain shares. The service team used these as examples for the legal team, so that they could start to rebuild service contracts to produce a set of different contract forms that reflected the firm's value propositions.

The firm recruited a commercial manager who had experience with advanced service contracts and, using examples from the market and teaming up with legal, started to design new service contracts. The aim was to design contracts that matched with the value propositions and aligned performance with payment. This was a major change from the existing approach, which started with the view of limiting liabilities. They ended up redesigning their

(continued)

existing contract terms – before then it was considered "the small print" – and created different advanced service agreements. To help achieve this, the commercial manager bought access to the New Engineering Contract (NEC) (https://www.neccontract.com), which had many examples (and templates) of contract form.

Bringing the legal department onside was a big win. The firm learned to design contracts that matched their value propositions and aligned them with customer outcomes. It was much harder than expected, and the service management spent time teaching counterparties' procurement teams about the benefits of the contracts they were proposing. The firm used the lessons to teach its sales teams how to deal with contracts and to stop considering them "the small print" but rather something that was important commercially. They learned to integrate performance metrics into all of the service contracts.

Case 56 Measuring Performance Is More Than Just Financials
All businesses need to be financially minded and make profits on what they do, but there is a point where measuring only financial performance as a way of evaluating success becomes self-defeating. Every project in this firm was booked on net present value (NPV), contribution margin, and 12 months' sales volume and was measured quarterly against these figures. However, having these is just part of measuring the project and its contribution to the business. The numbers that were being captured were important but missed important aspects – like customer satisfaction and the likelihood of contract renewal. They were also not something that could be openly discussed with the customer.

The firm assumed that payment of invoices was a measure of a successful relationship and, from this, that the business' financial measures were the most important metrics. Yet, they had customers complaining about service, but it was not taken seriously because they had paid their invoices. One explanation of this was "if they were really cross, they'd have withheld some of the payment to get our attention – that's what we would do." The product business used a number of nonfinancial metrics, like on-time delivery and the number of noncompliance reports (NCRs) to measure performance, but they did not seem to fit the service business very well, so they were not used. Still, the firm needed to measure the outcomes from their service work.

Meeting with customers to talk about outcomes from the work the firm did for them was a revelation. They had different measures for success than "just getting the work done." For many of them, safety metrics were important and key in deciding contract awards: with others, the key was turnaround time;

(continued)

with others, annual availability; and for others, the reports or daily meetings. This revealed many aspects, some key to individual customers and others having broader applicability. There was no magic bullet, but what was key was to capture the hard and soft outcomes or metrics in a quantitative way from the customer (at least five people) and integrate this into the project management system for each contract.

Initially, it was a mess of extra work from having many Excel spreadsheets with different metrics. This system had to be standardized and provided for all projects, large or small. These were the internal financial metrics (e.g., contract value, final sales value, pre/post margins) and the performance measures (e.g., on-time delivery, lead time, quality issues). The service team also added safety to the assessments and then provided additional customer-centric performance measures so that the customers could use these figures. This had a very positive effect as it allowed the customers to measure our performance directly in their business. Finally, the firm added net promoter score to the metrics to get a final semiquantitative performance measure.

2.5.7 How Do We Work with Installers?

Installers are important ecosystem actors for many manufacturers (Fig. 2.45). They take the equipment and make it useable for the owner, installing and commissioning it at the owner's facility. Installers often have different names: EPC, (ship)builders, distributors, system integrators, etc. They tend to have the direct relationship with the asset owner and can, unless well managed, limit the manufacturer's direct

Fig. 2.45 Firms that install the equipment you sell are your extended sales force (illustration by Annick Holland, authors' work)

2.5 Competitors, Suppliers, and Partners

connection with the customer. This can cause major problems, where the installer feels more like "piggy in the middle" as they pass issues back to the manufacturer, leading to the apparent poor performance of the equipment supplied. In this case, the manufacturer works to limit its liabilities, while the installer works to limit its costs. Poor equipment performance can be the fault of the installer due to poor selection of equipment or below-the-standard installation. For these reasons, the installer may work to prevent or limit direct customer contact.

Installers can be an important and helpful channel for service delivery, because they are often technically experienced and have direct relationships with the end-users. They may also be considering how to expand their offerings to their customer base. They can support service delivery in the same way as new product sales.

> ...Installers are hit and run, they are always chasing the next project and only care about getting past warranty unscathed!...

On a more advanced level, they can provide services directly to the end-user with the support of, or even on behalf of, the OEM. The level of performance may be limited to more basic inspections or in other cases provision of more advanced installation and repair services using OEM parts and remote support. So, proper collaboration with the installer can result in high profitability. What is critical is engagement: it is important to understand what drives each party and how a relationship can be mutually beneficial for the end-user, the installer, and the OEM.

The key lessons from the two cases are based around collaboration and understanding what motivated others to improve your services. Installers' businesses models are short-term project-focused: service businesses are long-term relationship-driven. This creates a paradox that firms need to learn to deal with and allows them to learn to provide services for both, in effect, segments. Collaboration can mean that all parties win in the end. However, it is essential to remember that not all installers want or understand cooperation and have to learn to deal with both types of behaviors.

> ...Working with installers collaboratively is not always possible but when it works the value for all is higher...

Whichever form of collaboration firms have with the installer, they need to be ready to deliver new service solutions after the warranty phase. It would help if firms were prepared with a value proposition that supports the equipment's long-term operation to allow them to gain a recurring revenue.

The tools that help to explore the barriers and to build actions to overcome them are:

- Avatar map.
- Case/actor matrix.
- Cradle-to-grave lifecycle map.

- Cradle-to-grave lifecycle visual mapping.
- Customer value proposition.
- Metric cascades.
- Service blueprint.
- Visual journey map – high level.
- Visual journey map – detail level.

Details of the individual tools are given in Chap. 3.

Case 57 Cleaning Up the Mess that Installers Leave Behind
The firm manufactured high-quality products that were then installed by technicians. They had no control on the quality of the installation, and worse, the installers may have selected the wrong products that would not do the job required. The challenge the firm then faced was that customers blamed them for the products' poor performance. The products had the firm's brand name on them, but in most cases, the problems were not the firm's fault. Trying to explain this to the customers was hard, as was telling them that they needed to go and ask their installer. Post-installation warranty, life got easier as the firm could support customers directly and for the long term.

The challenge was in two parts – one contractual, the other cultural. The manufacturer was effectively the subcontractor to the installer and had no direct customer relationship until after the installation had been completed and warrantied. The installers went in for the project and then moved on: "here-today-gone-tomorrow." Digging deeper, it became clear that the installers also found the situation "annoying." For them, the warranty handling was complex and could cost more in management fees than the remedy. They also confirmed that post-warranty, they had no further interest in the customer.

The firm considered the four phases separately:

1. Sales were to support the installers earlier with the selection of the best products for each project.
2. The firm would provide training on the installation of the products for a fee.
3. A post-installation audit would be made to check the quality of the installation.
4. At the end of warranty, the firm would visit the customer to offer them ongoing services and spares support.

This was a change in the approach that needed the manufacturing firm to integrate more closely with both the installer and the end-customer. The objective was to provide customers with both an improved experience and better support.

(continued)

> It worked better than expected. The end-users found out how they could get replacement products, spares, and consumables direct from the manufacturer. They also realized that the initial installation may not have been what was really needed, and the firm was able to adapt the equipment to suit their individual situations. The installation audit helped both the installers and the end-users to confirm the status of the handover; it also showed up areas where additional training was needed to prevent issues in the future. The sales support is taking longer to develop, but where the OEM firm has good relationships with the customers, it looks more promising.

> **Case 58 Using Installers to Extend the Sales Force**
> The firm sold to "end-users" via system integrators and installers. Sales were predicated on those partners' ability to sell what the manufacturing firm makes and to understand what to buy from the firm to meet end-users' requirements. They were not distributors, so the firm had limited control over what they did. So, in effect the firm could only be successful if the integrators and installers were successful, and they were often viewed as the main route-to-market and service channel. The challenge was that they also bought from competitors, and often the firm only knew this later. Moreover, the firm continued to sell traditionally using traditional sales approaches based on sales brochures. They were not sure how well this suited the new Internet-enabled business they were in.
> Over the past years, the firm had failed to update, and although it made high-quality products, it continued to support customers in the same ways. They mapped out a number of offers though the sales process and realized that, for some of the installers, the firm was offering a full service where they made the full offer, while other installers did most of the sales process themselves, often based on prior work. Both installers were charged the same for the products. In effect, the manufacturing firm was giving away free sales support to help some installers close their deals. How could the firm help and charge for the services they were providing for free sometimes, and how could they integrate the installers into the sales process to get a higher hit rate?
> The firm wanted to transform the sales system. They looked at the processes involved and realized that a benchmark budget figure was needed early on, with basic performance data. The installers needed this for budgeting purposes, and the firm needed the installers to have the appropriate budget to afford the products it sells. To get the offer in at the right budget, the firm needed the customer's information, and this helped them to understand the real number of projects the installers were working on.

(continued)

> The firm then developed a free online self-configurator or a sales manager-based configuration to produce a quote for a fee. The quotes were set up based on the project and its delivery schedule. The firm worked hard to enable the installers to directly integrate this data into their offer to their customers.
>
> The sales department said that it could not be done. But some customers liked it and others accepted the segmentation. Sales slowly transformed to a consultative selling approach, working with the customer to understand their real needs rather than pushing products. The two-stage quoting process allowed the firm to understand in detail the number of real projects; in many cases, they were bidding on the same project three or more times. The firm helped the installers to ensure they had sufficient budget to buy from them early on and confirmed this with binding offers. The binding offers were well-liked, as installers could quickly integrate them into their offers to their customers, either themselves or with the support of the sales managers.

2.6　Society and Environment

There are different levels of expectations in different locations. In some regions, relationships are considered primary; in others, friendship is usually separated from business. For instance, the behavior of employees at a Starbucks in the USA is quite different to that of a Swiss or French franchise, even where the product remains the same.

For some people in industry, engineering is the real business focus; for others, it is production and customer experience. In some areas, it is considered that service should not be charged for; in others, charging is normal. The local environments for service are also different; as local labor laws change, so do import tariffs and taxes. Imagine you had a service contract for a client in the UK and you served them from France – what happens to the service contract once the UK leaves the EU? This is a minefield compared with equipment businesses. In our research, this has been confirmed by interviews; the quotes present it more clearly than we would be able to.

> ...some regions were harder, because some managers do not think of service as the real business. However, some other regions were easier, because management support came...

> ...we have to offer free of charge solutions to support the loyalty of final customers and help to strengthen our relationship with the front-end partners...

> ...tax is becoming a major problem for transfer of pricing...

Service is a real business and the real cash generator for the majority of manufacturing firms, and without it, there is no real long-term sustainability for business. However, a service adopting the same approach cannot be delivered in

2.6 Society and Environment

Fig. 2.46 The relative importance of the barriers around "society and environment" (illustration by Annick Holland, adapted from West et al., 2018)

every country, as society and the wider environment present the service manager with many problems that require different capability and processes and have different rhythms. Therefore, a variety of solutions may be needed for diverse regions where attitudes and values can vary widely. Understanding and respecting these differences, both parts of the business can flourish. Dealing with the cross-border issues that service businesses create is complex and requires different approaches to ensure that costs and delays do not occur. The relative importance of the barriers around "society and environment" from the survey data is shown in Fig. 2.46.

When referring to "society and environment," the top issue is the common concern of moving to charge for services from the prior position of delivering them for free. The "think local, act global" approach that was pioneered by ABB in the 1990s remains an open issue and a problem for many firms, and more work is needed to address this, even with the application of modular approaches to service design. Also, the management of advanced service contracts and maintaining compliance with local laws and corporate requirements, clearly related to the "standardize/localize" paradox, is still a key challenge for many service managers.

However, as legal and tax issues associated with service delivery scored significantly lower than the other barriers here, more research is required to understand if this is associated with ignorance or is in fact the reality. It seems that what supports a business to overcome this type of barrier is the presence of the finance and control function from the pre-sale phase and the adoption of business plans to evaluate the internal costs and estimate the value added by the services, together with the adoption of economic and financial analyses. At the same time, the use of cost and pricing schemes based on standard modular components allows variable cost and pricing plans to be built and, consequently, provide the basis for a more accurate and reliable profitability control system.

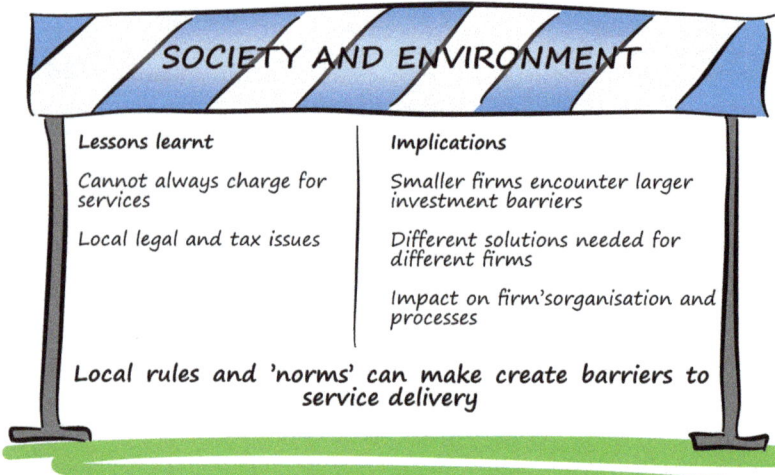

Fig. 2.47 The lessons and implications for the society and environment barriers (illustration by Annick Holland, adapted from West et al., 2018)

Finally, all the people we interviewed stated that market reactivity to accept new forms and types of services was easier than expected, and in some cases, servitization was a result of customer pull. Moreover, the case studies suggest that an effective strategic approach must reflect the local reality even if they appear contrary when compared to servitization logic. In particular, legal and tax issues associated with a local delivery of services were poorly considered by most of the firms. For small firms, this can be onerous, whereas larger firms may have the resources required. In summary, the implications for "society and environment" are:

- Businesses cannot always charge for services.
- Act according to local legal and tax issues.
- Smaller firms encounter larger investment barriers.
- Different solutions are needed for different firms.
- Recognize the impact on your firm's organization and processes.
- Introducing finance and control functions from the pre-sale phase.
- Adopt business plans and economic and financial analyses to evaluate the internal cost and estimate the value added by the services.
- Use cost and pricing schemes based on standard modular components.

Figure 2.47 describes some of the lessons learned and the implications from the interviews.

To help you better understand how to navigate the barriers, we will provide insights from cases to help you understand how others overcame the barriers, the barriers we identified (in order of importance) were:

2.6 Society and Environment

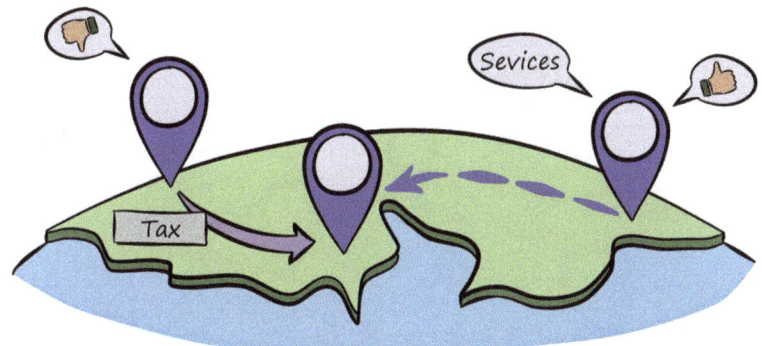

Fig. 2.48 Taxes and local laws can have a major impact on an international service business (illustration by Annick Holland, authors' work)

1. How can we convert free to fee (change internal and external mentality)?
2. How can we deal with the conflicting demands to standardize (for efficiency) and localize (for effectiveness) at the same time?
3. How can we manage long-term contractual commitments done at corporate level with local laws?
4. What are the main legal implications for our organization?
5. How can we understand tax and transfer pricing issues?

Taxes and local laws can have a major impact on an international service business, and this is shown visually in Fig. 2.48.

2.6.1 How Can We Convert Free to Fee (Change the Internal and External Mentality)?

In the past, many firms have not charged for service (Fig. 2.49) as they have considered it as part of the product or customer services that they have to provide, which may be appropriate with simple products with short operational life spans. This behavior rapidly converts the service activities into a pure cost and one where service is there to prevent the product or equipment being returned under warranty to the manufacturer. When service becomes a compliance activity, service gets a little respect within the firm, which often leads to poor customer experience, because the organization's commitment to service activities and responses from the customers can be very poor. This approach also leads to loss of information about the installed base and consequent loss of customer contact and potentially new business. Many service managers have expressed their frustration at being "just a cost center" and the problems that not being able to charge customers creates.

Moving from free to fee-based services leads to a positive change in behaviors on both sides of the service customer-provider relationship and begins with the

Fig. 2.49 The business and your customers gain when you move from free to fee in services (illustration by Annick Holland, authors' work)

perspective that people only value what they pay for. It takes time but brings great benefits.

> …Not yet completed in my specific case but with a great result to date…

As it is often not easy to implement, this step must be taken in small steps.

> …Free to fee can be digested well by the commercial part if it is proposed as a service to be offered as a substitute for discounts or promotions. This is the first step…

Visibility is everything: an additional customer visit has an associated cost, and someone has to pay – for this reason every non-warranty customer visit should always be billed to make the fee transparent to the customer. However, a credit note can be issued to cancel out the bill at any time Even with warranty work, the costs should be recharged to the equipment business, because as they say, "there is no such thing as a free lunch." Fees should nevertheless be based around customer value rather than simply supplier costs, and here some aspects need very careful consideration so that they do not cause difficulties with the customers. For instance, charging for travel time may be considered unnecessary in some cases.

It is an important lesson that customers pay for what they value and do not value free service. It is therefore essential to make fees visible in the pricing and billing process. A credit note that describes the "freebie" can be a useful tool in setting pricing expectations in the future. This is necessary where others often hide price relevant issues in the scope and charge for them as variations.

The tools that help to explore the barriers and to build actions to overcome them are:

2.6 Society and Environment

- Business model canvas.
- Business process mapping.
- Cradle-to-grave lifecycle map.
- Cradle-to-grave lifecycle visual mapping.
- Customer jobs-to-be-done.
- Empathy maps.
- Job-to-be-done insights.
- Job-to-be-done outcomes.
- Metric cascades.
- Service blueprint.
- Visual journey map – high level.
- Visual journey map – detail level.

Details of the individual tools are given in Chap. 3.

> **Case 59 Learning to Charge for Free Services**
> The firm had been providing many services free at the point of delivery to its customers, yet at the same time, it had more and more price pressure from those customers. On one hand, they said that they liked the services, but on the other, they took advantage of them as they were free. The sales department said that they had to give the services for free, but something felt wrong about not charging and the service team were always told to watch costs, even though the team told the product business that they were the ones who were generating those costs.
>
> The firm really had no idea what customers valued or why. Because the company focused on product design, the service aspects got overlooked. For example, cable would be shipped with the products, and customers would then at some point return the unused cable and expect a refund, perhaps over a year from the initial delivery. Worse, the firm was often unaware that the customer had held on to materials that had been supplied to them – not very professional, as everything has a cost.
>
> The management team spent time walking through the customer journey from pre-pre-sales to post-post-sales. This was very helpful as it started to identify many service tasks they did for customers, many of which they did not realize were done or were valued. The team then started to segment the services to estimate how important each one was for the customers and also checked how satisfied customers were with the service delivery. To do this, the service management team tried to work with sales, but they were reluctant to offer support.
>
> The team identified over 20 hidden services and were able to define them clearly. Customers had complained that some of these services were delivered very poorly and hinted that they might be willing to pay for them if they were

(continued)

delivered in a more professional way. The team also identified some services that could not be fully untangled from product sales. Sales pushed back and were not supportive as they were using the "free" services as a negotiation tool. Still, the team documented and priced the less contentious services and moved them out of the "vanilla" offers. They were confident that there was a hidden service business with sustainable revenues that the firm was missing out on. In much the same way, airlines have unbundled baggage from their basic tickets.

Case 60 First Steps of Changing for Services
In this firm, the sales team stated that it would not be possible to charge for hidden services. It was impossible. They had a list of services with fees but were blocked from unbundling them from product sales to start to charge for them. But this was something that customers had said they actually wanted to do.

The service team needed to find a way around the sales team, to try to unbundle the services with a small group of customers. Bypassing sales was a dangerous approach, and it created friction between two groups within the business. Fortunately, the head of the business stood behind the approach and provided support. New offers were produced with the product and the services separated and made visible for the first time. This allowed the firm to reduce the product price in many cases and increase margin as it was not providing services for free. Not all of the services were fully stripped out, but rather, the firm time-limited them and, where they went over the limit, the customer was charged.

The firm started to get returns of excess materials sooner; some of these were related to (expensive) shipping containers. For others, they started to bill customers and realized that because of this, the firm's service team knew where its products were geographically (well, they did create a bill) – something that had been hidden in the past. When people brought in repairs, if they were stored for longer than 30 days, again, the firm started to bill them. Sometimes the bill was enough to remind the customer to collect the equipment or have the firm ship it back to them. This saved storage space and therefore reduced costs. Interestingly, some customers asked for equipment to be repaired and then stored until they needed it returned. This was something new that has since grown into a new service business. Customers pay the firm to store their equipment; it is inspected every year and the warranty on the repair work is extended. However, the firm has not yet started to store new equipment for them. It seemed that the firm was unable to store and manage

(continued)

> their own inventories in the past. The firm has another advantage from this, as when the customer asks for the equipment, it normally means that they have an unplanned failure and may need field service and later parts and repairs.
>
> The sales function, after being slow to adapt to the new unbundling approach, has been very keen to help extend the services the firm now offers.

2.6.2 How Can We Deal with the Conflicting Demands to Standardize (for Efficiency) and Localize (for Effectiveness) at the Same Time?

There is an ongoing challenge to be flexible to customers' demands for services and yet build a standardized service offering (Fig. 2.50). Most likely, this will continue as we move closer and closer to a lot size of one and individualized bespoke manufacturing. Certainly, standardization (of services rather than service modules) makes it easier for the sales team to explain what it is they are selling and easier to deliver the services. The service modules are centrally adapted, reframes as required, and all the necessary documentation can be changed via the intranet at the push of a button. In effect, the customer can get a service for a lower fee when it is delivered in a standard way, while the service supplier can improve their margins.

> …Standardization vs. efficiency: it is a continuous process of trial and error…

In this regard, the airlines have been very successful creating packages that are well understood and well-defined for their customers.

> …Creating standard service modules (or building blocks) allowed us to improve our efficiency and the quality-of-service delivery…

Fig. 2.50 It is important to allow local adaptions to local conditions (illustration by Annick Holland, authors' work)

When providing flexibility (within the triangle between customer requirements, normative specifications, and standardization) it is essential to understand what the core blocks are that are non-negotiable for the services. The blocks that must be standardized, typically, are the project management blocks, billing, cost control, and spares definitions. The other blocks are often built around field services, repairs, and "conversions, modifications, and upgrades." Therefore, when designing the blocks, it is fundamental to consider what could be made the responsibility of a customer or dealer. One way to consider the approach is to use the extremes and a midpoint: do-it-for-me, do-it-yourself, and do-it-with-me. Remember that liabilities change as responsibilities change. This is important in the innovation process as it encourages different modes for delivery, ones which may be outside the traditional approach taken by the firm. Such considerations clearly emerge from the cases that suggest it is possible to "have your cake and eat it," that is, standardize as much as possible to drive efficiency and simplicity and use standard building blocks (or modules) to give the flexibility you need while speaking the customer's language. This approach allows sales to build a customized solution effectively. The tools that help to explore the barriers and to build actions to overcome them are:

- Business model canvas.
- Business process mapping.
- Case/actor matrix.
- Cradle-to-grave lifecycle map.
- Cradle-to-grave lifecycle visual mapping.
- Customer value proposition.
- Metric cascades.
- Service blueprint.
- Understanding your business.

Details of the individual tools are given in Chap. 3.

> **Case 61 Standardizing Service Modules to Provide Flexibility**
> The firm had standard repair profiles for every service it provided. They built them up for every job from the last version rather than from scratch, because it was quicker to take the last one and edit it than to create a new one each time. It made it difficult to add flexibility to the work, while the firm needed be more adaptable, as customers were demanding more and more. It became essential that the firm consider what customers wanted rather than sticking to its standard "menu."
> Internally, the firm had no real standards. The sales team said the service engineers could do anything, but they ended up saying one thing and then doing something different. There was a mismatch between the services and
>
> (continued)

what was in the enterprise resource planning system. The firm knew it needed to offer more flexibility but kept getting tied up within its standards.

The firm mapped out all of the services it offered and categorized them into field services, equipment repairs, and spares. They started by assessing the high-level journey or process map for the work and found that this quickly became generic. They then mapped out the individual tasks for services and started to find that some tasks were also similar in many respects. What they discovered was that the firm had many standard modules that they could build together to create new services, which they could quickly adjust for both the offers they had to make (high level scopes) and for detailed workorders.

Up until this, the firm had thought that everything they offered was different, but by looking at the similarities rather than focusing on the differences, they started to see common processes, which were used to help standardize the services offered. This was possible in the office functions as much as the operational areas of the business. Rather than ending up with less flexibility (something that everyone had feared), they gained more by having clearly defined modules. The standard service models improved costs, quality management, and the turnaround times of the service work.

Case 62 Developing Competencies and Capabilities for Modular Services

The firm has been selling repairs into the market for over 30 years based on the work it does. The engineers and technicians take great pride in their work and their quality standards. The challenge that the firm faces more and more with new customers is that they just do not understand what the firm does and how it does it, and some of the customers do not seem to care. They just ask for references and whether the engineers have repaired X or Y before. They do not seem to understand that skills are transferable from one repair to another.

After some surveys and customer interviews and some long periods of internalization of the problem, the firm realized that people were not buying the engineers' competences or capabilities, but rather the outcome of their work. In effect they wanted to know that the team could repair a machine and that following the repair it would run safely again. Analysis established that there were several layers needed to get to the high-level outcomes customers wanted, based around machine availability. In general, they were built up from the firm's basic competencies and capabilities, which could be mapped to the repairs and the outcome of the repairs.

The firm realized that it was mixing many things together and missing the point of why "people buy a drill" as the customers really were "buying a

(continued)

solution." Because of this, the team made three changes: (1) they changed their marketing language to that of the customers, speaking their language; (2) they made a list of repairs based on machine OEM/type; and (3) they mapped the repairs to the team's underlying competencies and capabilities. This allowed the firm to view potential repairs based on different modules, and it could also then separate out the standardized back end and the service options. This helped confirm that the engineers could do a repair and assured the firm that it had the wherewithal to deliver the outcomes the customers required successfully.

They moved to a more flexible yet standardized operational model; this helped to cut costs while being able to "pick-and-mix" capabilities and competences to deliver the outcomes that were key to customers. It also allowed them to add or remove additional adjacent services that they either wanted or did not require.

The use of the customer's language was powerful, as the firm learned how to back up customer-facing statements with a more detailed level of technical capabilities and competences. This was far more powerful than just offering to extend the warranty, wade through pages of technical documents, or just show the ISO certificate.

2.6.3 How Can We Manage Long-Term Contractual Commitments Made at the Corporate Level with Local Laws?

Long-term agreements need to be made with a competent team who understand risk management, but they are often made centrally by a small team that have limited experience of execution yet pass the contracts to the local businesses for execution. Conversely, the local execution teams do not have the commercial skills to negotiate complex multiyear advanced service contracts. This can create a lack of local ownership for an agreement and a lack of local empowerment with the agreements.

> ...Corporate agree these long-term agreements and we have to execute them, often without local buy in...

Such agreements also contain inflation escalators, embedded exchange rate risks, or delivery commitments that the local business may not fully understand or be able to control. Therefore, balancing the control and responsibility between the center and the regions can be a tough job (Fig. 2.51).

> ...The impact of tax law on daily action is often difficult for the individual to understand without help from the tax department...

Fig. 2.51 Balancing central control with regional freedom is a never-ending task (illustration by Annick Holland, authors' work)

There must be buy-in locally for a long-term agreement, and in some firms, this is easier to achieve than in others, depending on the early involvement of the local entity. Moreover, the underlying cost model must be understood by all, as it is the plan the local team will execute. Therefore, the handover of the agreement to the local execution team is critical so that they understand what their obligations are. Making the local team a cost center does not work – service shop managers are expected to be business leaders, and business leaders have a profit and loss sheet. Also, risks should be apportioned appropriately, while the finance department that provides the exchange rates or escalation indexes should take ownership of these; the execution team should be responsible for their scope; from all of this, margin can then be allocated accordingly.

The most important lesson is that with long-term service agreements (often advanced services) a specialist commercial team should lead the acquisition of advanced service contracts – the local service shops should be responsible for their fulfilment or delivery. The handover from the commercial team to the execution team should be a phased process with clear allocation of responsibilities. The local team that delivers the advanced service contract will also need ongoing commercial team support during the delivery of the services.

The tools that help to explore the barriers and to build actions to overcome them are:

- Business model canvas.
- Business process mapping.
- Case/actor matrix.
- Customer value proposition.
- Service blueprint.
- Understanding your business.

Details of the individual tools are given in Chap. 3.

> **Case 63 Cleaning Up the Mess that Corporate Created**
> Corporate dumped a service contract on a regional service center that they were not involved in drafting, making the regional team responsible for the delivery of the agreement that they had been signed up to. The team soon found they did not understand all of the contract terms and were uncertain of how they would deliver the services. They also found some of the cost assumptions were incorrect, and they were unsure how to deal with the performance commitments in the agreement. What the team understands is their rates for particular tasks.
>
> The team were not involved in the contract negotiations and have limited understanding of performance and use-based advanced services. They found that they just did not have the commercial project management capabilities to deal with the contracts both internally and externally (e.g., with the customer). This led to frustration and the regional team feeling that they needed to clean up the mess that corporate had created, although it did appreciate the effort that corporate had gone to with winning the contractual services.
>
> Unused to dealing with POC-based (percent of completion based) contacts, the team agreed with corporate that they needed a contract performance manager for the advanced service contracts and that they needed to be costed into the project – not something that had been done before. Then, the regional service center ended up hiring a contract performance manager to interface with the customer and to coordinate internally to ensure that the right services were delivered at the right time and to deal with the contract reporting. That said, the team saw that sales costs were lower as they were leading the sales process rather than the sales managers.
>
> Hiring a contract performance manager was tough and getting them to fit into a very technical/action-oriented business was really hard. Contract performance managers need to think and behave differently to achieve their goals – they do not care about the technical details in the same way as engineers do. It took time for the service team to learn how the new manager behaved and thought, as much as they had to learn how the team operates – this was a big step.
>
> The regional service team required that the contract performance manager was involved in the later stages of the contract negotiation process. This was a big help with understanding the contract scope and structure. For their part, the contract performance manager helped to translate the work into the service team's standard language.

Case 64 Tax in Service Is Really Hard to Get Right

The firm won a project over 10,000 km from their service shop. This was great as they had found a new market to sell into, and the work initially started with the selling of spares. Quickly, the agent asked the firm to provide field service. Working in-country for an extended time for a major overhaul and upgrade on the equipment was well within their normal scope of supply, but they had not considered the local tax issues for temporary workers and withholding tax.

In other words, the firm had been pulled into a full upgrade project after initially only being asked to provide some service spares. However, as they are a company that like to do the right thing, they said "yes." They then discovered there are work permits to get (the customer agreed to help with these and pay the costs), and as the engineers were on-site for longer than initially planned, the local tax authorities claimed that the firm had a "permanent establishment." This situation quickly started to unravel, as they could also be liable for the local social security payments for the engineering staff, even though they were being paid in their home locations.

The company hired a local tax expert to first get them out of the hole they had dug for themselves and second to provide guidance for future projects.

The tax expert created a dossier on the tax implications for the project, and the firm used this to understand what they had done wrong and the range of the tax bill they could face. With this information in hand, they spoke with the local tax office and the customer company. An agreement was brokered that was satisfactory (well mostly) to all parties.

The tax experts looked at the business and the risks around tax and gave guidance on how to prevent this problem occurring in another location. The firm worked with corporate tax as well as the local Finance and Control department (F&C) to build a set of operational guidelines that identified what was acceptable, where risks lay and what to do about them, and, perhaps most useful, who to contact.

The tax bill paid was much lower than the firm had feared it was going to be. Proactively opening up the discussion with the tax office was a very useful act, made more helpful by having a local tax expert and corporate F&C supporting these discussions. The tax office was not impressed but equally was pleased that the firm had initiated the discussions and had not hidden anything from them.

Creating a tax guidance note for sales was really helpful, as it allowed the firm to highlight tax risks early during the bidding process. They also found ways to become more tax efficient as part of the review process.

2.6.4 What Are the Main Legal Implications for Our Organization?

A limitation on the liability of contract value is often the case in new equipment sales, but what does this mean for service? What happens if an inspection on a machine leads to several millions' worth of damage? What happens when a customer incorrectly installs a spare part and it fails? There are many legal aspects that are completely different for services than for new equipment sales, often caused simply by working on a machine that is on the end-user's site. Acceptance of customers' terms and conditions can mean that there is simple acceptance of legal responsibilities that were written for buying new equipment and that liabilities are being accepted that the service business has no control over. Often, to accept an order, the service sales department is willing to accept "the small print" and move on; when things go well, this works, and when work does not go according to plan or when a customer's behavior changes, it may not be the best approach to take (Fig. 2.52).

> ...Sales consider terms and conditions 'the small print' and never read them, we just accept the orders and hope everything is fine...

A balanced set of service terms and conditions should be created, referring to a wide range of service activities, from providing advice to inspecting equipment on site, to repairing equipment off site, to transporting equipment, to providing spares, and to providing performance improvements. Also, different aspects, such as third-party liability, limit of liability, warranty obligations, etc., must be considered.

> ...We consider risks in a pragmatic way; this is on a project-by-project basis and through considering which legal system to apply to a contract. The business must not be allowed to fail because of one bad contract...

Sales then needs to understand the importance of service-applicable terms and conditions and to be able to explain them to their customers. This is, and has to be, the first line of defense, and it is likely that the buyer may be unaware of the potential

Fig. 2.52 When making long-term agreements with customers, always have a good lawyer on the team (illustration by Annick Holland, authors' work)

problems as well. When accepting equipment for repair, it should be logged into the enterprise resource planning system, and the terms and conditions given, as this can prevent future problems.

The two cases show the importance of the "small print," and managers have been known to forget that signing up to a bad set of terms and conditions means you can lose the whole business. Therefore, it is essential to have early involvement of commercial, risk, and legal teams to reduce the risks and allow time to build more robust solutions. Moreover, a pragmatic risk assessment allows for the contract review process, and it should be commercial-led rather than legal-led, as the business must lead here.

The tools that help to explore the barriers and to build actions to overcome them are:

- Business model canvas.
- Business process mapping.
- Case/actor matrix.
- Service blueprint.
- Understanding your business.

Details of the individual tools are given in Chap. 3.

> **Case 65 Sales Needs to Learn to Negotiate Service Terms and Conditions**
> Sales always talked about the "small print"; it was on the back of the offers in 9pt text that was virtually unreadable. They then always accepted the customer's terms and conditions (T&Cs) when we received a purchase order (PO) from the customer, no matter what the T&Cs said. The firm lost its commercial protection with this approach.
>
> The sales managers had never been taught about T&Cs; they only focused on the "technical offer" (e.g., the scope) and the "commercial offer" (e.g., the price). They virtually always overlooked other important aspects, such as limit of liability. They did not view the whole offer as the written form of the value proposition that the customer was buying.
>
> The team created new versions of the T&Cs for its service offers, which helped move away from the bland documents that came out of the enterprise resource planning system. It looked like the firm cared; it was also structured to describe the customer's problem and the firm's approach to correcting it. The pricing and the T&Cs were integrated into the document and could be read easily, and a "sign off" was also included within the offer, allowing customers to easily return the document.
>
> Combined with the new offer document, the service management team trained the sales team to start to understand the core contractual terms so that
>
> (continued)

they would not just give them away. As part of this, a simple offer checklist was created that they could use to raise offers and accept orders.

The integrated offer was liked by the customers, and the team tweaked it to improve its usability as not everything was right at first. It was close enough to help improve the hit rate and to reduce the number of POs the firm accepted without first questioning the T&Cs. The sales team slowly started to understand the importance of the document and the legal team saw that service management was taking more care with contract management than they did in the past. There was now always a written offer and confirmation of each order – this was something that had not happened in the past. Finally, the sales team now understand why the limit of liability is important for a service project.

Case 66 Service Risk Management that Creates Opportunities
Risk management was all about a tick list with a score. Nobody took it seriously. It was just one of those things that management said you had to do. It took quite a lot of time, and the service team did not understand what it was meant to bring them.

The real problem was that the team did not manage work commercially; they just looked at the scope from a technical perspective. They thought this was everything that was important. Clearly, this was wrong. The firm needed to look at risk as an opportunity and help to take some of it from the customers to allow both the customers and the firm to achieve important outcomes. The main issue was that the firm had become reactive rather than proactive, and because of this it had missed opportunities that were often staring it in the face.

The service management team moved to a position that commercial risk management in service needed to create opportunities for the firm rather than problems to hide behind. This was done to try and align value creation and value capture rather than it leading to loss of margin.

It was agreed that every new or larger service project would have a review of the risks at the bidding phase, at the contracting stage, and then during execution. The project leader was asked to lead the risk identification and then as a team everyone would work to find opportunities or mitigation for the risks. They stopped using an approach to risk using a matrix but rather identified the risks and then collectively looked for opportunities.

Margins started to improve, and actually margins at the end of the work ended up being closer to (or above) the bid margins. This was a major step forward. There was also more additional work coming out of the services. This was because the team was now dealing with the out-of-scope work, which in

(continued)

the past they just accepted. Importantly, doing it at the bid stage helped to highlight the risks to customers and made agreement with the extra work easier.

2.6.5 How Can We Understand Tax and Transfer Pricing Issues?

...The uncertainty of the position of the UK post-Brexit has highlighted the risks of not understanding the issues...

Tax is "taxing," and for many firms this is compounded with transfer pricing rules that were designed primarily for their manufacturing supply chains (Fig. 2.53). Service has different requirements to manufacturing and has a strong "people" component, as global and distributed equipment requires technicians performing their work in multiple countries. This means that tax issues around employees can become an issue that needs to be dealt with. With service, it can feel as if tax was designed just to cause problems, such as import/export formalities and tariffs, and changes to employee taxation. These prerogatives bring additional costs, take management attention away from the customer, slow down service delivery, and, worse, can involve fines from the authorities. How can these important issues be dealt with, without consuming excessive amounts of management time? One option is to only sell into your home market; however, today this is not a realistic option.

Being proactive is the only option. You have to assume that services are required on equipment that has been sold and is outside your "home" market. For spares, a solution can be to partner with a logistics firm that knows and understands the import/export regulations. This can give you pre-warning as well as provide solutions for some instances, e.g., how do you manage temporary import/export of tools to Russia? The same approach should be taken for employee aspects, e.g., what do I need to do to send a team to Australia for a 6-month project? Getting the

Fig. 2.53 Tax can be very taxing to deal with in an international service business (illustration by Annick Holland, authors' work)

temporary import/export procedure wrong means that your tools will remain in Russia, while getting the visa issue for Australia wrong means the employees can be deported and the firm fined. Similarly, cooperating with a partner who understands transfer challenges and costs allows you to better target your transfer pricing choices. Nevertheless, effective transfer pricing needs a set of simple and transparent guidelines to be implemented within the firm, but to do so needs the finance community within the business to understand the service processes and what this means for margin sharing.

> ...We have a simple margin splitting agreement to deal with transfer pricing, before we had to defend every price we offered...

The lessons seen in the two cases demonstrate the importance of transfer pricing for intracompany trading and how it can create tax issues. The problems of tax should never have been underestimated, as the tax office was relentless, and really these issues need to be expanded to include the paperwork aspects. The cases highlight that expert input on understanding tax and cross-border matters is necessary, especially when working and operating in new countries, where there are always additional costs and delays associated with tax, duties, and transfer pricing.

The tools that help to explore the barriers and to build actions to overcome them are:

- Business model canvas.
- Business process mapping.
- Case/actor matrix.
- Service blueprint.
- Understanding your business.

Details of the individual tools are given in Chap. 3.

Case 67 Learning to Deal with Political Risks from Brexit

For this large firm, most service work in Europe included shipping the spares and repairs to the customer's site. They had never seen a risk here and it was normal as the European Union (EU) provided a very stable trading system. The firm's large outcome-based service contracts were similar to one-off contracts, and the company used the EU as a single marketplace, allowing them to ship spares and repairs to and from countries as they saw fit. Then Brexit happened...

The firm has never had to deal with increasing regulation as disruptive. Its multiyear agreements were based on local deliveries, and it might now have to pay import duties and complete certificates of origin. This had cost implications of 3% plus paperwork to complete. They also realized that for

(continued)

2.6 Society and Environment

some of the field work, they needed to send specialists from outside of the UK to the UK – the working arrangements here were unclear and therefore the impacts on the contract delivery were also unclear.

This was a major change in assumptions for the long-term contracts and, depending on the remaining duration of those contracts, the impacts could be greater. The loss of clarity with the use of foreign field service and specialists was rather less clear; there was a risk of needing to use "illegal" staff on site. The team needed to sit with each of the customers with existing contracts and to change the contracts to take account of the uncertainty.

The firm added to all new and existing contracts a clause that would cover future changes in the membership of the EU, placing the risk on the shoulders of the country withdrawing, making the contract clause independent of customer or supplier.

Contracts with a few years of term were left and the firm accepted the loss of margin on the spares. For contracts with longer remaining durations, there were tough negotiations with the customers, starting with the position that they would have to pay the additional costs, although the firm generally fell back to a 50/50 cost share position with the customer taking responsibility for export/import clearance.

Labor was much more complex and, in all cases, required the customer to support the acquisition of the correct permits. Some customers tried to push back and make the firm take responsibility, but without its engineering staff, the work the customer needed could not take place. Not generally a satisfactory outcome for either party but one where both parties needed each other to ensure the work could be performed successfully.

Case 68 Building Transfer Pricing that Is Competitive and Compliant

The service department had a set of transfer pricing rules in place that were given to them by the larger product division. The rules had been agreed by the firm's tax experts and were set up to pay the correct levels of tax in each country. The product business was based on large production sites that were generally independent of each other on an operational basis. The service centers often cooperated and bought spares together from the different manufacturing sites. As prices came under pressure, the duplication of margins meant that the service centers were becoming uncompetitive.

The transfer pricing was based on an arm's-length relationship between the contracting locations. This meant that as margins became tighter, the main contracting site started to look for other solutions, as internal cooperation meant that the costs built up would be higher than the market price. Finance

(continued)

were unwilling to change their proven rule book just for a "small number of service sales."

The service department wanted to encourage the service centers to collaborate with each other and with the manufacturing sites. To do this, they needed a simple approach to transfer pricing that was both acceptable to finance and the tax authorities. Doing this, they put in place a service center cooperation agreement that defined the anticipated gross margins from each service center based on the historic margins and set these as the guide for cost-plus pricing. They also agreed to share any excess margins based on the cost-plus proportions.

The changeover helped the service centers by stopping the margin-on-margin pricing that had been developed in the past. The objective of achieving a price that was market-based was delivered, and it was compliant with the tax rules. Formerly, the sharing of excess margins was complex and often needed additional adjustment; where input from others was less than 20% the sharing was not implemented. This was considered too complex, and excess margin sharing was used for all intracompany cooperative service work.

2.7 Economic and Finance

Cost calculations and pricing provide barriers for every firm in services – they can be much harder than for equipment businesses. In many cases, there will not be a bill of materials; in some, there may be costs that are unknown. Therefore, pricing in services is not a simple calculation of summing up the costs and adding a margin. This can worry controllers from manufacturing business who like to have full cost disclosure.

Another important different is that in service, blue-collar employees are one of the key drivers of revenue – the more skilled manual workers you have in the business, the more resources you have to sell. On the contrary, in manufacturing, there are always reasons to reduce blue-collar employees. Therefore, trying to convince management, in particular the manufacturing part of the business, of the value of services is essential.

> ...we need to work more to be efficient and that is the plan over the coming years: growth in sales with no growth in white collar full time equivalent...

Manufacturing and management need to appreciate that service creates customer retention, increases margins, and generates additional sales, although it may reduce the gross margin percentage. If, for example, your company's aftermarket business was previously 100% spares, with additional services the gross margin percentage

2.7 Economic and Finance

Fig. 2.54 The relative importance of the barriers around "economic and finance" (illustration by Annick Holland, adapted from West et al., 2018)

may reduce, but experience has shown that other indicators improve (in particular, cash generation).

> ...analyses carried out by the commercial department demonstrated that service increases customer retention and margins...

Convincing management means using examples from other similar businesses that show how cash generation from services will help to support the manufacturing business.

> ...giving the top management the growth story of service business was the best argument to convince them to get on-board...

It is important to collect metrics that will confirm the customer retention and increase in revenue per customer. Improvements in cost estimation and customization of enterprise resource planning systems to better support service businesses only come with time and experience. The relative importance, based on the findings of the survey, of the barriers around "economic and finance" is shown in Fig. 2.54.

Sharing benefits and obligations from a win-win perspective is a good example of a shared strategy tool. Indeed, the economic-financial perspective of the service is not only another important element for servitization success but also a potential barrier.

Our study reveals that the main problem derives from the difficulty of reviewing and rethinking the logic of calculating margins and, consequently, pricing policies, moving from a cost-plus vision to a perspective based upon the concept of customer value. The latter depends on different factors, as suggested by the respondents, such as time saving, better exploitation of assets, increased productivity, and the general competitive advantage. Importantly, the organization often underestimates certain activities that apparently do not generate value (because they give reduced or no margins), forgetting that in fact they are crucial to the creation of margins generated

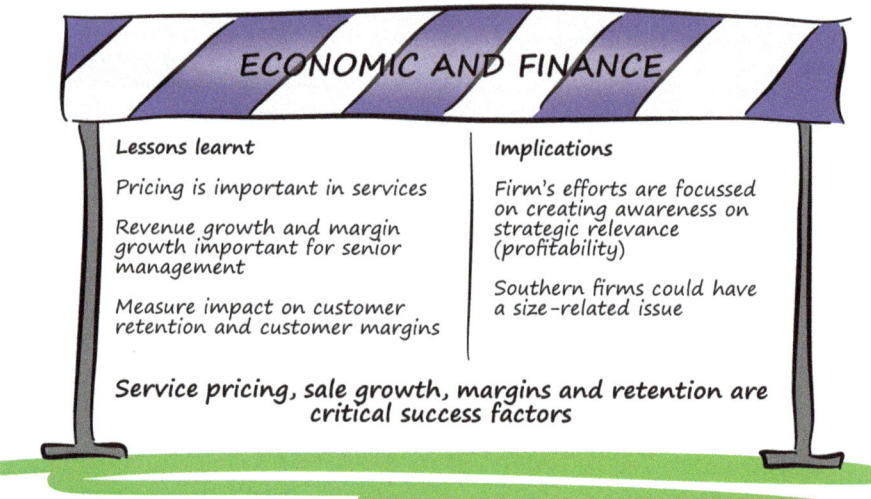

Fig. 2.55 The lessons and implications for the economic and financial barriers (illustration by Annick Holland, adapted from West et al., 2018)

by other activities and/or services. Figure 2.55 describes some of the lessons learned and the implications from the interviews.

Although in our interviews pricing was considered important and difficult, a few answers suggest that the culture of pricing models/tools is still at a preliminary stage. Moreover, in-line with the literature we looked at, the firms confirmed that service scalability emerges as essential to sustaining the required investments in technology, infrastructures, capital assets, and knowledge base, as well as people and training. Specifically, monitoring service value growth through different indicators, considering orders, sales, profits, revenues, customer retention, and loyalty, can help managers to get a much better understanding of the real value of a service and verify its long-term sustainability. Some metrics were considered different to manufacturing operations, where operational excellence dominates decision-making (Fig. 2.56). The implications for this barrier are that:

- Pricing is important in services.
- Revenue growth and margin growth are important for senior management.
- Measurement of impact on customer retention and customer margins is needed.
- The firm's efforts are focused on creating awareness of strategic relevance (profitability).
- It is necessary to introduce finance and control functions right from the pre-sale phase.
- It is advisable to adopt business plans and economic and financial analyses to evaluate the internal cost and estimate the value added by the services.
- Use cost and pricing schemes based on standard modular components.

2.7 Economic and Finance

Fig. 2.56 Service improves the business performance – be clear with the message (illustration by Annick Holland, authors' work)

To help you better understand how to navigate the barriers, we will provide insights from cases to help you understand how others overcame the barriers (in order of importance were):

1. How do we move away from cost-plus/hours-based?
2. How should we consider margins? How to price effectively?
3. Spares have high margins and more service will reduce the margins; how do we manage this?
4. How can we develop our service business when we have no cash to invest?
5. How can we manage dealer discounts better?

2.7.1 How Do We Move away from Cost-Plus/Hours-Based?

We often hear that service is based on labor hours and therefore is a cost-plus business – the margin is then made on the spares. This approach comes from the manufacturing approach of taking all the costs into account and then adding a simple margin to create the price. Once the business has moved away from free to charging a fee, often the next challenge is to move away from cost-plus and labor hours to a more value-based pricing approach (Fig. 2.57). Cost plus (and *open book*) does not necessary provide the best price for the customer, and it does not provide the best earning approach for the service supplier either. A price built simply from hours worked encourages the supplier to keep working for longer than is absolutely necessary, so the desired outcomes are not aligned. There is therefore a need to change perspective and review pricing logic.

Fig. 2.57 Try new revenue models that are based on customer value rather than your costs (illustration by Annick Holland, authors' work)

The two questions that need to be considered are the following: What other revenue models exist? How can they help to align the supplier and the customer so that when the customer gains value, the supplier gains too?

> ...How to educate customers to a new pricing system (value added) when they are used to an old one (cost plus)...

> ...In spite of all the attempts made by accounting/finance and controlling to abolish it, we have continued to maintain flat rates...

The simplest option is to move from "time and materials" to "fixed price." This way, any cost overruns are borne by the supplier, with out-of-scope work being charged back to the customer. Other, more complex arrangements can be developed where target price is used, and for extra works, the time-and-materials approach can be effective. For example, with the target price method, some of the risk is shared between both parties, normally to set limits. Here, the pricing remains mostly focused on input rather than the key outputs that are important for the customer.

Moving to more outcome-based payment structures, many firms take additional risk-and-reward-based approaches, with outcomes based on metrics that are important to the customer, often aspects such as availability, reliability, efficiency, and safety. The base fees can be further modified so that they are built upon customer inputs, per hour of operation, or customer outputs, per barrel of oil pumped. At each different level, there is a risk transfer between the supplier and the customer, and where you end up is based on the market and the risk appetite of the supplier.

The lessons from the two cases are that it is necessary to start to charge and move to value-based pricing that is closer to the customer's willingness to pay than just based on costs. The cases show that fixed prices move risks to the supplier and can provide better value for both parties; nevertheless, the use of "cost plus" will always remain in the system, where the value being added is low (e.g., for travel costs, although here a per-day charge can be simpler to manage). Moreover, pricing should always be in-line with the customer's outcomes, and when building a revenue model, it is good to consider some form of pain/gain sharing; finance can help create new revenue models.

2.7 Economic and Finance

The tools that help to explore the barriers and to build actions to overcome them are:

- Business model canvas.
- Business process mapping.
- Cradle-to-grave lifecycle map.
- Cradle-to-grave lifecycle visual mapping.
- Customer jobs-to-be-done.
- Empathy maps.
- Job-to-be-done insights.
- Job-to-be-done outcomes.
- Metric cascades.
- Service blueprint.
- Visual journey map – high level.
- Visual journey map – detail level.

Details of the individual tools are given in Chap. 3.

Case 69 Teaching Buyers that "Cost Plus" Does Not Deliver Value

The firm wanted to move from a "time and materials" approach to service to use more "fixed price for fixed scope" methods. They knew that this would put more pressure on them to estimate the cost for the scope accurately, but it would give much more price certainty to customers. The team had been told by the budget holders in customer companies that they were fed up with not being able to budget for the cost of work, as there were many different costs added to the basic rates. The firm explained this was because by law overtime had to be paid at different rates and the travel and living costs were different for each job. The budget holders replied that Club Med had the same issues but charged for their holidays on an all-inclusive basis – so why could not this firm?

The move to fixed pricing required the firm's service team to assess a number of projects they had worked on. What was the invoice value? What were the hours? And what was the scope? They tried to work out what was going on and to strip down the work that had been done. They broke the jobs up into the core work, the extra works, and the mobilization costs. Extra work was the largest challenge, as some was generated by the customer in terms of waiting time, and some was associated with additional scope. Having done the exercise, the firm appreciated the problem customers were facing in estimating the total costs to them. The firm had always been very transparent, but they realized that that transparency was actually making their life more complex.

The first few times the team tried the fixed price approach, there were problems with a customer's budget holder's procurement office. They wanted to know the specific rate for the work and how many people were providing

(continued)

the service. They were only interested in the hourly rate and failed to read the scope the firm was providing. If the customer was given an indication of the number of people working on the job, they then divided the price by the hours and told the firm it was too expensive. They always tried to break down the cost to an hourly rate. The firm released that these customers only bought on the lowest day rate rather than focusing on the scope. This is how their procurement team was showing value to the business – the problem was that the budget holder was then feeling the pain of the decision to try a new way of billing.

The firm took a gamble with one important client and offered them both options – one fixed price and one based on rates. The team said they would accept either and would compare the outcomes of both options. The customer's procurement department liked it as they thought they could not lose and decided to stick with the traditional pricing model.

Once the work was complete, the firm wrote the invoice for the rate-based approach and compared it to the fixed price offer. The rate-based invoice was higher, even after they stripped out the extra work that was in addition to the original scope. They moved forward with the customer to develop a hybrid solution: a fixed price for mobilization and the core scope plus a "blended" hourly rate for day working and for night shifts and a cost per day fee to cover hotels and meals.

Case 70 Working with Finance to Build New Revenue Models

The finance departments were always a pain, telling the service team what to charge for their services. They had a 10% ROS target, so the team simply took the costs and added 30% to them to get to the price. It is an easy calculation but it seemed to encourage inflating the hours in a project to show bigger contributions. The team was looking for new approaches to pricing, and this cost-plus revenue model did not seem to reflect the value that they were creating for customers. All it did was make sure that the firm recovered its costs and made a modest margin. The service team realized that it did not match with the customers' operational models and thought that this might in the longer run mean the firm would lose their competitive position.

The real problem stemmed from the fact that the firm had no idea on market norms for particular tasks, and because of this, they fell back on basic cost-plus pricing. Without understanding the market benchmarks, it's hard to understand if the price is appropriate for the job or not. There were also other customers asking for a change to the firm's revenue model, to better match their cash flows. Following an order from a distressed customer, the service

(continued)

team management met with finance to see what could be done. There were two objectives: to understand the market rate for the job and to change the service revenue model.

The customer needed the repair work to be done and they were almost bankrupt due to weak cash flow. Normally, the firm would invoice at the end of a project and ask for (but not usually get) a 25% advanced payment for the planned work. Instead, the firm offered a 5-month turnaround on the work, payable monthly in advance. Extra work needed to be identified by the service team within the first month; otherwise, the monthly payments would be fixed.

The new model worked; the customer wanted to pay monthly as this matched their cash flows, because they had issues with large cash payments. It also helped the service team, as it would be cash positive over the duration of the work, which meant that the team did not have to make risk provisions for the customer failing to pay for the work. The service team simply warned the customer that, if they missed a payment, the customer's equipment would be taken out of the workshop and placed outside in the parking lot and that remedial work would be needed to repair the weather damage, unless they paid a storage fee, in which case it would be stored undercover.

Since then, the service team has been working more with finance to design new revenue models for larger projects. They can be really helpful.

2.7.2 How Should We Consider Margins? How Do We Price Effectively?

Equipment businesses most often base their prices on the "market" price for the equipment, and in a highly competitive commodity environment, this is likely to be the most appropriate model. However, a service business has a wider range of options available to it when it comes to "how to price" than an equipment business, and you need to use a range of tools to help you price "correctly" (Fig. 2.58).

A service business can offer new ways of pricing, based on models where more money is made when the customer's performance is improved or where more money is made by helping the customer perform when they need to.

> ...With cluster analysis we can understand how to redefine the margins of spare parts to meet the needs of the market, with test systems we can test the hypotheses made and adopt the best possible solution...

This approach comes from the concept of "value-in-use" and helps to prevent the service firm from overcharging on price, which could have a detrimental effect on the relationship. Conversely, it helps to avoid underestimating those market segments for which too low prices risk depleting the value of the service.

Fig. 2.58 Pricing is no science – but analytical tools can help you find the correct price (illustration by Annick Holland, authors' work)

> ...We developed a multi-perspective pricing model to address the grey market for OEM spares with the lower prices associated (cut in margin)...

The lessons learned from the two cases are that margins are necessary to consider when setting the price and that pricing should not be based on the costs plus the target margin. The market generally sets the price itself, but some buyers will use inappropriate benchmarks to lead customers to poor decisions. Understanding the appropriate benchmarks to use, and the benchmarks that your customers use, is essential in service when building a price. Therefore, with pricing, it is necessary to find ways to share and communicate the outcomes you are creating for your customers (gain/pain share).

The tools that help to explore the barriers and to build actions to overcome them are:

- Avatar map.
- Business model canvas.
- Cradle-to-grave lifecycle map.
- Cradle-to-grave lifecycle visual mapping.
- Customer jobs-to-be-done.
- Customer value proposition.
- Metric cascades.
- Service blueprint.

Details of the individual tools are given in Chap. 3.

> **Case 71 Deal with Premium and Budget Pricing Models**
> A growing gray spares market was starting to impact on this firm's OEM aftermarket spares business and was starting to damage its margins. It's
>
> (continued)

2.7 Economic and Finance

understandable for people to buy non-authorized spares, but there are obvious risks involved, such as the potential for substandard spares to damage the equipment they are trying to repair.

Until then, the spares strategy was based on the installed base and the operational hours of a machine per year. The firm identified the long-term average spend customers should have with their service department and used this to help with sales targets as well as to gauge which customers were faithful and identify those who were not. Even if the company had two clear segments, they treated them identically, all as loyal customers. On the contrary, many customers were shopping around to get spares, initially for consumables, and then would move to more expensive parts in a more do-it-yourself approach to machine maintenance.

But what was driving these customers to shop around? Often, it was to do with lead times on spares, and other times, they said the reason was high pricing. It costs the firm money to hold stock and some commodity spares they held were very expensive; for example, a customer could buy an M6 bolt online for 20% of their price direct.

The firm's response was to create an authorized gray market. This felt quite revolutionary, and it needed the firm to integrate their supply chain directly with their suppliers and customers. They did this by creating an online marketplace that provided direct access to authorized suppliers. This was linked with the customers' equipment, to make it easy for them to buy the right parts. And to ensure customers could get the part they needed when they needed them, the marketplace confirmed stock levels and delivery times. The firm charged the suppliers to be on the marketplace and skimmed off a percentage from every sale, but the payoff for the sellers on the marketplace was that the OEM firm covered the warranty on the parts as if they had been supplied directly by them. It was all quite revolutionary.

Most customers who were buying from the gray market switched, while some, but not all, suppliers were willing to join the marketplace. In effect, overnight the firm killed the gray market and at the same time made spares pricing more competitive while also making more money per sale. The online marketplace turned out to be cheaper than the existing warehouse but was more expensive to set up and maintain than expected.

Case 72 Introducing Proactive Spares Pricing
Spares pricing was managed by the supply chain; they just took the cost and multiplied it by three to get to the price. Spares were not made by the OEM and the objective was to be consistent with pricing, because every time the

(continued)

customer was charged a new price, which was often related to the volume bought. The firm knew it needed to do something, because it lacked consistency to the customer, but the system "kind of" worked.

By pricing spares on supply chain costs, the firm had lost an opportunity to optimize and control the price it sold them for. Customers were coming to the firm, as the OEM, but it was behaving worse than a distributor. There were two causes for this – selling spares was profitable but it was not the core business, and they did not have a spares price book or catalog.

One of the supply chain team worked on building a solution and, in doing so, confirmed that there is an aftermarket niche to supply spares. An online catalog was developed with an underlying logic: access to the catalog was given to all owners of the equipment the OEM firm sold, but customers lost access if they did not buy from the firm within a 12-month period and sales were told to make direct contact with them. Each customer was assigned an individualized discount on the list prices, as the firm knew they'd all share the prices but not their level of discount. Sales and supply chain agreed together on the level of discounts or rebates based on five criteria.

The "Amazon" effect worked and made buying spares easier for customers. The OEM had a more structured, long-term approach to pricing spares, and this helped them to deliver consistency. The online tool helped the firm to proactively adjust prices where competition entered the market, although they tried to only adjust prices twice a year. Using the catalog, the firm started to push updates on machines that had limited long-term support. They linked spares sales with "what others bought" and flagged abnormal spares consumption to ensure that a field service technician would follow up. A big step forward was achieved.

2.7.3 Spares Have High Margins, More Service Will Reduce the Margins, How Do We Manage This?

When margins are associated with new spare parts from an OEM firm, any service is likely to reduce the return on sales (ROS) as a percentage of total sales (Fig. 2.59). This is a simple mathematical calculation and can cause problems with the whole business as well as with finance.

Providing services in addition to spares along with the product lifecycle improves the customer experience and therefore satisfaction, which leads to increased customer retention.

> ...We bundle spares and services into a prime equipment sale over a period of years beyond the warranty period...

Fig. 2.59 Spare parts have been seen as the "gold mine" for service – but if we do more services, parts last longer and margins reduce (illustration by Annick Holland, authors' work)

The result is that the service business increases, because more spares are sold to end-users while, equally importantly, there are many more touchpoints with customers. These are not just contact with spares sales but also deep service touchpoints that lead to improved retention and customer understanding.

> ...Providing field services and spares reduces the aftermarket margins but increases our spares sales capture rate...

What is important to measure is the increase in spares sales, but they must not be lost with other service sales. Reporting the breakdown of sales separately allows a like-for-like comparison of business performance.

The lessons from the two cases are that quality-of-service margins are essential. Moving to more services will most likely reduce the contribution margin percent while increasing the absolute contribution margin. Mathematically, you will reduce the margin as a percentage, but the cash generation will increase. When considering the contribution from service to the firm, it is important to consider margins, sales volumes, and cash generation as well as the customer retention through superior experience. Also, the cases suggest that bundling of spares and service with new equipment leads to reduced margins and lower prices and that unbundling them from the new equipment sale generally increases the margins and the sales volumes. So, field service is a channel for spares; however, this needs to be carefully managed, as field service must remain in the customer's trust.

The tools that help to explore the barriers and to build actions to overcome them are:

- Avatar map.
- Business model canvas.
- Cradle-to-grave lifecycle map.
- Cradle-to-grave lifecycle visual mapping.
- Customer jobs-to-be-done.
- Customer value proposition.

- Metric cascades.
- Service blueprint.

Details of the individual tools are given in Chap. 3.

Case 73 Spares Sales with New Equipment Belong with the Service Business

The firm considered spares to be a "sweetener" for the deal, and they were heavily discounted. The OEM then had the challenge of making money from service and recovering the spares pricing levels. This meant that the firm was losing margin in service and was fighting to return prices to realistic levels.

The cause of the problem was the margin expectations: equipment sales margins were low (0–5%), whereas service margins were higher (20–40%). The equipment sales team considered that the service sales team were "overpricing" on the spares.

Responsibility for spares sales transferred from product sales to the service business. The objective here was to establish the service sales contacts much earlier and manage the spares pricing. It was a specific change on one level but one with a significant impact on the firm's culture.

Product sales said that it would not work, because spares were needed to sweeten the deal. Service sales said that customers, in general, understood that they needed to pay for service if they wanted a professional level of service. The customer's sales message was that spares would be delivered as part of the service contract; this had the added benefit for the customer as the service contract provided additional warranty cover for the spare parts.

Pricing discipline within the firm was improved, and contribution margins increased.

Case 74 Focusing on Service Cash Generation Not Just Return on Sales

Moving into field service from just providing basic services to ensure that the firm sold spares meant that margins (ROS) would become eroded. This was not something that management wanted, as they expected the aftermarket business to grow at the existing margin levels. Field service had a lower margin expectation than spares, and through basic mathematics, this led to an erosion of ROS even with a growth in cash generation for the business.

The management did not want to understand the basic arithmetic. That was the challenge that had to be overcome. At the same time, they wanted to grow the service business.

Finance was key to helping to change the focus from unreasonable margin expectations to a more balanced approach to cash generation and margin

(continued)

levels. Segmentation of the services combined with benchmarking allowed the firm to set expected and minimum margins for each of the aftermarket activities and from this could then set the targets for the service business. The team also focused on cash generation in the aftermarket as the product business was a sink for cash. They measured this in the number of days to convert a project to cash, in much the same way they considered "debtor days."

The new model allowed management to set the total margin expectations based on a simple budgeting model. Finance supported this, as they understood the model and the value of cash in the business. Within these guidelines, the team grew the service business while maintaining control on price levels and cash generation. It was a steep learning curve for everyone, but it was beneficial.

2.7.4 How Can We Develop Our Service Business When We Have No Cash to Invest?

This is really an odd barrier given that the margins in service are generally higher than for new equipment sales. There are a limited number of options for developing a business without internal investment.

> ...The managers are brave and try new things. However, the financial constraints quickly bite...

The initial phase of service development will suck up cash, and this could be worse where there is a low density of installed base in a particular region. This makes it even more complicated to find sources of investment, because it is difficult to know how much you can get from the new investment.

> ...How can we invest in services if a return cannot be calculated in advance?...

The options are to outsource the frontline service delivery: to agents, to the customers, to competitor, or to other third parties. For example, CAT delivers services via its equipment dealerships, so outsourcing can work very well. Here, the services need to be delivered, but it can be more than the delivery mechanism that needs to be designed, because the correct control and payment schemes need to be developed so that everyone can win. This can mean that customer paid for innovation can be a tool to help develop the service business (Fig. 2.60).

Without investment, it is hard to build a new business. Startups burn cash and opening a new service business (or service center) will require investments, but there are approaches that can overcome the initial disadvantage. Agents can be trained (and billed) to provide the first line of service support locally. This can lead to an increase in aftermarket sales, improve relationships with the customers, and reduce

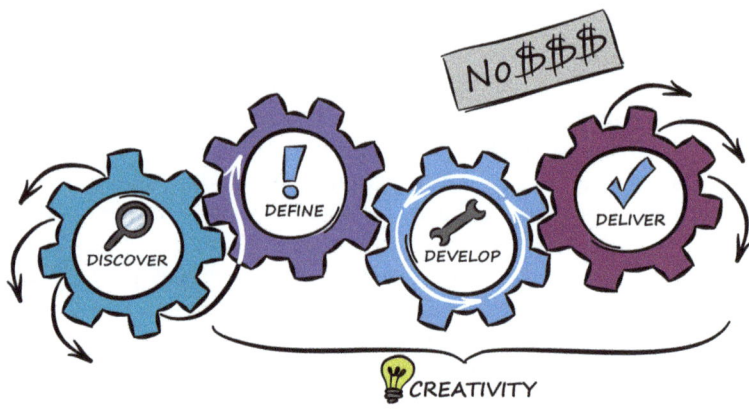

Fig. 2.60 Learn to make innovation in services with the customer to directly support new service development (illustration by Annick Holland, authors' work)

costs because less time is spent supporting simple issues. Customers can be certified (and billed) to deliver more than just routine maintenance, which reduces the service sales volume but leads to increased spares sales and better relationships. Even competitors can be given the service work to deliver, which can also work, but it obviously needs a number of legal aspects to be considered first.

The key lesson from the cases is that it is possible to develop a service business with limited cash for investment. Not having money for investment makes life more challenging and means that a service manager must be more entrepreneurial. Creativity can bring new capabilities and resources to the individual service centers. It means that the different local partners may need to be engaged on a project basis. When collaborating with others, it is crucial to weigh up the value for the customer or your partners and estimate the value you receive, as equality can be important.

The tools that help to explore the barriers and to build actions to overcome them are:

- Avatar map.
- Business model canvas.
- Business process mapping.
- Case/actor matrix.
- Cradle-to-grave lifecycle map.
- Cradle-to-grave lifecycle visual mapping.
- Customer jobs-to-be-done.
- Customer value proposition.
- Ecosystem mapping.
- Job-to-be-done insights.
- Job-to-be-done outcomes.
- Metric cascades.
- Understanding your business.

Details of the individual tools are given in Chap. 3.

Case 75 Investing in Service Without a Clear ROI
The firm wanted to provide more services but there were many gaps in the business plan. This meant that they could not confirm the return on investment (ROI) from the investment that was needed for the project. This was strange, as NPD did not seem to have this problem. How can you be sure what return you will make on an investment? There were customers asking for services, yet management still seemed to be unwilling to invest.

The problem was that the team was not being creative enough with the business plan. They were building up the business plan as if it was for a new facility rather than an extension to an existing business and an investment that could be redeployed in another facility – they really had limited fixed assets. Service also had more flexibility than production, since a service center could be set up within an existing building to run a test of the local market. This would all help to better define the potential ROI.

The service team took over one of the existing production facilities as a "pop-up" service center. Very little investment was required, and the production facility in question was going to be closed in any case. The workers knew that they had an extra period of employment to keep their jobs, which increased the flexibility from the labor force and helped the team cooperate with the workers' council. On this backdrop, they opened a new service center with a local customer base to prove the concept.

The company ended up hiring more staff. The model worked and finance started to understand the business model and the expected ROI that service could deliver to the business. The firm also learned how to set up and run a brownfield service shop at a site it was going to close, so there was nothing to lose. This helped to justify the trial business, reduced the investment costs, and in effect made the ROI an obvious choice.

Case 76 Getting the Customer to Pay for Innovation
How can you do innovation if you do not have an R&D budget? The service team was constantly developing new repairs and finding ways to manufacture new spares to complete their services in economical ways. This meant that the team was in the lead with additive machining as they were supporting small batch sizes rather than large batches. Yet, they were told it was not innovation.

The repair project's development work was being put through as expenses rather than following the product division's "stage-gate" approach. It was straightforward in many respects, as the team had the capabilities to develop

(continued)

the processes. They had just never actually done it. Often, they were only adjusting the work instructions for repairs, but they charged the customer for all of the development work, and the firm kept the intellectual property rights. It's just that the reporting system did not view this as innovation.

The firm moved its internal definition of R&D (generally based around product development) to one based on innovation. There was much discussion about what should be considered "new" and therefore innovative. So, the firm also started to log what was new, and this enabled others within the firm to share in the innovation and copy what they had done, reducing risk and costs while at the same time allowing them to widen their offering.

The team kept to the rule of expensing development costs on single projects unless a customer would require more repairs. This was financially prudent and was based on the assumption that the work would not be duplicated. They kept a "book" of repairs that was open to sales and production within the business, and this was helpful as it gave the price paid and some of the technical information. Sales used it to help sell and set prices, and operations used it to repair the details. This meant the service team did not invent the same repair independently in several locations.

The firm ended up with lower costs, lower risks, increased sales, and more margin.

2.7.5 How Can We Manage Dealer Discounts Better?

Where the aftermarket is dominated by the supply of parts, dealership discounts are often used and applied to price lists often on a regional basis (Fig. 2.61). The level of discount is commonly based on market norms and can be characterized by very considerable differences.

> ...Extremely difficult when using international distributors and when large pricing differences exist in different regions...

Here, the manufacturer and the dealer have very different goals: the equipment business wants to sell as much into the deal as possible to make the required sales revenue, while the aftermarket business needs to have parts available for the end-user with a known availability and lead time. Unless there is a good tracking system, parts can get lost within the dealer networks due to a lack of visibility in the system for the end-user. Moreover, dealers tend to order more than required to get better discounts on the price per part. This increases inventory costs and reduces turnover, and it increases the risk of obsolescence of parts in the warehouse, again running the risk of poor customer satisfaction.

Often price lists become escalated and unrealistic and therefore larger and larger discounts are applied. This can then become the new norm. On the contrary, price lists should be carefully managed and reflect the difficulty in manufacturing the

Fig. 2.61 Ensure that pricing is coordinated and that there is a sound logic applied to discounts (illustration by Annick Holland, authors' work)

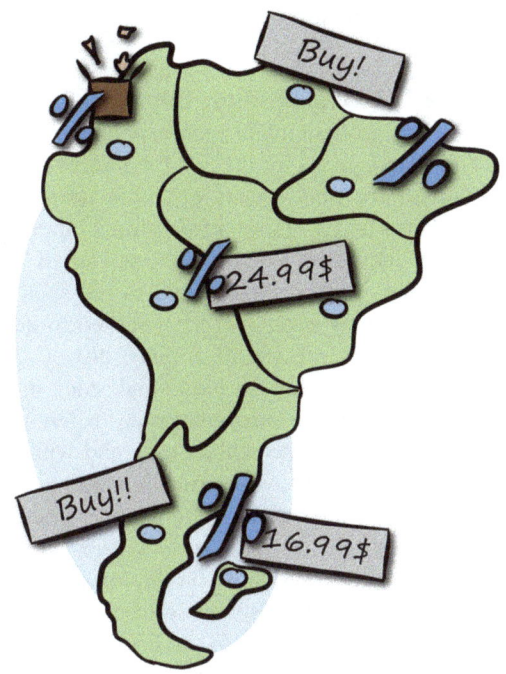

parts: other aspects can then become the dimensions that dictate the final price to the customer – more intangible dimensions such as delivery time, lead times, stock availability, ordering simplicity, and stock levels. Further, with the advent of advanced additive machining (3D printing), dealers may be able to reduce inventories further and print-to-order, which might offer the service firm different business models and more opportunities.

The lesson from the two cases is that managing discounts is a pain and that it is important to be consistent and to have a clear overview of discounts. List prices can be helpful but need to be realistic and reflect market norms; expect dealers to know your list prices and standard discount rates.

> ...Consistency is important here and it is always important to understand the bigger picture...

Using list prices as a reference point and applying discounts prudently can put the service manager in a commanding position.

The tools that help to explore the barriers and to build actions to overcome them are:

- Business model canvas.
- Business process mapping.
- Customer value proposition.
- Metric cascades.
- Service blueprint.

Details of the individual tools are given in Chap. 3.

Case 77 Global Business but Local Process
The firm thought it had been very clever with pricing as it had different service and spares prices for different markets and different customers. This approach worked for many years but with more acquisitions taking place in these markets, and a more professional approach to procurement, the pricing model they have been using has started to get the firm into trouble. Some customers have been shocked to see such a variation on pricing among the countries they serve and have started to demand that the firm meets the best commercial terms for all of their sites.

Pricing was left to individual sales managers with no oversight on the divergence of the prices between different customers and different markets. This was where the problem lay and what had led to an inconsistency of the pricing model. Moving prices up was considered a "no-no" by many of the commercial team and setting a single price for all was also not responsible.

The service team moved to a price list, similar to the product division. The list prices were set based on the top end of the archived prices, and separated labor costs from the spares' prices, to reflect each market's local norms. They then created a discount to the list price and set up customer KPIs to help drive it. This left the final pricing up to the local team and gave them guidance. Service management also provided market and customer discounts as reports to the commercial teams to help them with pricing.

It took time to start to adjust the prices. Part of it was helped by a move from rates to fixed prices for individual jobs. This allowed the team to take more risk by including all of the scope in some services; it also allowed them to charge more easily for out-of-scope items, something that had been a problem in the past. This approach was preferred by both the technical engineers and their buyers.

The application of special discounts helped the team to confirm the value that it was providing and in some cases the value that their procurement was able to create. It really helped achieve better margins in services with a higher degree of consistency.

Case 78 Dancing with Ambiguity by Having Transparency
By having price lists that listed every cost, the firm thought it would be able to provide a fully transparent or "open book" level of transparency that customers would like and appreciate. They'd only have to say what they wanted and there was a fee against it. Somehow, they were often surprised at the final invoice and said on many occasions that they were unable to budget based on the list of

(continued)

fees provided. They explained that it was simpler to understand the pricing model in a London taxi than use the list provided.

They were right. The system of prices, fees, and rates made it really complex to estimate the final invoice value. There were all sorts of added costs (particularly on labor) that made it really complex to estimate the final price. The team looked at Uber and the airlines for some help here and started to provide a target price for a particular job to allow the customer to budget. Above or below this price, based on a simplified set of rates, the firm and the customer would share the gains or the pains. For non-scope items, they would move back to a greatly simplified rates sheet.

Combination of target price with measures based on scope and rates was a big step forward. It was new in the industry. The simplification of the rates was tough to achieve, as finance wanted to cover all of the costs in the price and push these on to customers, which was very naïve of them and needed to be controlled carefully as the approach to pricing was set up. Finance only wanted to see full absorption of the costs, whereas the team looked to get a better price when they delivered more value to customers.

The customers liked it; the target price provided a budget that they could understand. The service team would have some initial argument with the fulfillment of the scope based on the now-simplified rates, but to help here, they put in a daily review process to help both parties gauge where they were against the scope.

The finance department were slow to be converted, saying all the time that the service team needed to increase the overhead rates as they were not covering all of the costs, but they found that with the target pricing and the clear rates, sales started to rise. This meant that the under-absorption of labor stopped, and the service team actually made it into profit.

References

Anderson, J. C., Narus, J. A., & Narayandas, D. (2008). *Business market management: Understanding, creating, and delivering value* (3rd ed.). Pearson Prentice Hall.

Baines, T., & Lightfood, H. (2013). *Made to serve: How manufacturers can compete through servitization and product service systems*. London: Wiley.

Kowalkowski, C. (2016). Service innovation in industrial contexts. In M. Toivonen (Ed.), *Service innovation, translational systems sciences* (Vol. 6). Cham: Springer. https://doi.org/10.1007/978-4-431-54922-2_11.

Valtakoski, A. (2017). Explaining servitization failure and deservitization: A knowledge-based perspective. *Industrial Marketing Management, 60*, 138–150. https://doi.org/10.1016/j.indmarman.2016.04.009

West, S., Gaiardelli, P., Bigdeli, A., & Baines, T. (2018). Exploring operational challenges for servitization: An European Survey. In A. Bigdeli, T. Frandsen, J. Raja, & T. Baines (Eds.),

Proceedings of 2018 Spring Servitization Conference "Driving Competitiveness through Servitization" (pp. 9–17).

West, S., Stoll, O., & Mueller-Csernetzky, P. (2020). 'Avatar journey mapping' for manufacturing firms to reveal smart-service opportunities over the product life-cycle. *International Journal of Business Environment.* https://doi.org/10.1504/IJBE.2020.110906.

Open Access This chapter is licensed under the terms of the Creative Commons Attribution 4.0 International License (http://creativecommons.org/licenses/by/4.0/), which permits use, sharing, adaptation, distribution and reproduction in any medium or format, as long as you give appropriate credit to the original author(s) and the source, provide a link to the Creative Commons license and indicate if changes were made.

The images or other third party material in this chapter are included in the chapter's Creative Commons license, unless indicated otherwise in a credit line to the material. If material is not included in the chapter's Creative Commons license and your intended use is not permitted by statutory regulation or exceeds the permitted use, you will need to obtain permission directly from the copyright holder.

Methods and Tools for Overcoming the Barriers to Servitization and Service Excellence

3.1 How to Build Your Service Excellence Roadmap

This section is intended to help you define where you need to get to and how you are going to get there. For every firm the starting point is different, and the end point will be different, so the route has to be different: this is because context matters (Dmitrijeva et al., 2020).

The development of services in an industrial context is always an evolution: we all have different starting points and different destinations. Your roadmap has to fit within your firm's vision and its longer-term strategy but also remain actionable. And that is not an easy balance to achieve.

What is important is that you first sketch out your service excellence roadmap, so you know what you are planning, when, and why. Find your preferred partners to work together with – this can be inside your own firm, as well as suppliers and customers.

To do this effectively, we think it is best to agree a service vision, and once you have this, you can then brainstorm the issues that are preventing you from delivering services (use Post-its). These can then be segmented by the different categories and individual barriers. From there, you can start to prioritize them in a two-by-two grid. Then, and only then, you can start to build up a roadmap based on your priorities and the challenges you face. Start with the easy/high-impact improvements, and then move down the list; be careful as some may be dependent on others. Review every 9–12 months and adjust, because the more you change, the more you will learn, and you will then want to fine-tune your approach.

If you pass on the tasks to others, hold a short regular call with your team to ensure progress is being made. If not, listen to understand where the barriers are and how you could help them overcome what is causing the problem.

With your roadmap, make sure you find people outside of your business and your firm who you can talk with and discuss your plans. It's a tough business change to make, and you will need the support of others to find ways to break though barriers (Fig. 3.1).

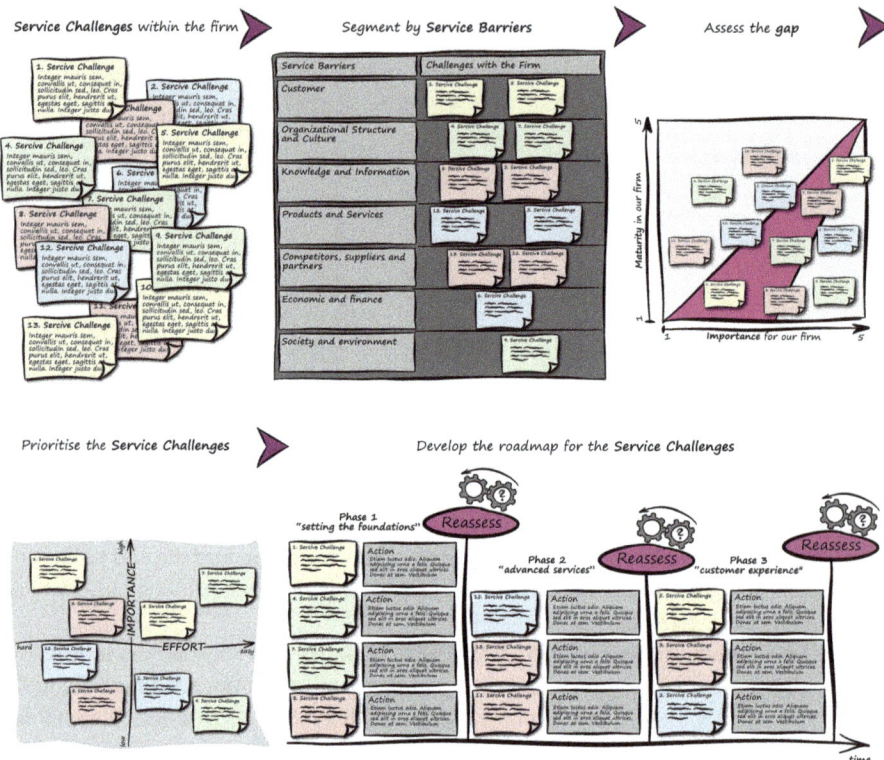

Fig. 3.1 A process to help build your service excellence roadmap (illustration by Annick Holland, authors' work)

3.2 Service Methods and Tools

This section contains a brief description of methods and tools that we have found are useful in creating or delivering services, both from our direct experience and from the feedback on our interviews with businesses. Specifically, Table 3.1 lists some general business tools as well as specific tools that are associated with the product-service system (PSS) implementation. The tools that we also found useful as general management tools are marked *.

Avatar Map
The avatar map is core to understanding the equipment or products that you sell to your customers. It is in effect the "persona for the machine." It's a tool that engineers find easy to complete as they can understand the inputs, possible data flows, wastes, and value.

Several avatars can be used to represent a flow within the customer's plant, allowing you to quickly figure out the relationships between the machines. The

3.2 Service Methods and Tools

Table 3.1 Cases and tools (compiled by authors)

	2.1 Customers						2.2 Organizational structure and culture						2.3 Knowledge and information					2.4 Products and activities				
	2.1.1 How do we get our sales to be effective in services?	2.1.2 How do we coordinate with our customers/end-users?	2.1.3 How can we reach the end user when the equipment it sold via…	2.1.4 How can we promote our solution to the end user when the…	2.1.5 Our customers ask us for new services, eXplicitly?	2.1.6 How can we manage our delivery when our customers want do…	2.2.1 Some managers do not think of service as a real business…	2.2.2 How do we get R&D to consider the whole equipment lifecycle?	2.2.3 How do we get top management involvement?	2.2.4 How do we get the firm to see service as a real BU with a P&L?	2.2.5 How can we reduce resistance to developing service business?	2.2.6 How can we educate HR/employees?	2.3.1 How do we better share know-how?	2.3.2 How can we better share service feedback with the equipment…	2.3.3 What new project management skills are needed for services?	2.3.4 How can we better learn about the equipment operation?	2.3.5 How can we mix know-how from installers and customers?	2.4.1 How do we understand the installed base?	2.4.2 How can we professionalize service delivery?	2.4.3 When can we start to design and deliver advanced services?	2.4.4 If customer ask for digital service, where do we start?	2.4.5 How can services support new equipment sales?
Avatar map						X	X	X			X	X	X	X		X	X	X	X	X	X	
Business model canvas					X		X		X	X			X			X		X		X		
Business Process mapping								X	X				X			X						
Case/actor matrix		X	X	X		X	X						X		X	X		X	X	X	X	X
Context map																						
Cradle-to-grave lifecycle map					X	X	X	X			X	X		X		X	X	X	X	X	X	X
Cradle-to-grave lifecycle visual mapping		X	X	X	X	X	X				X	X	X			X	X	X	X	X	X	X
Customer jobs-to-be-done	X	X	X	X	X		X									X	X	X	X	X	X	X
Customer value proposition	X	X	X	X	X			X	X							X	X		X	X	X	X
Decision matrix																						
Ecosystem mapping		X											X	X	X							X
Detailed empathy card	X		X	X	X							X	X	X	X							X
Empathy maps		X	X	X								X		X						X	X	
Feedback grid																						
Feedback sheet																						
Five whys																						
Job-to-be-done insights	X			X	X	X	X								X			X	X		X	X
Job-to-be-done outcomes	X			X		X	X									X		X	X		X	X
Keeping focused	X				X	X																
Metric cascades							X	X						X	X	X	X	X	X	X	X	X
Personas	X	X	X	X	X	X					X				X	X	X		X	X	X	X
Pitching planning																						
Problem breakdown with the five Ws																						
Service blueprint	X	X			X	X	X	X	X	X	X	X	X	X	X	X	X	X	X	X	X	X
Storyboarding																						
Understanding your business							X	X	X	X	X		X			X			X			
Visual journey map – high level	X	X	X	X			X	X	X		X	X	X		X				X	X	X	
Visual journey map – detail level	X	X	X	X		X		X	X	X	X	X	X		X				X	X	X	

(continued)

Table 3.1 (continued)

	2.5 Competitors, suppliers and partners							2.6 Society and environment					2.7 Economic and finance				
	2.5.1 How can we expand our capabilities?	2.5.2 How do we coordinate cooperation in the supply chain?	2.5.3 How can we transform agents and distributors into service…	2.5.4 How can we transform our partners into a service force?	2.5.5 How can we develop a common (business) language?	2.5.6 How can both (we and our partners) manage measurement…	2.5.7 How do we work with installers?	2.6.1 How can we convert free to fee (change internal and …	2.6.2 How can we deal with the conflicting demands to standardise…	2.6.3 How can we manage long term contractual commitments done…	2.6.4 What are the main legal implications of our organisation?	2.6.5 How can we understand tax and transfer pricing issues?	2.7.1 How do we move away from cost plus/hours-based?	2.7.2 How should we consider margins? How to price effectively?	2.7.3 Spares have high margins, more service will reduce the margins…	2.7.4 How can we develop our service business when we have no cash…	2.7.5 How can we manage dealer discounts better?
Avatar map	X	X			X	X	X						X	X	X		
Business model canvas			X	X	X			X	X	X	X	X	X	X	X	X	X
Business Process mapping			X	X	X			X	X	X	X	X	X			X	X
Case/actor matrix	X	X	X	X			X	X	X	X	X					X	
Context map																	
Cradle-to-grave lifecycle map	X	X			X		X	X	X				X	X	X	X	
Cradle-to-grave lifecycle visual mapping	X	X			X		X	X	X				X	X	X	X	
Customer jobs-to-be-done	X					X		X					X	X	X		
Customer value proposition					X	X	X	X	X				X	X	X	X	
Decision matrix																	
Ecosystem mapping	X	X	X		X											X	
Detailed empathy card					X												
Empathy maps	X	X	X		X			X					X				
Feedback grid																	
Feedback sheet																	
Five whys																	
Job-to-be-done insights	X	X						X					X		X		
Job-to-be-done outcomes		X						X					X		X		
Keeping focused																	
Metric cascades	X		X	X	X	X		X	X				X	X	X	X	X
Personas		X	X														
Pitching planning																	
Problem breakdown with the five Ws																	
Service blueprint	X	X	X	X	X	X	X	X	X	X	X	X	X	X	X		X
Storyboarding																	
Understanding your business								X	X	X						X	
Visual journey map - high level	X	X	X	X	X	X	X	X					X				
Visual journey map – detail level	X	X	X	X	X	X	X	X					X				

3.2 Service Methods and Tools

Fig. 3.2 An example of an avatar map (illustration by Annick Holland, adapted from West et al., 2020a)

avatar can be the focus of a journey mapping exercise or a lifecycle analysis. Here short- or longer-term insights can be obtained from the visual tool (Fig. 3.2).

Business Model Canvas
This is a great tool for describing and sharing your business model with others. Always start with the value proposition and connect it to customer segments. Remember that you will need more depth than you see on the canvas itself.

With services you will need to learn to integrate different revenue models into value propositions to support a specific segment. Cost models are dependent upon what you do and what you outsource (and here you could outsource to your customers) (Fig. 3.3).

Business Process Mapping
Business process mapping allows you to understand the steps that a process must go through from start to finish. It provides a clear view of what is happening and who should take the lead. It is closely related to a service blueprint and a journey map.

A business process map should be read left to right and should describe who is involved in the process and their roles. You may like to link this to jobs-to-be-done and empathy maps or personas to get deeper insights. Remember first to create an overview process map, and then create the detailed maps. It is best done with a long whiteboard and many Post-it notes (Fig. 3.4).

Case/Actor Matrix
This tool helps you understand who is involved in different situations. It shows you quickly and in one form who takes the lead and who are the other actors involved.

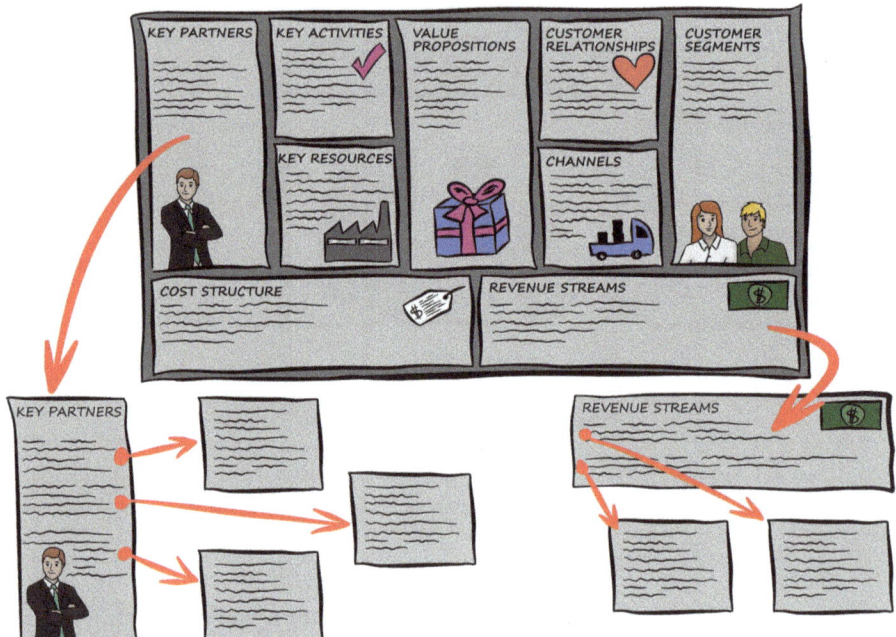

Fig. 3.3 Depth is often needed to understand the business model in sufficient detail (illustration by Annick Holland, adapted from Osterwalder & Pigneur, 2010)

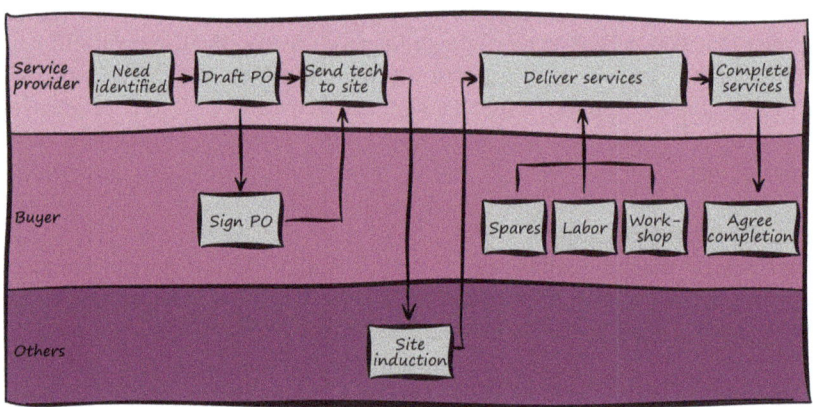

Fig. 3.4 An example basic business process map (illustration by Annick Holland, adapted from Tseng et al., 1999)

This tool can be powerfully insightful for service, as individual service events are all involved and based on interactions between individuals.

3.2 Service Methods and Tools

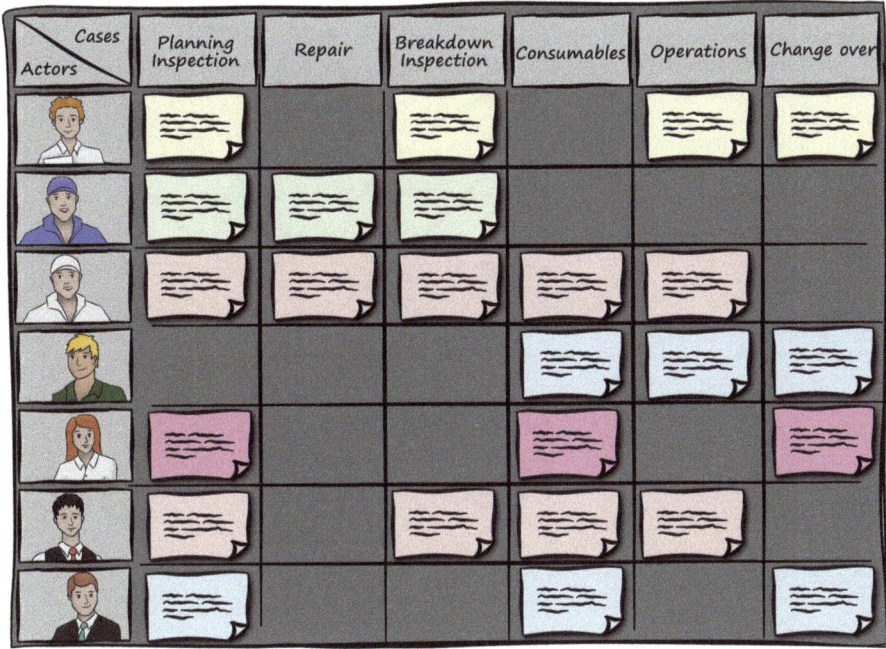

Fig. 3.5 An example of a case/actor matrix (illustration by Annick Holland, adapted from Stoll et al., 2020)

Make the matrix visual, and remember that for every firm this will be different. On aggregate, you will see common roles taking the lead responsibility. You might like to spit the actors into suppliers and customers, and then create a detailed journey map for every case (Fig. 3.5).

Context Map
The context map forces you to identify the dimensions of your problem or opportunity space. Using the context map, you are limited to eight dimensions; this is hard to deal with and focuses your attention on the real issues. Several context maps can be created from different points of view. However, the focal aspect must always be placed in the center (Fig. 3.6).

Cradle-to-Grave Lifecycle Visual Mapping
The cradle-to-grave lifecycle visual mapping tool helps you as manufacturers to understand the whole life of your equipment or products. It creates a storyboard of what each avatar will "experience" over its entire life. However, the avatar's lifecycle is not limited by the PLM cycle defined by the manufacturer but that defined by the asset owner. For example, the B52 bomber is still in operation today even though it is 70 years since it first flew.

Fig. 3.6 An example of a context map to help you focus on the problem (illustration by Annick Holland, adapted from Carleton et al., 2013)

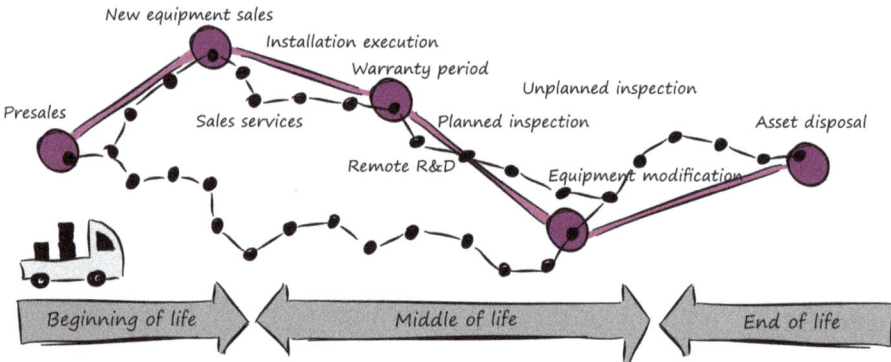

Fig. 3.7 An example of a cradle-to-grave lifecycle visual map (illustration by Annick Holland, adapted from West et al., 2020a)

The tool has three lifecycle phases and defines all the different services required to keep the avatar optionally functional for the owner. The tool can help you develop the total cost of ownership (TCO) based on the required activities and services. The model is best completed on a large whiteboard with customers, as there will be many activities that the manufacturer is unaware of (Fig. 3.7).

Cradle-to-Grave Lifecycle Map

Cradle-to-grave lifecycle activity mapping follows on from the visual mapping. Here, the purpose is to understand, on an annual basis, the costs associated with

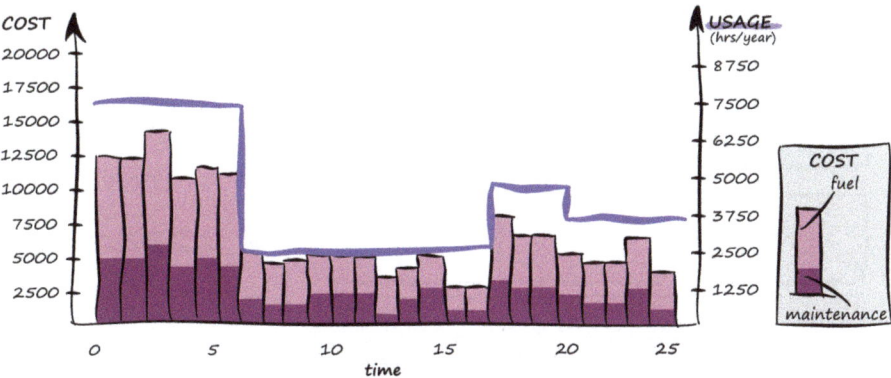

Fig. 3.8 An example of a cradle-to-grave lifecycle map (illustration by Annick Holland, adapted from West & Pascual, 2015)

the operations and maintenance of the machine or its avatar, to build up its total cost of ownership (TCO).

This tool will help you demonstrate to your customer the cost breakdown of the equipment and show the anticipated maintenance budget required over its full operational life. You will also learn from the customer about their costs, some of which may be hidden from you. Again, this is best when completed with a customer, and it is essential to understand the customer's cost drivers for the calculation. It can be done in the development phase of a new product to understand the total cost of ownership (TCO) or during the midlife phase to help with the assessment for an upgrade (Fig. 3.8).

Customer Jobs-to-Be-Done

Even trying to understand the job that a customer has to do can be very complex, it is essential for you to offer them the appropriate services. This is important, particularly where a product can have different applications in different industries, and critically some aspects (e.g., the value in use) can be very different, depending upon its actual application.

The customer job-to-be-done tool was developed to help you capture what is going on in a simple visual way, as reported in the example of Fig. 3.9. The visualization shows the core process and the supporting activities, linking them to business metrics. This tool is complementary to the avatar tool. Each step provides inputs to the next one; each needs inputs and creates an output. The steps need to have supporting activities and performance metrics or key performance indicators. The right-hand side of the tool is used to describe simply what the jobs-to-be-done are for the overall business. The statement should be straightforward, based on what described the purpose or mission of the business.

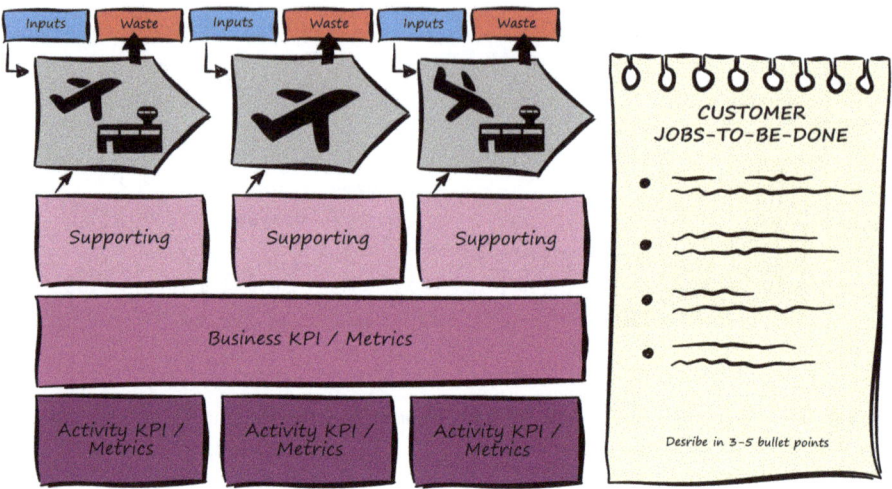

Fig. 3.9 An example of a customer jobs-to-be-done (illustration by Annick Holland, adapted from West et al., 2018b)

Customer Value Proposition

The customer value proposition is a very powerful tool to help understand what you are actually delivering to your customers and why they like it.

Use the customer side to explain the problems in a simple form. Then, fill in the solution description to describe what you are doing today. Now, you can begin to imagine new ways to fulfill the customer's problem description (more than one possible solution is always possible). Invent some very different ways to deliver it: consider a do-it-yourself model, models where you share the work with customers in new ways, or one where you deliver all of the services for them. The more solutions you are able to come up with, the better! You can then plot them out on a two-by-two decision matrix to assess which ones you will test with your customers. Remember not all customers are the same (Fig. 3.10)!

Decision Matrix

A decision matrix is a basic two-by-two analysis tool. The two axes are the basis of the decision-making and allow clustering and grouping of problems, ideas, or solutions.

Often the vertical axis is based around "value" or "importance" and the horizontal axis on "feasibility" or "effort." This helps you to make decisions based on these dimensions as well as share the decision-making process with mixed teams (Fig. 3.11).

Ecosystem Mapping

Ecosystems can be very complex to build and understand. However, they are very useful, as they provide essential insights into a firm's formal and informal processes.

3.2 Service Methods and Tools

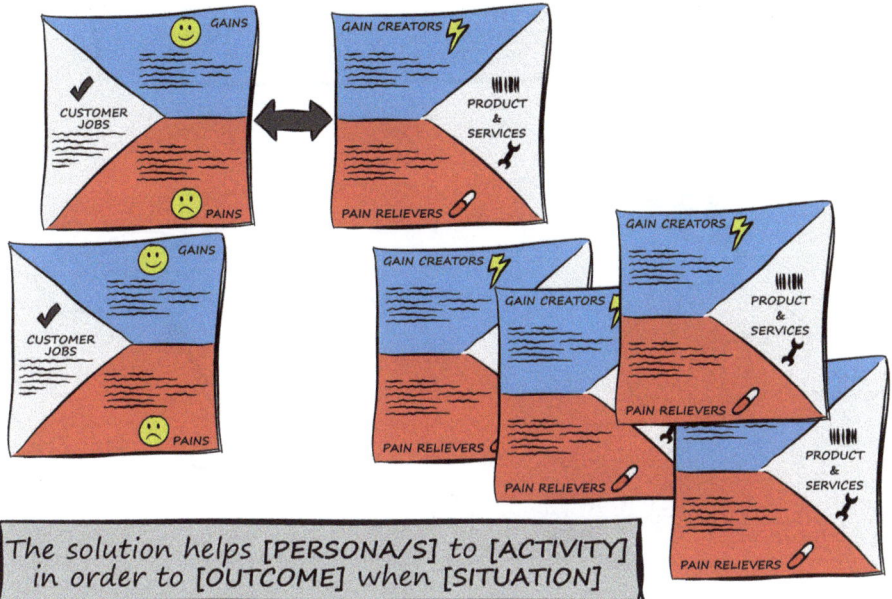

Fig. 3.10 Use the value proposition to help describe customer problems and create possible solutions (illustration by Annick Holland, adapted from West et al., 2018b)

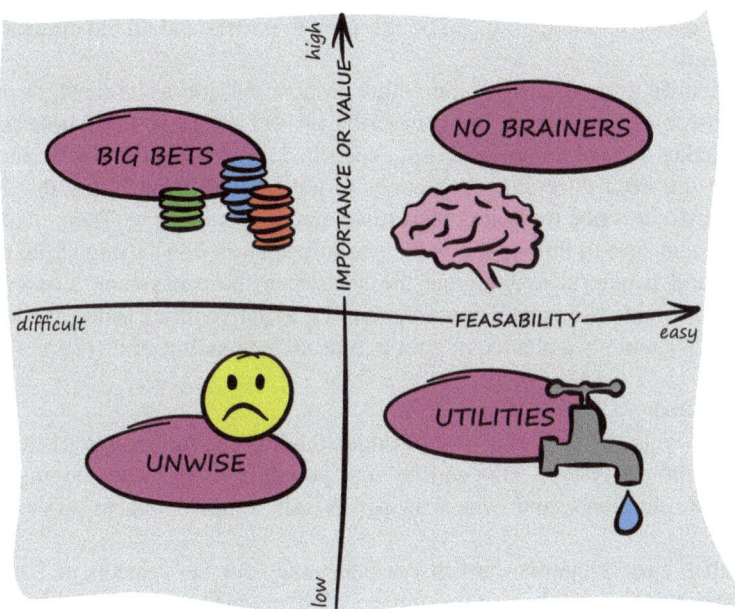

Fig. 3.11 A sample decision matrix (illustration by Annick Holland, adapted from IBM, 2018)

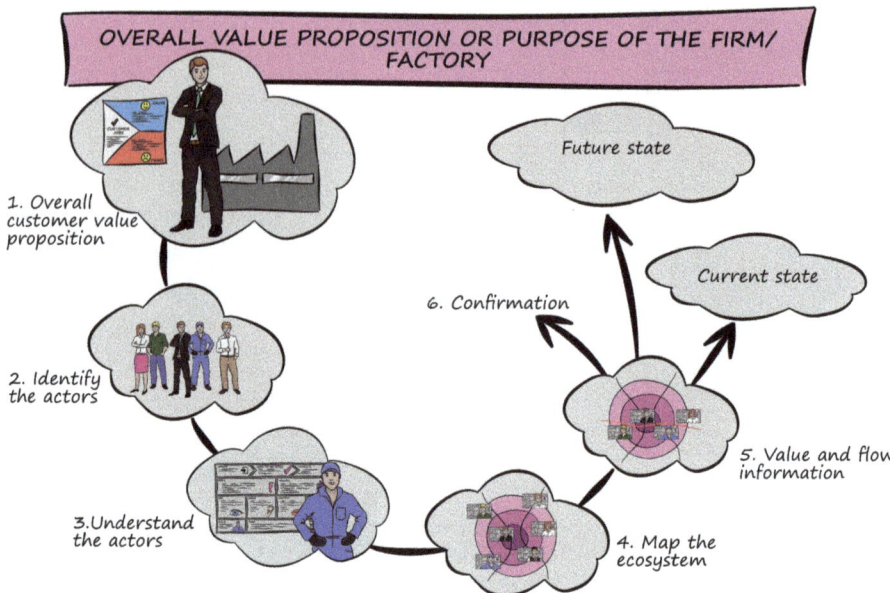

Fig. 3.12 Learning to navigate an ecosystem (illustration by Annick Holland, adapted from West et al., 2018a)

That's why ecosystem mapping can be essential to understand all the dimensions of your problem.

First, identify the overall customer value proposition, job-to-be-done, or purpose of your customer's business. Then, describe all the actors in the whole process; often, this takes several iterations as not everyone knows all of the actors, and, even if they do, you need different perspectives to get a full picture. Using the detailed empathy cards, describe the actors in as much detail as necessary. Then, place them on a board, and start to link up the value and information flows using string or tape. You may find it helpful to integrate the avatars in the ecosystem. You can then confirm the current state as well as start to build alternative future states. Building the ecosystem as a team is a chance to gain a joint understanding of it (Fig. 3.12).

Empathy Card

The detailed empathy card is a way of understanding the motivation of the people involved in the ecosystem. This can be very powerful, both in developing change management initiatives and when trying to sell a new concept of service to customers.

As with a basic empathy card, it considers the four key aspects of "see, hear, say/do, and think/feel." It also examines what people consider as "pains" and "gains." Additionally, it asks what the inputs are to their job-to-be-done and what the outputs are. Finally, it captures basic information on their role and the time they have (Fig. 3.13).

Fig. 3.13 A template for a detailed empathy card (illustration by Annick Holland, adapted from West et al., 2018a)

Empathy Maps

Empathy maps are a great way to get into people's shoes and start to understand and analyze the world from their perspective.

It takes time to get used to using this tool. It's a good way to understand the situation and learn how to react – this is why it is called "empathy." Detailed empathy cards are another very useful tool to help you go into more depth about particular people (Fig. 3.14).

Feedback Grid

The feedback grid allows you to get suggestions and comments from a group of people quickly. Four simple questions can be answered on Post-it notes to provide you with new insights that you can later put into action (Fig. 3.15).

Feedback Sheet

When developing new services (based on the blueprint or actual services), it is good to get feedback. Using this sheet allows you to do this in a structured way. Moreover, it supports the adoption of detailed journey mapping, and the two tools can be used together.

The test scenario describes the situation you are evaluating and what you are looking for. The reflections should be a mix of yours and the person you are testing. Try to keep it visual. This is best done using pen and paper (Fig. 3.16).

Fig. 3.14 An example of a basic empathy map (illustration by Annick Holland, adapted from Meinel & Leifer, 2015)

Fig. 3.15 An example of a feedback grid (illustration by Annick Holland, authors' work)

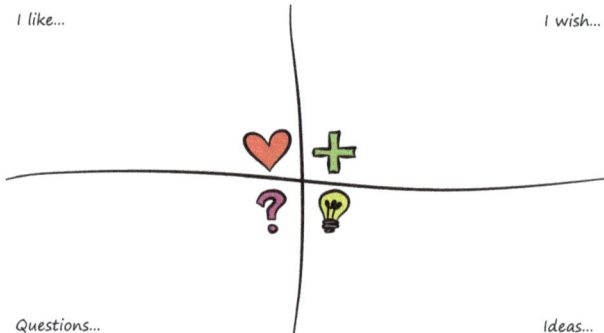

Five Whys
The five-why technique is used to get to the root cause of a problem. It is closely related to the five Ws. You should use them jointly when you are trying to understand a problem in depth. Too often, we do not get to the root cause of a problem but rather only consider the symptoms (Fig. 3.17).

Job-to-Be-Done Insights
Job-to-be-done insights allow you to get a detailed understanding of people and their actions. Based on the three main statements – when..., I want..., so I can... – it is a

3.2 Service Methods and Tools

Fig. 3.16 An example of a feedback sheet (illustration by Annick Holland, adapted from Kumar et al., 2020)

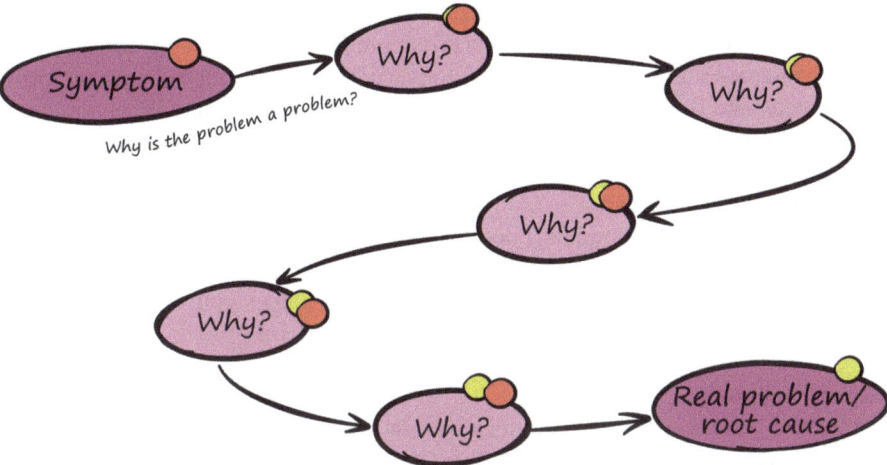

Fig. 3.17 Root cause analysis with five Ys (illustration by Annick Holland, adapted from Pojasek, 2000)

very simple approach to building a simple process and understanding where you as the service provider could help your customer.

It works as well within your organization as in other businesses (Fig. 3.18).

Fig. 3.18 Job-to-be-done insights (illustration by Annick Holland, adapted from Christensen et al., 2016)

Job-to-Be-Done Outcomes

Job-to-be-done is a great way to help make the innovation actionable. Too often, we just "score" innovation. Conversely, with this approach, you can get into the detail of what is being done through building a customer process map – considering the core process steps and the supporting services. From that understanding, it is possible, using the formula, to build a clear outcome that is statement based. Using the outcome statement, you can then ask actors if they are satisfied with it and verify how important it is for them.

The results of satisfaction and importance can also be plotted on a two-by-two decision matrix. You can then build a roadmap that helps you to identify what to focus on first and what you could do later. Finally, it shows you where you over-deliver and where you might be able to reduce cost (Fig. 3.19).

Keeping Focused

Keeping focused means understanding what your core services are and what are the "other services". It is important to track both, as some of the "other services" you may want to stop offering or redefine.

In both cases, you need to use customer data (e.g., sales volumes and margins) to provide you with the input (Fig. 3.20).

Metric Cascades

The metric cascade is helpful to understand how you contribute to the customer's outcome (or not). There is often more than one way to provide lower costs to the customer, and this method can help you see that your costs may be important, but they might not represent a major cost to your customer's operations. Moreover, developing a cascade can provide you with an understanding of what you do and

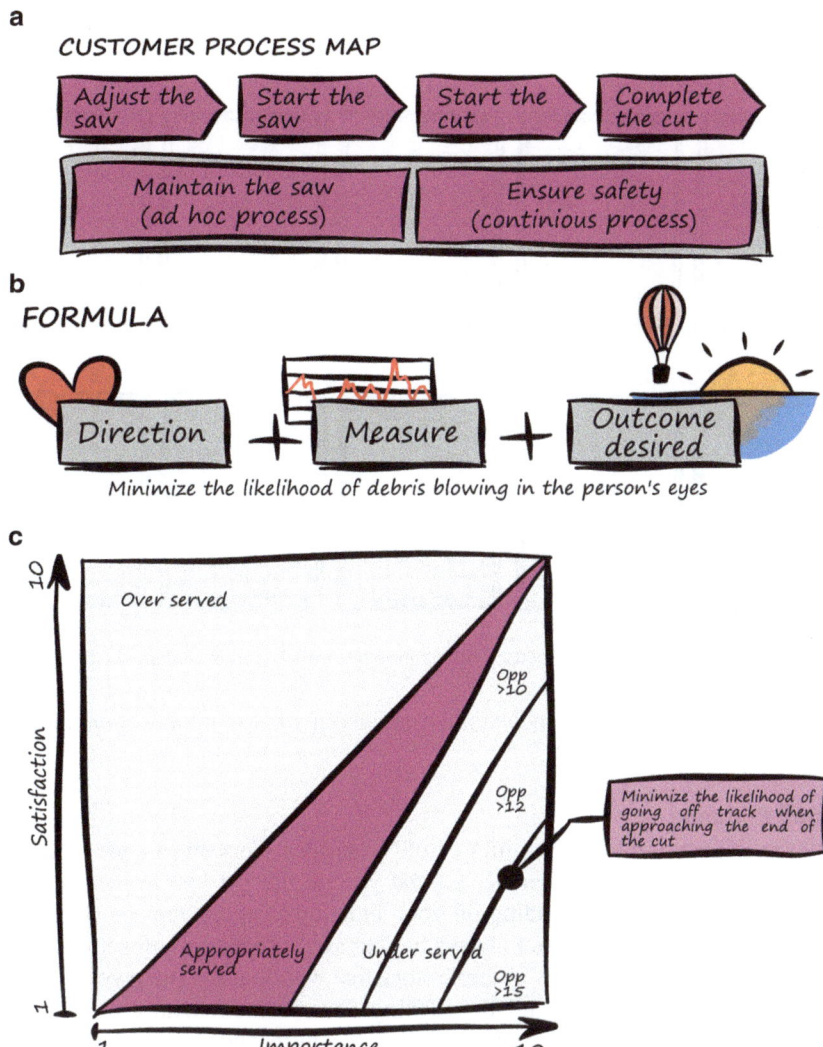

Fig. 3.19 Job-to-be-done outcomes (illustration by Annick Holland, adapted from Ulwick, 2002 and 2005)

affect and what it might do for your customer – there is always more than one way to skin a cat. This method can work well with understanding "customer jobs-to-be-done" and can help provide detailed insights into the operation (Fig. 3.21).

Personas
Personas give you a wider and deeper view of an actor than empathy maps. Therefore, an empathy map can be a good starting point to allow you to build a persona. You can start from it to create a detailed persona that allows you to get

Fig. 3.20 A template to help keep focused (illustration by Annick Holland, adapted authors' work)

under the skin of an actor to understand more about what motivates them and how they can contribute (Fig. 3.22).

Pitching Planning
Making an impactful pitch is helpful to "sell" your idea. This seven-slide model can help you put your thoughts together so that you do not get lost in the problem's details and the solution. Depending on your situation, you can replace slides (e.g., the business model slide may not always be required). Pitching is closely related to the storytelling tool, as it adopts a simple story line with focus, to help you to end up with less conflict when it comes to reaching an agreement with colleagues and managers. To make this tool more efficient, the intro slides should contain the purpose of the pitch (e.g., why are we here?), while the key messages and the feedback should be on the slides that you are using – not hidden in the text but clearly presented on the slides. Moreover, the summary slide should include a statement that confirms the agreement. After the meeting, issue the slides as notes and, in pen, state the agreement that was reached. Adjust the structure depending on the situation – always confirm the purpose of the pitch, and provide a clear view of the next steps. Rather than taking detailed minutes, attach the final agreement to the pitch, and share it quickly with the team (Fig. 3.23).

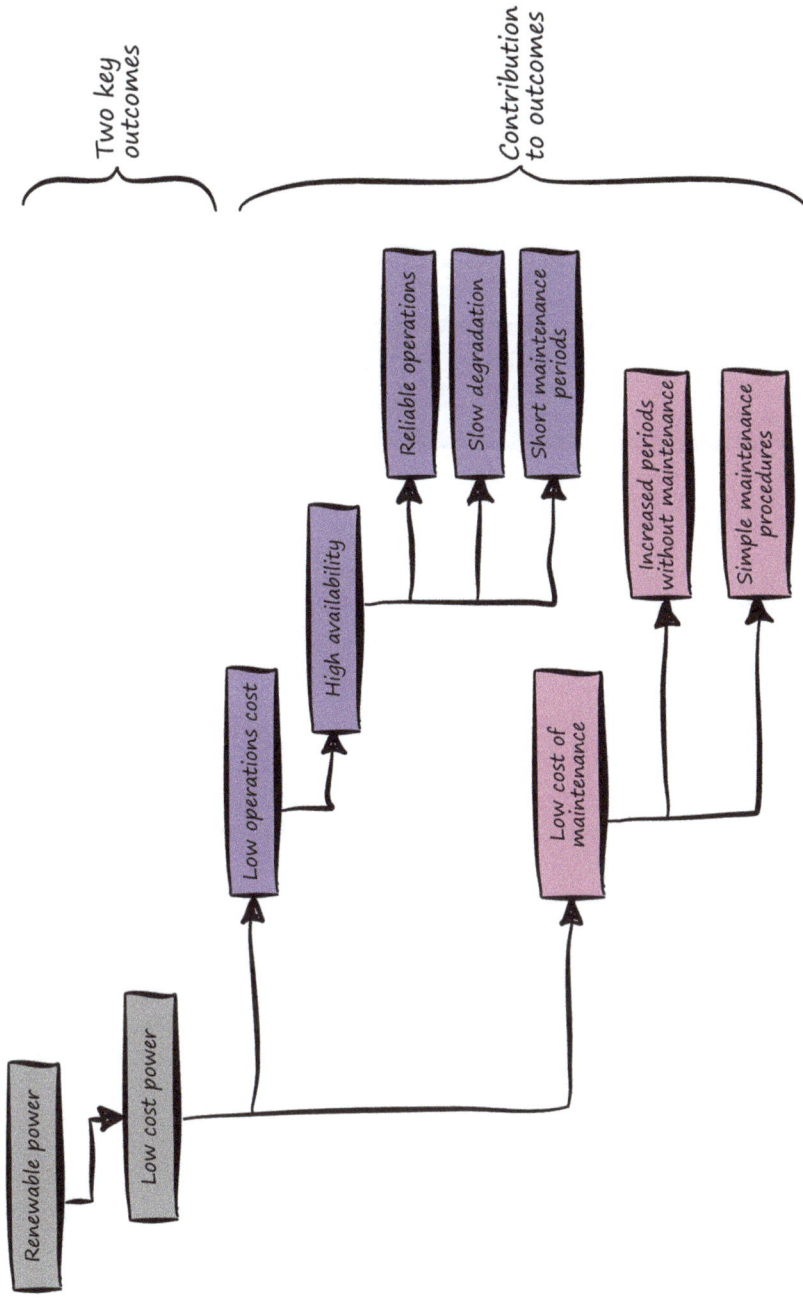

Fig. 3.21 An example of cascading metrics (illustration by Annick Holland, adapted from Eckerson, 2009)

Fig. 3.22 An example of a persona (illustration by Annick Holland, adapted from Harniess & Harniess, 2020)

Problem Breakdown with the Five Ws
Using the five Ws provides a comprehensive analysis of many problems. The tool is complementary to the five-why tool and gives you more contextual information on a problem (Fig. 3.24).

Service Blueprint
The service blueprint can help you to understand the connections between different individual tasks. You can get insight into the tasks and people who are normally hidden from view. Moreover, it allows you to sequence the service journey as you imagine or design it. For simplicity, it is best to use the same template for a service blueprint (the planned or designed service) as well as journey mapping (actual state).

You need to understand the use case (e.g., the service and its value proposition) and the involved stakeholders (direct and indirect). Adding high-level phases to the blueprint always helps develop better understanding. You should always start "too early" and end well after the service has been delivered. Graphics really bring the blueprint alive and make it easier to understand (Fig. 3.25).

Storyboarding
Stop before you work in PowerPoint to create a presentation, and first create a storyboard. By doing this, you will improve the clarity of your communication. By creating a simple visual narrative supported with some text, you will have more impactful and more clearly communicated messages. Focus on the "beginning," "middle," and "end" (Fig. 3.26).

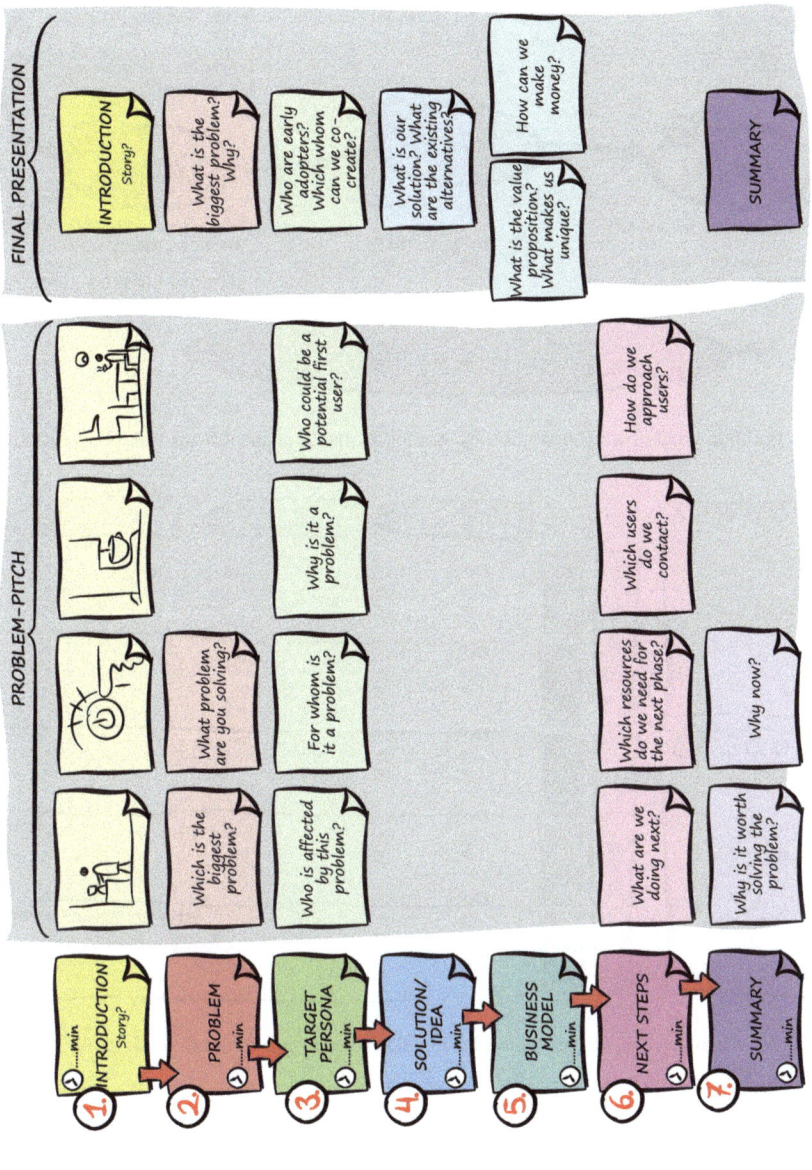

Fig. 3.23 An example of how to plan a pitching presentation (illustration by Annick Holland, authors' work)

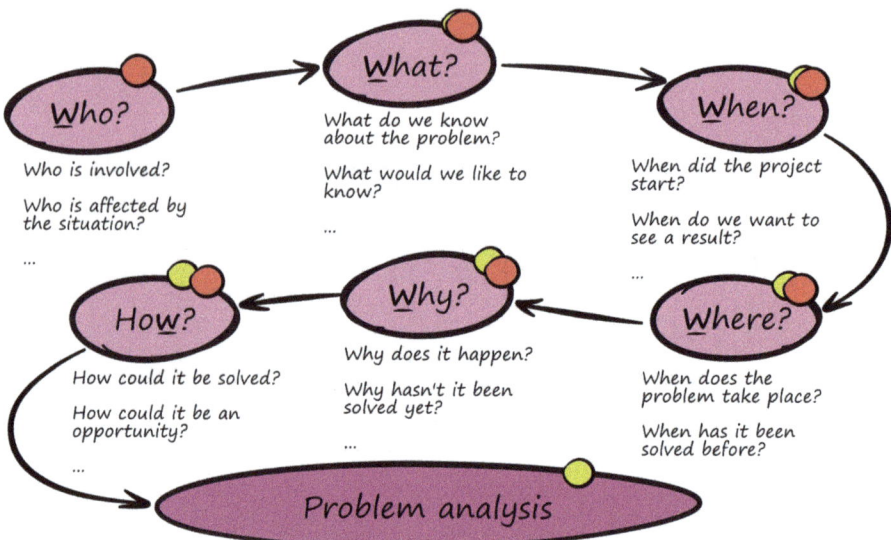

Fig. 3.24 Problem breakdown (illustration by Annick Holland, adapted from Wikipedia, 2020)

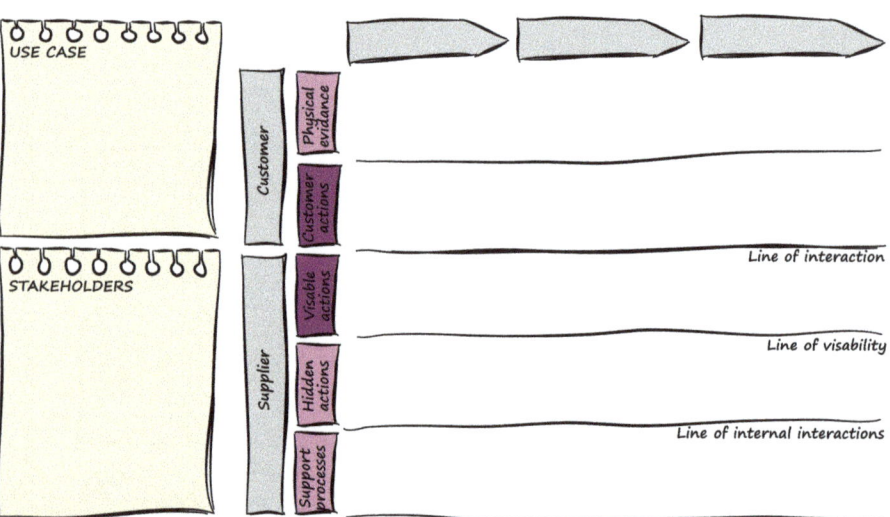

Fig. 3.25 An example of a service blueprint template(illustration by Annick Holland, adapted from Lynn, 1984)

Understanding Your Business

It is important to understand your business, and this tool allows you (with your team) to do this in more depth and with more objectivity. It supports the business model canvas tool. As a team, this model helps you to share what the firm does, why, and

Fig. 3.26 An example of storyboard planning (illustration by Annick Holland, adapted from Wikström et al., 2013)

how. Often, we found it necessary to make two loops to get a shared understanding (Fig. 3.27).

Visual Journey Map: High Level
When a visual journey map is drawn, it allows you to understand the problem better at a high level before you dive into the details. A whiteboard with Post-it notes is often a good way to create this kind of map. Very quickly, you start to see and understand a problem from many perspectives.

This can form the first part of a detailed journey map for a customer. In addition, it can help you to understand the equipment lifecycle from the asset management perspective rather than the manufacturer's perspective. To make it really effective, every touchpoint here should have a value proposition clearly defined. Moreover, every person identified (customer and supplier side) should have an empathy card or a persona developed, to further deepen the insights (Fig. 3.28).

Visual Journey Map: Detail Level
By detailing out an individual journey map, you will learn what people like and, importantly, dislike about the services you deliver. Therefore, this is a tool that allows you to get direct and actionable feedback from a customer and learn more about how they act and behave.

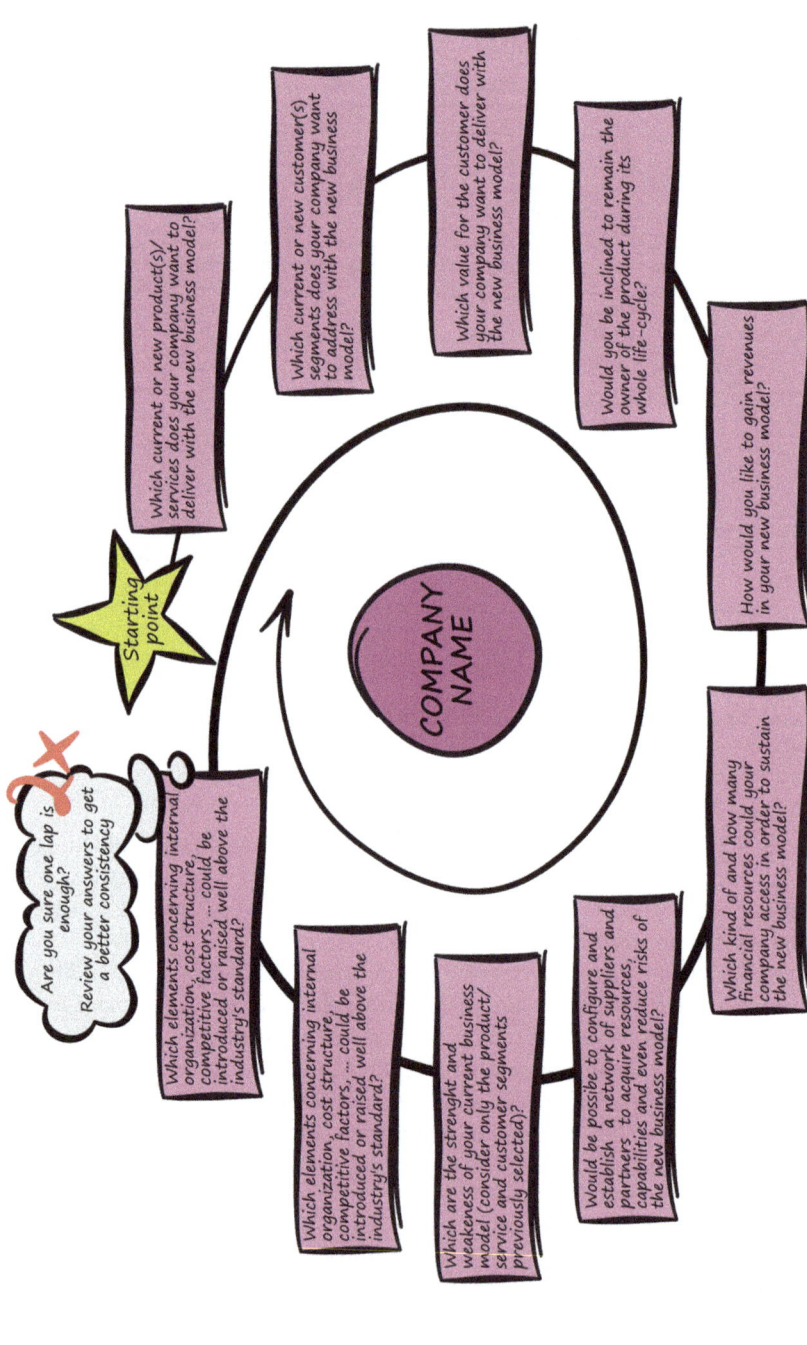

Fig. 3.27 An approach to help you understand your business (illustration by Annick Holland, authors' work)

3.2 Service Methods and Tools

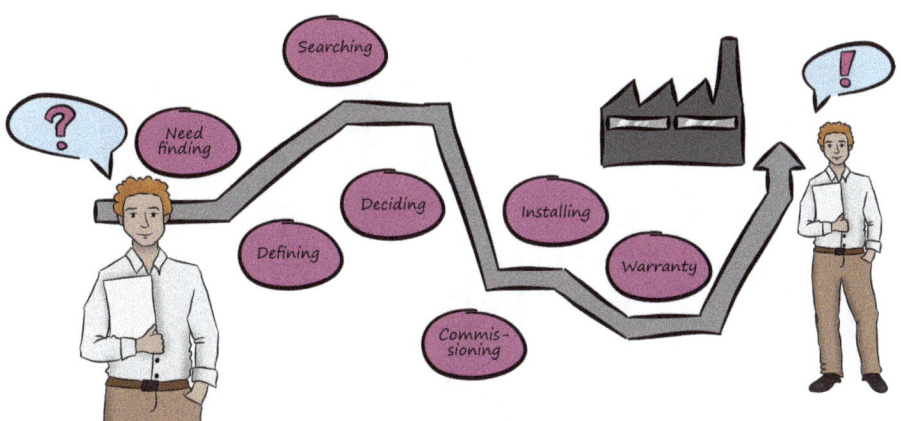

Fig. 3.28 An example of a visual journey (illustration by Annick Holland, adapted from West et al., 2020b)

Pen and paper work best, and keep the scope limited by looking at single interactions. You can use it internally as well as externally with your customers (Fig. 3.29).

Other Tools

In addition to the tools provided in this section, we suggest the book *This is Service Design Doing* (Stickdorn et al., 2018), which offers many examples of how firms have created or improved services in a highly practical way. The book is supported by a website (https://www.thisisservicedesigndoing.com). The Service Design Tools website (https://servicedesigntools.org) is also helpful with tools and tutorials. Again, Polaine et al. (2013) wrote an excellent book on service design entitled *Service Design: From Insight to Implementation* that provides more insights into the design and delivery of services. Even SAP scenes are an excellent tool kit, as they allow you to easily create storyboards and service prototypes. These are freely available on the Internet from SAP and need little introduction (https://community.sap.com/topics/fiori). Finally, IBM's enterprise design thinking website (https://www.ibm.com/design/thinking/) provides more tools and a handy PDF that can help you with developing services in your business.

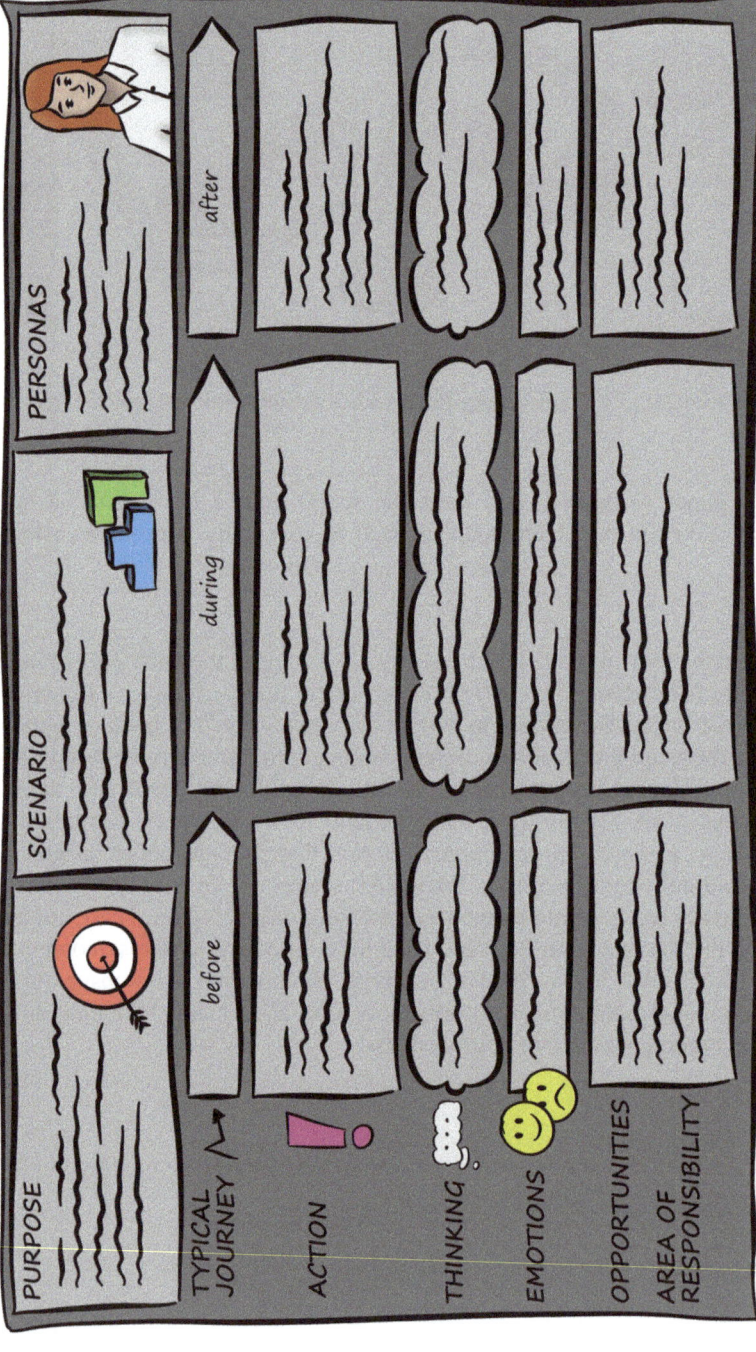

Fig. 3.29 An example of a customer journey map (illustration by Annick Holland, adapted from Polaine et al., 2013)

References

Carleton, T., Cockayne, W., & Tahvanainen, A-J. (2013). *Playbook for strategic foresight and innovation*. Accessed December 30, 2020, from https://www.innovation.io/playbook

Christensen, C. M., Hall, T., Dillon, K., & Duncan, D. S. (2016). Know your customers' "jobs to be done." *Harvard Business Review*.

Dmitrijeva, J., Schroeder, A., Ziaee Bigdeli, A., & Baines, T. (2020). Context matters: how internal and external factors impact servitization. Production

Eckerson, W. (2009). *Performance management strategies: How to create and deploy effective metrics*. The Data Warehousing Institute. Accessed December 30, 2020, from ftp://public.dhe.ibm.com/software/data/sw-library/cognos/pdfs/analystreports/ar_peformance_mgmnt_strategies_how_to_create_and_deploy_effective_metrics.pdf

Harniess, W., & Harniess, W. (2020). Personas. In *Red, white and radical*. Routledge. https://doi.org/10.4324/9780429054198-3

IBM. (2018). *Enterprise design thinking – Field guide*. IBM Studios. Accessed December 29, 2020, from ibm.biz/fieldguide-public

Kumar, K., Zindani, D., & Davim, J. P. (2020). Introduction to design thinking. In *SpringerBriefs in Applied Sciences and Technology*. https://doi.org/10.1007/978-3-030-31359-3_1

Lynn, S. G. (1984). Designing services that deliver. *Harvard Business Review, 62*(1), 133–139.

Meinel, C., & Leifer, L. (2015). Introduction – Design thinking is mainly about building innovators. In H. Plattner, C. Meinel, & L. Leifer (Eds.), *Design thinking research. Understanding innovation*. Springer. https://doi.org/10.1007/978-3-319-06823-7_1

Osterwalder, A., & Pigneur, Y. (2010). *Business model generation - Canvas*. Wiley.

Pojasek, R. B. (2000). Asking "Why?" five times. *Environmental Quality Management*. https://doi.org/10.1002/1520-6483(200023)10:1<79::AID-TQEM10>3.0.CO;2-H

Polaine, A., Løvlie, L., & Reason, B. (2013). *Service design: From insight to implementation*. Rosenfeld Media.

Stickdorn, M., Lawrence, A., Hormess, M., & Schneider, J. (2018). *This is service design doing*. O'Reilly Media.

Stoll O., West S., Rapaccini M., Barbieri C., Bonfanti A., & Gombac A. (2020). Upgrading the Data2Action framework: Results deriving from its application in the printing industry. In: Nóvoa H., Drăgoicea M., Kühl N. (eds) Exploring Service Science. IESS 2020. Lecture Notes in Business Information Processing, 377. Springer, Cham. https://doi.org/10.1007/978-3-030-38724-2_20

Tseng, M. M., Qinhai, M., & Su, C. (1999). Mapping customers' service experience for operations improvement. *Business Process Management Journal, 5*(1), 50–64. https://doi.org/10.1108/14637159910249126

Ulwick, A. W. (2002). Turn customer input into innovation. *Harvard Business Review, 80*(1), 91–98.

Ulwick, A. W. (2005). *What customers want: Using outcome-driven innovation to create breakthrough products and services*. McGraw-Hill.

West, S. S., & Pascual, A. (2015). The use of equipment life-cycle analysis to identify new service opportunities. In T. Baines & D. K. Harrison (Eds.), *Servitization: The theory and impact: Proceedings of the Spring Servitization Conference 18–19 May 2015, SSC2015*. Aston University.

West, S.S., Müller-Csernetzky, P., & Huonder, M. (2018a). Ecosystems innovation for service development. *Practices and Tools for Servitization*. https://doi.org/10.1007/978-3-319-76517-4

West, S.S., Rohner, D., Kujawski, D, and Rapaccini, M. (2018b). Value-scope-price: Design and pricing of advanced service offerings based on customer value. *Practices and Tools for Servitization*. https://doi.org/10.1007/978-3-319-76517-4

West, S. S., Stoll, O., & Mueller-Csernetzky, P. (2020a). 'Avatar journey mapping' for manufacturing firms to reveal smart-service opportunities over the product life-cycle. *International Journal of Business Environment*. https://doi.org/10.1504/IJBE.2020.110906

West, S. S., Stoll, O., Østerlund, M., Müller-Csernetzky, P., Keiderling, F., & Kowalkowski, C. (2020b). Adjusting customer journey mapping for application in industrial product-service systems. *International Journal of Business Environment, 11*(3), 275–297. https://doi.org/10.1504/IJBE.2020.110911

Wikipedia. (2020). *Five Ws*. Wikipedia. Accessed December 30, 2020, from https://en.wikipedia.org/wiki/Five_Ws

Wikström, A., Everskog, A., Forsberg Wallin, A., Hyltefors, M., Larsen, S., & Verganti, R. (2013). *Storyboarding - Framing the "frame" of opportunity*. In Proceedings of the International Conference on Engineering Design, ICED.

Open Access This chapter is licensed under the terms of the Creative Commons Attribution 4.0 International License (http://creativecommons.org/licenses/by/4.0/), which permits use, sharing, adaptation, distribution and reproduction in any medium or format, as long as you give appropriate credit to the original author(s) and the source, provide a link to the Creative Commons license and indicate if changes were made.

The images or other third party material in this chapter are included in the chapter's Creative Commons license, unless indicated otherwise in a credit line to the material. If material is not included in the chapter's Creative Commons license and your intended use is not permitted by statutory regulation or exceeds the permitted use, you will need to obtain permission directly from the copyright holder.

Lightning Source UK Ltd.
Milton Keynes UK
UKHW020938020222
398082UK00001B/23